Wesley for Armchair Theologians

WILLIAM J. ABRAHAM

ILLUSTRATIONS BY RON HILL

WESTMINSTER
JOHN KNOX PRESS
LOUISVILLE · KENTUCKY

Scripture quotations from the New Revised Standard Version of the Bible are copyright © 1989 by the Division of Christian Education of the National Council of the Churches of Christ in the U.S.A. and are used by permission.

Book design by Sharon Adams
Cover design by Jennifer K. Cox
Cover illustration by Ron Hill

First edition
Published by Westminster John Knox Press
Louisville, Kentucky

This book is printed on acid-free paper that meets the American National Standards Institute Z39.48 standard. ♾

PRINTED IN THE UNITED STATES OF AMERICA

07 08 09 10 11 12 13 14 —10 9 8 7 6 5 4 3

Library of Congress Cataloging-in-Publication Data is on file at the Library of Congress, Washington, D.C.

ISBN-13: 978-0-664-22621-3
ISBN-10: 0-664-22621-3

To
Siobhan Elizabeth

Contents

Preface   1

1. On the Road Again   3

2. Background Music   25

3. Life Is Nearly as Bad as You Thought It Was   45

4. Starting All Over Again   61

5. With God All Things Are Possible   83

6. Help Is in the Works   107

7. Making Moral Sense   123

8. Spiritual Hiccups and Measles   145

9. Providence and Predestination:
    Double or Nothing   159

Notes   181

For Further Reading   185

Index   189

PREFACE

This little volume on John Wesley is intended both as a contribution to the debate about his theology and as an introduction for the beginner. I offer a fresh interpretation of his theology, but I do so in a way that I hope proves interesting to the newcomer to Wesleyan studies. I also aim to draw folk into their own theological reflections today. My fondest desire is to make Wesley come alive for those who would truly love to become unpretentious armchair theologians. Wesley is a friend who can ably launch them on a wonderful intellectual journey in faith.

I confess at the outset my own ambivalence about Wesley. In the early stages of my own intellectual and spiritual journey, Wesley was pivotal for me. After my conversion in my teenage years through the ministry of the people called Methodists in Ireland, I read Wesley avidly. I did not then know that I was supposed to be bored by his writings. While I was at university the lively biography of Wesley by

John Wesley Bready, *England before and after Wesley* (New York: Harper, 1938), was a godsend during a period of backbreaking summer work in a cement factory in East Anglia in England.

When I took up the formal study of theology, Wesley suddenly went dead on me. I found him not so much archaic as surreal. I thought I would never come back to my first love, even though the hymns the early Methodists let loose in the world remain a spiritual treasure that I still sorely miss in the move from Ireland to North America. Happily, listening to some purloined audiotapes on Wesley by Albert Outler during a bad dose of the flu arrested this journey away from Wesley. Yet Wesley remains a figure who is both near and remote. He is clearly an extraordinarily interesting figure in the history of Christianity; but it is far from easy to know what to make of his life or his theology. So I write this volume with a certain fear and trembling.

Wesley clearly has a distinctive theology. I hope I have offered a persuasive rendering of that theology. My thesis is that Wesley's theology is an intellectual oasis lodged within the traditional faith of the church enshrined in the creeds. This move dictates the ordering of the material up ahead. I begin with two chapters on Wesley's life and context in the eighteenth century. I then provide a chapter that picks out one component of the classical faith of the church that is critical for understanding his theology as a whole. The next five chapters provide the meat of his theology. I then circle back up into the wider faith of the church and take up a topic that has always been a source of comfort and curiosity to me. I hope the reader will find a pleasing symmetry in the work.

William J. Abraham
Dallas, Texas
December 11, 2004

CHAPTER ONE

On the Road Again

A Fortunate Family Row

John Wesley began life as a happy by-product of a family dispute in the local Anglican parsonage in Epworth, England, in 1702. His parents had had a royal row over praying for the current king. His mother, Susanna, had refused to say amen after the family prayers for the reigning monarch William III. As she remembered the event, her husband, Samuel, had "immediately kneeled down and imprecated the divine vengeance upon himself and all his posterity if ever he touched me more or came to bed with me before I had begged God's pardon and his."[1] So Samuel had gone off in a huff. When he at last decided to return, John Wesley was conceived. He was number fifteen in a family of nineteen children.

Both Susanna and Samuel Wesley were formidable in their own way, and they both left their mark on John, who was born on June 17, 1703, and lived until March 2, 1791. They began life as Dissenters, that is, as those who rejected the vision of Christianity developed by the Anglican Church after the Reformation. Independently of each other, they had examined the theological issues of the day for themselves and been converted to the Anglican tradition. Susanna was the daughter of a distinguished Dissenting preacher and had made ample use of her father's library for her research. She made the move to the Anglican tradition when she was twelve. As long as Susanna lived, she had a powerful influence on her son, beginning with intensive homeschooling in which Thursdays were devoted to the intellectual and spiritual care of John. Samuel Wesley had gone over to Anglicanism as a young man, went up to Oxford to study for the priesthood, became a minor churchman of his day, and devoted forty years of his life to his contrary parishioners.

Given this background, it is no surprise that John Wesley was steeped in the Anglican Church of his day. While he led a renewal movement within it that ultimately went its own way, he never wavered in his own sense of loyalty. He loved the Church of England dearly, gloried in its treasures, pined over its faults, and worked mightily to goad it into a deeper spirituality and into a more effective service to God.

John Wesley inherited a rich theological tradition, and he was steeped in its ways of piety and ritual. From the age of eleven in 1714 until he sailed for Georgia in the New World in 1735, he spent most of his life in Anglican educational institutions, first as a student and then as a lecturer in logic and Greek. As a fellow of Lincoln College, Oxford, he received a living from the Church of England until he married. He was totally immersed in his church's worship and prayers, shaped in a host of ways by its wonderful intellectual balance, its openness to truth, its stately presence in politics and country, its internal linguistic beauty, and its sense of humble grandeur and confidence. While Oxford University was in his day something of a glorified high school crossed with a finishing school for grandees, he gained a priceless education there as a student and teacher that served him well throughout his career. He learned well how to articulate and defend his ideas even when they were daft and irregular. When he reluctantly abandoned the university to work as an itinerant preacher, he took with him an abundance of skills and self-assurance.

In his late thirties Wesley tended to underestimate the depth of his early spiritual life, but there can be no doubt about the genuineness of his faith. He was an ardent servant of God, becoming first a priest and then an enthusiastic missionary. In preparation for his ordination as a deacon in 1725 he devoted himself to a life of holiness. He read avidly in the literature of personal sanctity, working across the theological spectrum that was available to him. When his brother Charles and some friends began a small-group ministry at Oxford University devoted to Bible study, prayer, and service to the needy, he readily joined, becoming the natural leader. He was not afraid of hard names or opposition and later came to see this experiment in small-group ministry as the nucleus of his Methodist Societies. Such was his commitment and diligence that he became a missionary to the New World. He persuaded his brother Charles to go with him. Wesley's personal prayers, his obsession with spiritual discipline, his rigor in matters of church law, and his sermons display a man who was bent on a quest for real Christianity.

Below the surface, however, John Wesley was far from

settled spiritually. While his father lay dying on April 25, 1735, he urged his son to seek a truly personal encounter with God through the work of the Holy Spirit. On the way to Georgia, Wesley fell in with a group of Moravian missionaries whose vibrant faith challenged his own inner uncertainties. He was so impressed with their assurance in the face of death in the storms at sea that he learned German so as to better understand their spiritual secrets. He met regularly with their spiritual leaders, one of whom, Peter Böhler, challenged him back in England to the very core of his being about his faith in Christ. Working in and around Savannah, he failed as a missionary. His efforts to impose his rigorous vision of church life on a mixed bag of immigrants came to naught in the end. He fell in love with one of his parishioners, but like many a rural Irish bachelor, he dithered when it came to the time for commitment. When Sophia Hopkey married a rival, he barred her from Communion on flimsy grounds and landed himself before

the grand jury for misconduct. Protesting his innocence and accurately calculating his slim chances of a fair trial, he slipped out under cover of darkness and headed back to England in December 1737. He had been gone for twenty-two months. He came back a failure in love, in missionary service, and in his own search for a truly inward relation to God.

Turning Up the Heat

The year 1738 was a very important one for John Wesley, as it was for his brother Charles. The debate about what happened in that year remains intense, but the central development is secure. Wesley found an initial assurance of the love of God for himself. It took him years to reach a settled account of his spiritual experiences, but there can be no doubt that he caught fire within in his love for God. The human agent who more than anybody acted as a catalyst in this was Peter Böhler. He and Wesley started a religious society together in London called the Fetter Lane Society, so they had ample time to talk. Böhler introduced Wesley to a vision of the Christian life that put enormous emphasis on personal, inward certainty about forgiveness and victory over sin here and now. Böhler argued that it was possible to experience the love and power of God as something tangible, that one could enter into this experience instantaneously, and that it was imperative to do so. Wesley was reluctant to buy this spiritual package, but he checked it against Scripture, mulled it over, listened to pertinent witnesses, stuck to his spiritual routines as a good Anglican, and wandered off on occasion to find spiritual resources in other pastures.

In the midst of the challenge presented by Böhler, the penny finally dropped, and Wesley found himself catapulted into a new world of faith. His brother Charles had been converted three days earlier. On Sunday, May 24, after the regular morning service in St. Paul's Cathedral in London,

> In the evening I went very unwillingly to a society in Aldersgate Street, where one was reading Luther's preface to the Epistle to the Romans. About a quarter before nine, while he was describing the change which God works in the heart through faith in Christ, I felt my heart strangely warmed. I felt I did trust in Christ, Christ alone for salvation: And an assurance was given me, that he had taken away my sins, even mine, and saved me from the law of sin and death.[2]

Wesley had met God for himself. Yet we must be careful how we understand this experience. This encounter with God did not take place in a vacuum. It was integrally related to his coming to a much clearer account of the Reformation doctrine of justification by grace through faith in Jesus Christ. Rather than do all he could to be worthy of God's mercy, he discovered that true faith must be directed outward to the work God had done in Jesus Christ for the salvation of the world. Here Wesley moved from a notional to a real assent to theological proposals that were already incorporated into his intellectual hard drive. Wesley went back immediately and resurrected theological material on justification that was available in his own Anglican tradition in a set of normative sermons called the *Homilies*. The Aldersgate encounter with God was more than some sugary, pious experience; it was a profound spiritual and intellectual reorientation. At one and the same time, Wesley found assurance in his relationship to God, saw acquittal in the courts of God as the critical door to true holiness, and was flooded with zeal to share what he had discovered with others.

Since his days at Oxford in the 1730s, he had been experimenting with new ways of helping people find faith for themselves. His collaboration with Böhler led him to take a study tour of the Moravians in Germany. They refused to give him Communion, not really accepting him as a true believer. Even as he wobbled his way into his new spiritual world, he had a keen eye for effective innovation that would bring spiritual renewal within the boundaries of his Anglican heritage. At the same time, Wesley was fascinated by the reports coming from New England about the religious awakening in and around the ministry of Jonathan Edwards, a tough-minded intellectual who was taken aback by the work of the Holy Spirit operating through his tight, carefully constructed sermons. Thus, just as Wesley was sorting through his new encounter with God, he was also wrestling with how best to hold together the need for effective forms of new ministry with the mysterious presence of God in religious awakening.

Wesley was not alone in this journey toward God and effective evangelism. A friend from his Oxford days, George Whitefield, was much more radical in his readiness to innovate. Drawing on antecedents in Wales initiated by a remarkable layman named Howel Harris, Whitefield had taken to preaching in the open air. Called away from Bristol to Wales in March 1739, he asked Wesley to fill in. After casting lots, Wesley reluctantly launched forth. On Monday, April 2:

> At four in the afternoon, I submitted to be more vile, and proclaimed in the highways the glad tidings of salvation, speaking from a little eminence in a ground adjoining to the city, to about three thousand people. The scripture on which I spoke was this, (is it possible any one should be ignorant, that it is fulfilled in every true Minister of Christ?) "The Spirit of the Lord is upon me, because he hath anointed me to

preach the Gospel to the poor. He hath sent me to
heal the broken-hearted; to preach deliverance to the
captives, and recovery of sight to the blind: To set at
liberty them that are bruised, to proclaim the accept-
able year of the Lord."[3]

The thousands who heard clearly benefited from his
preaching, and Wesley was launched into a new phase of his
life and ministry. The rest of his life was spent in caring for
and organizing the people who found him to be an effective spiritual director, an inspiring leader, an effective
organizer, a calm but fearless preacher, and a clear and
astute thinker. His theological work was always related to
his primary vocation of evangelism and spiritual direction.
By 1739 he was beginning to reintegrate all that he had
learned and experienced into a new vision of the Christian
tradition. He shied away from speculative theological
divinity, yet when it came to the theological and spiritual
issues that mattered to him and his converts he was picky,
shrewd, and resolute. He is rightly remembered for his
genius as an administrator and organizer, but his practical
and institutional work was always informed by a knowledgeable theological intelligence. We can readily see the
interaction between theory and practice in his long span as
leader of the people called Methodists.

Birthing a Movement

The term "Methodist" was used at Oxford as a pejorative
label for the student society Wesley had led in the early
1730s. Wesley simply co-opted it and used it positively to
name the movement that emerged under his leadership.
Whatever its origins, it gave the right impression, for it sig-
naled a readiness to be methodical in all things spiritual.

11

Wesley accepted the people who responded to his preaching as he found them, and worked out a complex arrangement of practices to foster their quest for genuine faith. Central to his method of working was the gathering of seekers into societies, bands, select societies, and recovery units that were truly effective in providing informal spiritual direction among friends. These groups provided space to hear the gospel and to try it on for size. Wesley simply adapted the available models on offer or made up the rules as he went along. He learned early on the importance of listening to advice from every quarter. Despite this, he was a benign dictator in his leadership style. This combination of careful consultation, omnivorous reading, and independence of judgment served him well over the years.

For five long decades he traveled England, Ireland, and Scotland to secure the welfare of the people who voluntarily joined him in faith and service. Clearly Wesley developed and changed over that period. He liked to think of himself as staying consistently on tune, but this was due in part to a natural self-delusion and in part to the need to answer critics who accused him of changing his mind and not coming clean about it to the public.

In the 1740s and '50s Wesley skillfully spent his time preaching the gospel and developing the institutional resources required to serve the spiritual and material needs of the people who came to him for help. This was a period of organization, of mob persecution, of theological conflict, of intellectual self-defense, and of fundamental theological

consolidation. Rebutting the rule on not interfering in another priest's parish, Wesley claimed a special dispensation as an Oxford scholar to treat the world as his parish. When the issue of preaching outside parish boundaries arose in Bristol, he met with the brilliant Bishop Butler to talk things over; they parted with neither side yielding an inch. Wesley was more interested in reaching the fun-loving, malicious mobs than in adhering to the objections of a bishop who put good order before effective ministry. There was a certain arrogant cheek in Wesley's attitude.

There was also a degree of intellectual arrogance in his decision to go to war with George Whitefield over their differences about predestination. Wesley detested the view that God simply chose some unconditionally to salvation and others to damnation. Whether Whitefield held to this version of Calvinism is a matter of dispute. The encounter between the two of them reminds one of modern academics who want to be good friends with colleagues down the hall who disagree with them but whose intellectual certainty and self-satisfaction get the better of them in public. Thus, they publish their attacks, and they do what they can to make up afterward. Wesley's handling with his critics within the Anglican establishment was no less self-assured and relentless. He published a series of *Appeals to Men of Reason and Religion* in 1742 and 1743 that argued that he was not out of line with the tradition of the Church of England. Together with *The Principles of a Methodist Further Explained* (1745), *A Plain Account of the People Called Methodists* (1748), and various collections of sermons, these furnished the new movement with the theological concepts and background assumptions that were essential for long-term success.

As the interest in personal religion spread, various volunteers attached themselves to Wesley to lend a hand in his labors. Wesley gathered this crucial group of coworkers, carefully designated as "assistants," into "annual conferences," where they hammered out their ideas and practices. They divided the work into "circuits" and invented new services of worship. By the end of the 1740s the Methodists had their own meetings for preaching, exhorting, and singing. Charles Wesley supplied a priceless means of grace in his hymns, and lay preachers were trained to keep up with demand. Wesley took over a school, the Kingswood School, and developed a curriculum that was incredibly demanding both intellectually and spiritually.

Making Provision for the Sheep

By the early 1750s Wesley had already established an evangelical order within the Church of England. Ever keen to provide intellectual nurture for his leaders and people, he published *A Christian Library: Extracts and Abridgements* in fifty volumes between 1749 and 1755; these made available a body of useful theological materials that were sparsely used. On the domestic front he dithered once again in his love life. He was attracted to a young widow named Grace Murray, who was a fine coworker. His brother Charles impetuously stepped in and had her married off to a friend. John was a mere half-hour late for the ceremony. He recovered from this devastating blow, and on the rebound he made a disastrous choice of partner in Mrs. Molly Vazeille, a forty-one-year-old widow with French Huguenot connections. This required him to resign his Oxford fellowship in 1751, thus removing once and for all his fig-leaf defense of his preaching in other priest's parishes. The marriage was in time a disaster.

One of the reasons for Wesley's failure as a husband was his resolution to travel and take care of business. One item

of business was that of taking care of dividers and schismatics. Given the inevitable dissatisfaction of some of his new converts with the cold reception they got from the Anglican Church, it is not surprising that some wanted to break from the church and go it alone. Wesley was ruthless in his rejection of separation from the parent body. This was not the last time he would have to put his foot down with force on an issue that was to drive him to drastic action thirty years later. In 1758 he published *Reasons against Separation from the Church of England* in order to explain his foot stomping.

Given this internal tension, Wesley clearly needed not just ironclad discipline but also an accessible vision of the positive theology that governed the movement he was leading. A close brush with death no doubt concentrated his mind in this arena. While laid up sick he took to writing. In 1755 he published *Explanatory Notes upon the New Testament*, a small book that became with his *Sermons on Several Occasions* his own designated account of the essentials of true religion. In 1760 the fourth volume of his *Sermons on Several Occasions* was published. To this day these four volumes of sermons are required reading for all preachers in the homeland of Methodism.

Once this material was in place the domino effects were predictable. On the one hand, Wesley had to face down the internal critics who felt that his position was far too tame theologically. Interestingly, some of his critics within Methodism laid claim to have experienced dreams, impressions, visions, healings, and the like, phenomena that would show up in one stream of Wesley's grandchildren, the Pentecostals. In the early 1760s he was confronted with hotheads who thought that he had underestimated how holy we might become. Given the perfection they had attained, they were the only people who had access to the truth about God, so they drifted into separation. Given their perfect understanding, they also knew when Christ was coming back, so they moved into the prediction business. Wesley was amazingly tolerant of this nonsense, but in the end he sent them packing. He was convinced that there was the need of a lady's hand as well as a lion's heart. Ever the preacher with an eye to the occasion, he showed up in time to preach a sermon entitled "Prepare to Meet Thy God" to those who were awaiting Christ's return, perhaps in the hope that they would come to their senses. One of the hotheads, George Bell, was dragged off to jail for holding meetings in an unlicensed meetinghouse and later lost his faith. The other troublemaker, Thomas Maxfield, took about one hundred followers and went independent, but many of those who left came back to Methodism.

On the other hand, Wesley faced opposition from his Calvinist colleagues in the revival. For a time he was very keen to see a united front for renewal and reform. He sent out a call for union in 1764, hoping that all involved in the work of revival might find a way forward together. Three out of fifty replied to his letter. Some repudiated his overtures because he was interfering in their local parishes; others did so because they thought he was not sound theologically. His most important publications in this period, most notably *A Plain Account of Christian Perfection* (1766), did nothing to assuage their fears. Yet Wesley really did want to make a common front with the Calvinists, so much so that in 1768 he collaborated in the founding of Trevecka College in Wales. There were domestic problems in the college from the beginning, and the theological differences soon ended the collaboration. Twenty years later the college moved to Cambridge and was renamed

Cheshunt College. It was closed in 1969, and its assets were transferred to Westminster College, Cambridge.

One suspects that Wesley's intentions for unity with other leaders in revival were not advanced by his readiness to use Sarah Crosby back in 1761 as an "exhorter" but not as a preacher. This sounds like a distinction without a difference. One leading public intellectual of the day once described women preachers as akin to dogs walking on their hind legs. Nor was Wesley's cause likely to be helped by his experiments with a property deed in 1763, the year in which the *Sermons on Several Occasions* and *Explanatory Notes upon the New Testament* were officially adopted as doctrinal standards governing the practice of preaching. So while Wesley was working for unity, he was also consolidating the theological identity, the physical holdings, and the practices of his renewal movement. To many it must have appeared that he was building his own growing sect inside the church and that he was far too independent in his judgments to be reliable. Indeed, because of the large numbers coming to Communion, he had hired an obscure Eastern Orthodox bishop called Erasmus to ordain one of his preachers and assistants. This was surely bizarre in the extreme. In time he quietly abandoned this way of finding proper credentials and returned for the moment to the true and tried way of the Church of England.

In the end Wesley could not prevent matters coming to a head in his dispute with the Calvinists. He bent over backward to try and satisfy his Calvinist opponents, even to the point where he allowed that God might irresistibly bring some select, chosen souls to salvation. He tried to keep his mouth shut and hold off on disagreements. So long as George Whitefield was alive, there was hope that they could avoid theological warfare. However, Whitefield died on September 30, 1770, in Boston; Wesley delivered

19

a fine eulogy for him on November 18 in London. Opponents carped at Wesley's spin on Whitefield. A theological crash was waiting to happen; when the collision did come, neither side wanted to leave the scene of the accident.

All hell broke loose after the publication of the Conference *Minutes* of 1770, in which the Methodists openly spoke of good works as remotely or indirectly essential to salvation. The Calvinists interpreted this move as diluting the place of God's action in salvation. The debate, led on the Methodist side by John Fletcher of Madeley, lasted for most of the 1770s, and by the end of it the lines were drawn in the sand. Wesley's course was set. He would have no truck with Calvinism because it undercut the motivation for holiness in the Christian life and because it was contrary to his core conviction that the ruling attribute of God was uncompromising love for all. In 1778 he launched the *Arminian Magazine*. In time most of the protagonists in the war kissed and made up, but there was now no question of any kind of substantial union. Wesley would have liked the differences to be buried below a common commitment to Scripture and the official doctrines of the Anglican tradition, but both sides were too passionate about their take on the truth for this to count for much.

Putting the North Americans in Their Place

In the meantime Methodism grew like a weed, not least in the New World. It had been brought there by Irish Methodists as early as the 1760s, with English reinforcements sent in the early 1770s. Richard Boardman and Joseph Pilmore had gone to the work in North America in 1769, and the great future leader Francis Asbury had sailed in 1771. On July 14–16, 1773, the first Methodist Conference in America was held in Philadelphia. The American

War of Independence began in 1775, and the Declaration of Independence was signed on July 4, 1776. These latter developments sent shock waves throughout the whole church scene. The upshot for Methodists was that they were deprived of the sacraments, as most of the ordained clergy had fled for their lives.

This absence of the sacraments caused an acute practical headache for Wesley, for Methodism depended critically on the background resources supplied by the Anglican Church. Wesley valiantly tried to get the bishop of London to ordain some of Wesley's assistants, but the bishop refused. Wesley noted that the good bishop "did see good to ordain, and send into America, other persons, who knew something of Greek and Latin; but who knew no more of saving souls, than of catching whales."[4] It did not help that Wesley himself had little sympathy for the rebel cause in America. The danger of American Methodists taking

things into their own hands and inventing their own spiritual resources came to a climax in the early 1780s.

The year 1784 was a critical one. Wesley had to solve the acute pastoral and institutional problems with which he was faced. The outcome was a mess intellectually and theologically, but it was not a mess from a practical point of view. Wesley managed to provide effective mechanisms of survival and transitions for both England and North America. For the English side of the movement he enacted in law a "Deed of Declaration" that made the conference a legal body. He created the "Legal Hundred" preachers as the supreme legislative body that would rule once he was gone. We can well imagine the jockeying and jealousy this evoked in the scramble to be in that inner ring. Yet Wesley managed to keep Methodists inside the Church of England, if only in the short term.

For the American side of the movement, however, he did two things that make it clear that he was creating a new church. He ordained two of his assistants to perform the sacraments, and sent a third, Thomas Coke, to become with Francis Asbury a general superintendent. Charles Wesley had a theological fit when he found out; John had talked the matter over with a group of leaders at the conference in Leeds, but not with Charles. It did not help when Charles also discovered that Coke and Asbury had been designated "bishops" in America. Wesley also sent over to America a revised version of the *Book of Common Prayer*. Within this he cut back the Thirty-Nine Articles to twenty-four. By ordaining and by supplying his followers in North America with official doctrinal resources, he had crossed the line and invented a new Christian denomination.

John Wesley lived for another seven years. He soldiered on as an incurable workaholic, preaching right up to the point where he had to be propped up in the pulpit. His marriage had failed in the 1760s, a fact that could in part be concealed by his constant traveling. His wife died in 1781, and he did not make it to the funeral. His beloved brother Charles died in 1788. To the end he was working to fix the world, founding the Strangers' Friend Society in 1786 to help folk lost in the cities and pressing the case for the ending of slavery in a famous last letter to William Wilberforce in 1791. In 1786 he endorsed a plan for missionary work abroad, a practice he had earlier opposed because of lack of appropriate resources. In 1787 he welcomed Sarah Mallet into the connection as a preacher; she was the first officially sanctioned female preacher of Methodism.

John Wesley died on March 2, 1791, surrounded by devoted friends and nervous allies who made sure that there was a clear record of his last words and wishes. Nobody wanted any fiddling with the arrangements that were already in place for the future of Methodism. He was buried in City Road Chapel, London, the Vatican of Methodism, on March 10. From the age of thirty-six he had traveled 225,000 miles and preached more than 40,000 sermons, some to more than 20,000 people. Now at last his work on this earth was done; he would no longer be on the road again.

CHAPTER TWO

Background Music

Dislodging the Standard Picture

John Wesley's life was one of tumult and extraordinary achievement. Setting out to fix the church he loved, he founded a renewal movement that eventually became the many branches of Methodism. Given the image of Wesley as a great organizer and spiritual leader, it is easy to dismiss him as a minor theological figure. He is small fry compared to other great theologians of the past. Wesley certainly is different from the standard theologian who sets out to provide a systematic ordering of Christian teaching. If we judge him by that standard, he does not fare very well. For that reason he has won a hearing not as a systematic theologian but as a folk theologian, a theologian for the common people.

Our concern, however, is to give him his due rather than worry about his place in history. If we are to be fair to his work, we need to undertake two things at this stage. First, we should take careful note of the wider context within which he operated. Much recent work on Wesley has been misleading at this point. As a result, the general tenor of Wesley's theology has been misread, and the very particular concerns he developed have been misunderstood. If we fail to get the background music right, we tend to mishear Wesley's very singular tunes. Second, we should note the theological watersheds in this career as a whole. Here we go beyond the overall story of his life we have already charted and identify those moments that display his deepest theological concerns and interests. We shall see that these fit nicely with the bigger background picture.

At the outset we need to dislodge the standard background story. The standard story of the background to Wesley runs like this. Wesley shows up, we are told, in history at a time known as the Enlightenment in modern Europe. The great intellectuals of the day had gradually been throwing aside the system of authority that had been so central in the Middle Ages. This process of liberation had started with the Reformation when Martin Luther and John Calvin broke from the Roman Catholic Church. They created intellectual and political space for freedom of conscience, and thus paved the way for the ultimate break with Christian culture. It is this break with the Christian past that brings us into the springtime of light after the long winter of darkness and corruption. Without fully realizing what they were doing, the great Reformers were digging their own grave. They set in motion a process of revision

that ultimately undermined their own foundations. As a result, we are now committed in the West to reason over against revelation, to doubt over against faith, to freedom of thought over against authority, to experience over against tradition, to tolerance over against coercion, to individual conviction over against community coercion, and to science over against theology. At the core of modernity is this conviction: We will now no longer be afraid to think for ourselves, and nobody will ever again tell us what to think or do. It is this revolution, it is said, that was well under way in the eighteenth century and that provides the pivotal background to Wesley.

Set against this backcloth, Wesley is often seen in the following way. He is the great exponent of personal religion, staying the course until he finds God for himself at the famous Aldersgate meeting. He is the mighty champion of creative innovation, breaking from the shackles of his Anglican tradition to reach out to those who are trampled aside by the established religion. While he reads voraciously and is fascinated by past history, he thinks for himself, writing in clear prose and with assured self-confidence. Whenever there is a choice between the demands of the political status quo and the needs of the poor and marginalized, he always sides with the latter, taking on the big battalions of business and vested interest. At heart he is a man of reason and experience, thus lining up with John Locke in philosophy and finding a way to express the Christian faith in a manner that is up to speed with the latest in the world of learning. While he is a traditionalist in his leanings in worship, he recognizes that fashions change, and that it is, therefore, urgent to make innovations in worship and evangelism. He is a whirlwind of energy, organizing self-help programs that meet the needs of the hour and providing structures that foster native leadership and cross-generational efficiency.

To be sure, we have to temper our enthusiasm a tad if we buy this picture of Wesley. He believes in ghosts and miracles. Politically he is a great champion of the marriage of throne, altar, and parliament. He is naive at times, too readily resorting to the casting of lots to decide issues and to putting his finger randomly in his Bible to look for direct guidance. Deep down he is a dictator when it comes to the final decisions that have to be made. And when it suits him he is reckless in destroying the good order of the church. However, what more can we expect from someone who is caught in the middle of the intellectual, spiritual, and political revolution we call modernity? Whatever Wesley's faults and weaknesses, he is on the side of the angels. He is the champion of liberty, freedom, tolerance, conscience, experience, and reason.

Somewhere between the sixteenth and twentieth centuries there was a massive revolution in the Western world. Whether we call this revolution the arrival of modernity or the Enlightenment, it happened, and there is no turning back the clock. However, we need to keep our wits about us in charting this change and in marking the timetable involved. Once we change the timetable, we change our picture of Wesley as well. The crucial facts to bear in mind as we read Wesley are as follows.

Official Doctrines Everywhere

First, Wesley lived in a world where there was a confessional state. To be a political somebody or to get anywhere in the English society of the eighteenth century one had to believe in the Trinity and effectively be part of the Anglican establishment. In reality, English theologians and politicians had co-opted the Enlightenment themes of reason and experience and used them to bolster the status quo at its foundations. This is not at all surprising, for they had seen the disastrous effects of bloody revolution in the seventeenth century. They had seen their king murdered and the country taken over by a group of Puritan fanatics. In the 1660s the monarchy was restored, the Anglican establishment was reconstructed, and the Puritans were put in their place. In the 1690s England went through a further political crisis, this time from the forces of Catholicism, and its leaders had sent them off to France by installing a stout Protestant king in William of Orange. Hence, from hard experience the powers that be had hammered out a theological vision of the state that required creedal subscription as the entry fee. To express the matter graphically, you could operate in politics only if you were theologically house trained. Puritans and Catholics had shown themselves unstable, violent, and unreliable; the only cure for this was not some secular state but a state that was theologically confessional and that laid down minimal theological commitments. You had to sign

on to the doctrine of the Trinity to make it in court and Parliament.

Second, there was also a sign-on fee for making it in the church, namely, accepting the official practices and beliefs of the Church of England. The beliefs were spelled out in a list of Thirty-Nine Articles that every priest had to accept by way of an oath of office. To be sure, enforcement was sometimes lax. Moreover, members of the clergy could always sign on with mental reservations, and who but God could know what they really believed in their heart of hearts? Yet the commitment to the Thirty-Nine Articles was deadly serious.

The proof of such seriousness takes us to a third consideration. In the late 1830s, John Henry Newman, the greatest English theologian of his day, was put on trial at Oxford University for arguing that the Thirty-Nine Articles could be interpreted in such a way as to be consistent with the teaching of the Roman Catholic Church. In the end he got off on technicalities, but his prosecutors were big-time academics, and they were deadly serious in their opposition. Thirty years later, brilliant young priests who had prestigious university positions were resigning their posts because they could no longer subscribe to the official creed of the Anglican Church. This was a hundred years after Wesley. In his day, Wesley lived and died in a church that had very clear and enforceable standards of doctrine. He worked in the pay of a church that was unashamedly confessional in ethos and practice. This same church was in charge of the only universities of the day, at Oxford and Cambridge. Hence, Wesley was the product of a university system that was shamelessly confessional in orientation.

Fourth, Wesley's day was profoundly Christian in its intellectual orientation. The picture of a freewheeling, secular world driven by science and reason and led by noble skeptics and unbelievers is simply false. On the contrary, a network of intellectual heavyweights, who had routed the opposition, had championed the Christian faith in the public arena with great skill and success. The challenge to orthodoxy had come at the highest levels of English society in the late seventeenth century. A network of brilliant anti-Trinitarian thinkers had called into question the doctrines of the incarnation and the Trinity. Among the opponents of Christian orthodoxy were figures as famous as John Locke and Sir Isaac Newton. Interestingly, these thinkers were very conservative in that they held a high view of Scripture and spent years poring over the text of the Bible to find the truth. In time they rejected the Trinity and became Deists, or, like Locke, they stayed indoors and kept their mouths shut. The threat they posed to the Church of England was massive. Yet they were met by a small army of Christian intellectuals who effectively routed them in the debate. Chief among them was Bishop Joseph Butler, whose *Analogy of Religion* showed that precisely the objections lodged against Christian orthodoxy could also be lodged against the scaled-down theology of their opponents. Thus, the critics of the faith of the Church of England either had to move further down the road into atheism or come back into the safe haven of orthodoxy. The critics stood their ground, but they were now placed between a rock and a hard place. Butler and his cohorts of defenders effectively protected the grand fort of orthodoxy in the public square.

It was this world of faith that Wesley inhabited. He was supported at every level in his work. The state, the church, the universities, and the intellectual giants of his day supplied him with a network of ideas and practices without which he would have been hopelessly handicapped. Wesley himself rarely saw this; like most reformers and renewalists

he had a keener eye for what was wrong than for what was right. He was so preoccupied with the problems of dry rot in the pulpit that he forgot how good the foundations were. He was so worried about the broken arms of his patients that he ignored how well they had already learned to walk. He was so busy adding new trains to the railway company and getting them to run on time that he overlooked his deep dependence on the network of track and railway stations that dotted the countryside. He was so taken with his piccolo trumpet and the tune he was playing that he disregarded the steady beat of the big drum at the back of the orchestra. Wesley's life and thought depended critically on the commitments of the state, the requirements of the Church of England, the theological presuppositions of university life, and the effectiveness of the intellectual work done by a host of scholars and writers. His genius was to note that these in themselves were not enough to secure the spiritual welfare of people. The church also needed to be an effective tutor in the spiritual life of its people; it needed to find ways whereby the love of God might find a way into the hearts and lives of its members. This is where Wesley pitched his tent and went to work.

Five Watersheds in Wesley's Intellectual Journey

It helps at this point to return to Wesley's life and look at it afresh from a different angle. We can readily identify five distinct theological watersheds in his career. The first took place in and around 1725 when he developed a passion for holiness. In the reading of theologians such as Jeremy Taylor and William Law, Wesley became convinced that holiness of heart and life is the heartbeat of Christianity. He was attracted by a vision of the gospel that put a premium

on personal transformation. Christianity, in this view, is inescapably inward and spiritual. The gospel changes people from the inside out and turns the world the right way up. Until his dying day this remained the theme song of Wesley's life and ministry. It launched Wesley into ordination and into a restless quest for authentic spirituality.

The second watershed was his experience at Aldersgate in 1738. Having been immersed in the Anglican tradition of his day, Wesley rediscovered the explosive effects of the doctrine of justification as taught by the Reformers. More particularly, he realized that there could be no deep growth in holiness if the problem of his own guilt and failure was not addressed in a radical fashion. This problem could not be put right by a benign combination of faith and works, the position he had tried to live out as best he could. Without forgiveness and pardon there was no way to be set free from the bondage of the past; liberty to become all that God wants us to be is not possible until we have been delivered from the burden of the past. The rediscovery of the doctrine of justification by grace through faith brought the relief he sought in this arena.

This liberating intellectual discovery was accompanied by a radically new theological insight that was mediated to him by his Moravian friends and that was not readily available within the Anglican fold. Faith was not just a bare assent to abstract theological notions, nor was it just a reliable trust in Jesus Christ dying for one's sins; faith was also a direct, experiential encounter with God through the Holy Spirit that brought awareness of the love of God in one's heart and released new moral energy to gain real victory over evil here and now. On this front Wesley stumbled into the doctrine of assurance through the internal working of the Holy Spirit in his heart. More importantly, he came to experience the love of God for himself; there was now a fire within that burned up the former sense of failure and fueled a new sense of God. He could now resume his former missionary labors with a new perspective and with a new flow of boundless energy.

The third theological watershed occurred in the year 1764. It is marked by the adoption of his *Sermons on Several Occasions* and *Explanatory Notes upon the New Testament* as the official doctrines of the movement he founded to form people in the faith. In these documents, Wesley put before the public the essentials of true religion as he saw them. While he continued to write sermons and to publish a vast array of materials, the *Sermons on Several Occasions* and the *Explanatory Notes upon the New Testament* remain landmark documents in understanding the core of his theology. To be sure, as historians it is important that we see the whole sweep of Wesley's writings across his lifetime. Even when we read the individual sermons in the *Sermons on Several Occasions,* it is wise to note where he shifted and turned over time. But it is a radical mistake to overlook the fact that Wesley identified a select body of texts that captured the core of his theology. Wesley was first and foremost an evangelist and spiritual director. He realized that there was no way ordinary folk could master everything he wrote. His target audience needed a meaty summary of critical issues that they could work through in a finite period of time. A set of sermons and a commentary fit this need very nicely, for they directed the reader to the fountainhead of Scripture and could be digested in sections and mulled over at will.

The focus of Wesley's self-chosen, canonical writings is obvious—namely, the quest for God, or better, God's relentless quest for lost souls. Wesley's clear concern was to help people be formed in the faith. He explained the crucial concepts needed and the pivotal doctrines that have to be understood. He provided relevant psychologi-

cal insight and commentary so that people could chart where they were on the journey of faith. He cleared up objections and undermined the intellectual charm of attractive but fatal alternatives. He described the moral content of the faith and the behavior that is appropriate. He outlined the proper relationship between law and gospel, between faith and works, between predestination and free will, and between justification and sanctification. Knowing that we all sin differently, he dealt head on with precisely the kind of temptation that befell those who were under his care.

His style is strong and sensitive, clear and efficiently organized. He warns, and cajoles, and persuades, and exhorts, and goads, and argues, and threatens. At times he plays the logician and lawyer, trapping and drawing the reader into the path to follow. At other times he plays the lover and friend, tenderly leading the stammering convert to a fine dinner on her first date. At other times he plays the army general, mobilizing his movement to reform the nation, especially the church, and to spread scriptural holiness throughout the land. To the end he was a father in God, helping his spiritual children and colleagues stay the course and keep the fire of love burning forever.

The fourth theological watershed was the publication of the *Conference Minutes* of 1770. In this material Wesley set the record straight with his Calvinist critics. On the one hand, he refused to shy away from good works as central in salvation. Any mention of the term "salvation by works" was totally unacceptable to the staunch Protestants of the day. On the surface, talk of salvation by works called into question the depth of sin in the human agent, undermined the sufficiency of the work of Christ, and seemed to open the door to schemes of merit in the sight of God. For Wesley, if salvation included holiness, then works were in some

sense essential. Thus, his bedrock commitment to moral transformation made an emphasis on works inevitable.

On the other hand, Wesley felt that the denial of good works was fueled by a vision of predestination that was disastrous at every turn. The standard Calvinist doctrine of predestination left next to no room for genuine human agency; thus, to insist on good works on the human side poked a gaping hole in its foundations. For his part, Wesley thought that predestination, unless properly understood, was a form of blasphemy because it cast a terrible shadow over the love of God for the whole world. Thus, his favorable attitude to good works was the positive expression of his resolute opposition to the Calvinist vision of predestination. Behind both of these ideas was a vision of God as unsurpassed grace, generosity, and goodness that was central to his conception of the gospel. God loved every single human creature he had made, and through grace every human agent could experience the washing away of their sins and come to live the love of God in the world. Hence, the publication of the controversial minutes of 1770 stands out in his public career as a landmark moment.

The fifth and last theological watershed year was 1784 and is marked by Wesley's decision to provide for the launching of a new church in North America. This decision stands in line with Wesley's primary commitment to the spiritual welfare of his people. He could not bear to see his sheep wandering in the open field without proper pastures, shepherds, and boundary markers. However, what matters here is not just the radical move to start a new denomination but the theological provision he put in place for its future welfare. The crucial element in his decision was the provision of a set of robust articles of religion that were to serve as the foundation doctrines of the new church. Wesley makes it abundantly clear that he was committed to the classical faith of the church as developed within the Anglican tradition.

The twenty-four articles sent over by Wesley were a revision of the Thirty-Nine Articles of Religion adopted by the Church of England. They contained the deep faith of the church as hammered out in the early centuries and updated at the Reformation. As we have seen, this material was critical background music for Wesley's own journey of faith. The Anglican articles provided the crucial context for the reception of his distinctive vision of the Christian life as expressed in his *Sermons on Several Occasions* and *Explanatory Notes upon the New Testament.* Thus, Wesley operated within the Trinitarian and incarnational faith of the church as a whole. If this material is elbowed aside, then all we have is a hopelessly reduced vision of the Christian faith. Even though Wesley's way of expressing himself some-times suggested otherwise, the decision of 1784 high-lights that Wesley had no intention of jettisoning the classical faith of the church. There is indeed a problem here; one can legitimately wonder if the great faith of the church was beginning to idle. However, what matters at this stage is that we see the bigger picture: Wesley lodged his distinctive contribution to theology within the con-tours of Christian orthodoxy.

Wesley the Evangelist and Spiritual Director

Two interrelated points suffice at this juncture. First, for the most part I will take the wider classical faith of the church as a given in what follows. To be sure, I will bring it up from time to time. I will indicate how Wesley relies on the great Christian narrative of creation, fall, and redemption. I will make mention of the doctrine of the Trinity, in which God is understood as three persons in one substance. I will draw attention where appropriate to Wesley's conviction that Jesus Christ is fully human and fully divine. I will set forth, as required, various ideas about how Christ atones for the sins of the world. The fact of the matter is that Wesley has nothing radically fresh or new to say on these issues. His strengths and insights lie elsewhere, that is, in theological materials he puts in place for his work as an evangelist and spiritual director.

Second, the primary source for the exposition that follows is *Sermons on Several Occasions*. These sermons are worthy of sustained attention because they represent Wesley's own choice of materials and constitute what he considered to be the essentials of true religion; they are what we might call the canonical sermons of Wesley. (I will bring in other material to clarify the wider horizon within which Wesley operated.) There is, in fact, an interesting inner logic to the *Sermons on Several Occasions*. They flow naturally from an early batch of sermons dealing with becoming a Christian, to a middle batch that deals with the Sermon on the Mount and lays out the content of the Christian life, to a last batch that picks up a rag bag of issues that arise precisely for those on the journey of salvation that Wesley so assiduously tried to unpack and make practically possible. In what follows I shall follow this general pattern of thought, but I shall pause and explore other proposals in Wesley that make sense of the crucial theological topics that he covers in this ordering of business.

Where does all this leave us in our general understanding of Wesley? Wesley was more a medieval theologian than he was a modern one. He inherited the robust Trinitarian faith that had been worked out in the early centuries of the church. He held a very high view of the sacraments. He believed in special revelation, and he was immersed in the Scriptures, using them as a kind of second language with ease. He was convinced that the Anglican Church had recovered the faith of the Fathers of the church, so that the Reformation was not a fresh start but a course correction. He lived in the world of the ancient church prior to the fourth century and was entirely comfortable there. His commitment to reason and experience makes him look as if he were a member of the Enlightenment fringe, but in reality this rationalist and empiricist streak was nothing new in the history of the church. The medieval theologians were brilliant logicians, and their commitment to reason and experience was without apology. Wesley, in fact, much preferred Aristotle's vision of experience to the one worked out by John Locke. In all he was a traditionalist, committed to the ancient doctrines and ways of the church.

What makes him different and unique was his search for the reality of God inside this inherited world. Here he reminds us of St. Bernard, St. Francis, St. Teresa of Avila, and even of Martin Luther. His theological abilities were bent toward working out a complex doctrine of the spiritual life. Here he was unashamedly supernaturalistic in his orientation. He believed in God as an ever-active agent drawing and working to bring the hurting, rebellious, sinful world back to its origin and destiny. He was a Catholic pietist with a bent toward the Pentecostal and with a passion for the poor and the needy. Because he was theologi-

cally conservative, he was a revolutionary in his ministry; he challenged the nominalism and complacency that are the sins of all establishments not with a liberal revisionism but by a radical retrieval of lost ideas and practices. He passionately and stubbornly believed that the whole of human existence should be brought immediately into line with God's will for creation. What God had required, God makes possible here and now, this very moment. Hence, he was intoxicated with a persistent optimism that kept him working day and night for the arrival of the kingdom of God.

What makes Wesley important for our day is precisely this combination of ancient commitment and present passion. His greatest strength was to put his finger on where people were hurting spiritually, take their pulse, and then set about connecting them to the God and Father of our Lord Jesus Christ through the agency of the Holy Spirit. He stumbled into a living faith in God, and then spent the rest of his life sorting through what this meant and sharing it with others.

Even with his faults and foibles, he provides a fine point of entry into the study of theology. He shows that theology is about God and his coming to us in Christ through the power of the Holy Spirit. We get up from our reading knowing that the claims advanced within theology can break our hearts in love for God and neighbor. In mulling over his proposals we sense in our bones that doing theology is both exhilarating and risky. We find our intellects reeling with a beauty and a disorientation that drives us forward in the quest for a clarity that is never complete. We are fortunate to be able to sit at his feet and watch his mind at work.

CHAPTER THREE

Life Is Nearly as Bad as You Thought It Was

Creation

John Wesley's distinctive and central theological concerns are housed very firmly inside the classical Christian tradition. Thus, he is unashamedly committed to the grand Christian narrative of creation, fall, and redemption, and he resolutely reads this narrative as centering on the agency of the triune God of Father, Son, and Holy Spirit. Wesley has little that is original to say on these topics. His interest lies in finding ways to connect ordinary people to this narrative and to the triune God so that God's purposes for human life get worked out to the full. The heart of his thinking is focused on getting into the kingdom of God, staying there, and making full use of the resources God has placed within it.

We might think of Wesley's theology as designed to help folk to come to God and then to grow up and become mature, functioning adults. The seekers have already had a tour of the household of faith; what they now need is to connect with the owner and find out their place in the scheme of things. More precisely, without being aware of it, the seekers have actually arrived in a hospital for terminally ill patients. They have perhaps been wandering around its wards and buildings, they have gotten to know some of the staff and even read some of the medical textbooks, but they have never really noticed that they themselves are terminally ill. Wesley's concern is to help patients come to terms with their illness and find a cure that really works.

Wesley, of course, sees the world as created by a God who is eternal, omnipresent, omniscient, and holy. Furthermore, God is totally wise, just in his dealings with the world, and altogether loving. And God is the sovereign governor of the whole universe. This is no teddy bear deity; this is not some human construct invented to suit our partisan interests and desires; this is a God who is a robust active agent. Hence, God has a definite hand in everything that happens; God both creates and preserves everything that exists. Human agents inhabit a spiritual and natural environment, which is designed by God for them, and which is a fitting place within which they can flourish and be deeply satisfied.

To be a human agent is glorious and wonderful. We are not simply complex configurations of matter with sophisticated computers at the top end; we are not merely the apex of some grand evolutionary scheme, beasts dressed up in fancy clothes and headed to market; we are not helpless patients knocked around by impersonal forces of chance and necessity. God has made us and sustains us with an

innate principle of self-motion; we are genuine personal agents, who can make real decisions, and who can know, love, and obey God. More specifically, we are made in God's image, an incorruptible picture of the glory of God. We are made, says Wesley,

> not barely in his natural image, a picture of his own immortality; a spiritual being, endued with understanding, freedom of will, and various affections;— nor merely in his political image, the governor of this lower world, having "dominion over the fishes of the sea, and over all the earth;"—but chiefly in his moral image; which, according to the Apostle, is "righteousness and true holiness." (Eph. iv. 24)[1]

Thus, God made human agents to a very specific design plan. Expressed differently, we were created for love:

> "God is love:" accordingly, man at his creation was full of love; which was the sole principle of all his

tempers, thoughts, words, and actions. God is full of justice, mercy, and truth; so was man as he came from the hands of his Creator. God is spotless purity; and so man was in the beginning pure from every sinful blot.[2]

The Human Predicament

Tragically, human beings have fallen from this exalted state. Originally given genuine freedom, we have abused this freedom, and as a result we have tumbled into a network of disastrous consequences. We suffer from the effects of original and ongoing sin in our lives. Wesley uses a wealth of images to depict our predicament. He speaks in terms of debt, bondage, and disease:

> Indeed we are already bound hand and foot by the chains of our own sins. These, considered with regard to ourselves, are chains of iron and fetters of brass. They are wounds wherewith the world, the flesh, and the devil, have gashed and mangled us all over. They are diseases that drink up our blood and spirits, that bring us down to the chambers of the grave. But considered, as they are here, with regard to God, they are debts, immense and numberless. Well, therefore, seeing we have nothing to pay, may we cry unto him that he would "frankly forgive" us all.[3]

This infection of our nature is manifest in the particular sins that we see all around us. We invent all sorts of theories about ourselves to hide the truth from sight. Our blindness, our deep failure in understanding the truth about the world and ourselves, reaps a bountiful harvest of evils. We see ourselves as the masters and mistresses of the universe; we are proud and egocentric to the core. We strut around looking for approval; we resist the authority of God over our lives; we are riddled with pride of heart, self-will, and love of the world. Given our rejection of God, we are caught in a network of particular evils that naturally arise from our pride:

> From this evil fountain flow forth the bitter streams of vanity, thirst of praise, ambition, covetousness, the lust of the flesh, the lust of the eye, and the pride of life. From this arise anger, hatred, malice, revenge, envy, jealousy, evil surmisings: From this, all the foolish and hurtful lusts that now "pierce thee through with many sorrows," and, if not timely prevented, will at length drown thy soul in everlasting perdition.[4]

The intellectual effects of sin are especially devastating. We like to think of ourselves as free, generous, upstanding moral agents; we like to congratulate ourselves on our

wisdom and goodness. If we are educated, we think of ourselves as reasonable, sophisticated, and untouched by vulgarity and prejudice; we pride ourselves on rising above superstition, prejudice, and credulity. In reality we are blind to the truth about God, the world, and ourselves.

Wesley is unrelenting in his depiction of the sinfulness of human situation. In spelling out his vision he deploys the traditional account of the disobedience of Adam and Eve in the garden of Eden. He clearly takes this material in Genesis literally. However, he effectively uses this narrative to lay bare the root cause of evil in the world, so for the moment we should not worry overmuch that Wesley speaks from within his live intellectual options. The story in Genesis of the creation and fall is not just an ancient story for him; it provides a causal account of the origin of evil in the universe. What Wesley is seeking is a vigorous analysis of what has gone wrong. He sees in the first parents of the human race a fall into corruption and decadence that cannot be put right by human agency. Even the natural evils that arise in creation are the just punishment of our rebellion against God. If there had been no fall into sin, there would be no nasty animals or dangerous quicksands; humans would have lived in harmony with God, with each other, and with their environment. Given our rebellion, the whole world is shot through with misery, disease, and suffering.

This grim picture of the world is pivotal in Wesley's theology as a whole. He considered the doctrine to be central in what is called "the analogy of faith." The analogy of faith, that is, the central teachings of Christianity, is for Wesley the sense of Scripture as a whole. So the doctrine of sin is one of the fundamental doctrines of the Bible, and hence of the very essence of Christianity. Indeed, he makes the doctrine of original sin an element in the very defini-

tion of Christianity. Deny it, and you are but a heathen still. Furthermore, Wesley is convinced that it is only by recognizing the depth of human sin that we can fully grasp how deep God's love and grace are. We have a deeper realization of God's commitment to us precisely because of the lengths to which God goes in saving the world.

Clearly, Wesley presents a very forbidding vision of ourselves. Yet this is not the last word for Wesley. The bad news is that we are in bondage to our own self-inflicted ignorance and evil; the good news is that God has already come to meet us to begin repairing the damage. God does this generously as a matter of unconditional grace without our asking for help. God has moved in "prevenient" grace, in the grace that comes before the actual deep healing made available in Christ through the Holy Spirit, to enable us to see our current predicament and to take the first steps toward recovery. In other words, God has stepped into everyone's inner life to help us see what is wrong with us and to awaken us to a positive response to the further saving grace that God is only too ready to make available to us. This "prevenient" work of God is universal, and it is irresistible.

Consider an analogy. In Wesley's way of thinking we are all like alcoholics. We are addicted to self-destructive ways of thinking and behaving. The only way out of our addiction is to recognize that we are in bondage and to form the initial desire to go and get help. However, the fateful problem for many alcoholics is that they cannot recognize how grim things are, and are unable to form the desire to go and get the necessary help; thus, they stumble along from drinking bout to drinking bout, still thinking that they are fine, and that they can take care of things. The initial breakthrough happens when they see that they cannot get out of the addiction on their own, and when they form that first faltering intention to get help. So the first step to health is a reordering of our understanding. The will, the emotions, the inner machinery of human existence are all affected by our vision of ourselves and the world.

Notice that on this reading of our situation we can well think of ourselves as free. Thus, the alcoholic can decide whether to drink Russian vodka, or Irish whiskey, or Australian wine, or American beer. The alcoholic is not an inert machine; there is an inward principle of self-motion at work, and real choices can be made. The problem is that the choices are set in a context of bondage to alcohol, so at a deeper level there is no freedom at all; the alcoholic is bound by his addiction to alcohol. It is likewise with sin. Within a life of sin we can exercise our free will. We can decide whether to express our jealousy by making a cutting remark or by a stony silence; we can punch our enemy in the teeth or kick him in the shins. So the initial problem is how to get through to that deeper level so that we recognize our problem and form the initial desire to go and get help.

Grace Is at Hand

Prevenient grace is the initial help God gives to everyone to see how grim things are and to form the first intention to get help. This grace is given to all universally and irresistibly:

> With regard to . . . irresistible grace, I believe, that the grace which brings faith, and thereby salvation into the soul, is irresistible at that moment: that most believers may remember some time when God did irresistibly convince them of sin: that most believers do, at some other times, find God irresistibly acting upon their souls: yet I believe that the grace of God, both before and after those moments, may be, and hath been, resisted: and that, in general, it does not act irresistibly; but we may comply therewith, or may not: and I do not deny, that, in some souls, the grace

of God is so far irresistible, that they cannot but believe and be finally saved. [5]

There is an air of artificiality about this way of thinking. Everybody inherits the disease of sin, but God immediately injects a small dose of prevenient grace, say, in conscience, to enable us to see and turn to God for help. Hence, there are in reality no real sinners; we have all already started out on the road to recovery. Things are not really as bad as we thought they were.

At this point it is crucial to see why Wesley and the Western tradition he inherited developed the notion of "prevenient" grace. Wesley is trying to solve an old problem in theology, the problem of freedom and grace. Given that human agents are thoroughly depraved, the theologian is faced with a dilemma. She needs to hold at one and the same time the following conflicting convictions:

1. Human agents are stuck in sin, unable to heal themselves.
2. God alone heals and saves.
3. Human agents can claim no credit or merit in their healing.
4. Human agents are genuinely free and thus responsible for their situation if they are not saved.

The problem is this: How do we hold to the fourth and last point if we also hold to the first three? Wesley attempts to relieve the pain in the brain by claiming that God intervenes in everyone's life, giving them the grace that empowers them to say yes to his healing work in Christ.

Consider our options here. We can modify our doctrine of sin and simply insist that things are not quite as bad as Wesley says they are. Wesley refused this option. He was utterly convinced of the depravity and corruption of human

beings. We can modify our vision of grace, attributing some of the healing to God and some to ourselves. Wesley refused this option too. Given how bad things are, only God can save us. We can salvage human responsibility by allowing human agents the power to say yes to God's saving action. Wesley refused this option also. If we are able to recognize our predicament and make the first move to go to God and get help, then we have not really hit rock bottom in sin; we have really denied the depth of the problem. Furthermore, if we can see the truth about ourselves and turn to God, then we have in some sense saved ourselves; we have added our ounce of action to our salvation, and we can then take some credit, however little, for our salvation. In taking credit we say that salvation is not really a matter of grace all the way to the bottom; we have to hold back on giving God the full credit for our salvation, and we can boast, however minimally, of what we have done to save ourselves. Wesley refuses to go down that road. Yet another solution is to say that God gives his prevenient grace to a select few and leaves the rest to stew in their sins. Wesley refused this option as well. It makes God look like an arbitrary tyrant who doles out grace to the few and lets the rest go their own merry way to hell.

What Wesley proposes is that God gives prevenient grace to all. Thus, Wesley makes God the empowering agent behind the recognition of our predicament and behind our first desire to seek the good. If we now fail to be healed, it is because we have refused the offer of God's further help in salvation. Thus, Wesley thinks he has been able to keep afloat four distinct ideas: a radical doctrine of sin, salvation through grace alone, giving all the credit to God for salvation, and human responsibility if we fail to gain salvation. So rather than in any way modifying the standard Western vision of sin, Wesley insists that the first moves back to sanity and health are, as it were, entirely the work of God. For this to work, the prevenient grace of God must indeed be universal and irresistible.

Getting the Balance Right

Frankly, ingenious and original as this solution is, I find it less than compelling. The critical problem is that Wesley is caught in a nest of confusion about the nature of causation that traps him in a set of false alternatives. Sorting through this cannot be undertaken in this work. It is enough at this stage to say that Wesley (or any other theologian) cannot deny the role of human agents in accepting the offer of salvation. Believers accept Christ; God does not do this for them. So some element of genuine human action is absolutely essential in salvation. As we shall see later, Wesley cannot avoid this move, and it eventually surfaces in his claim that works are remotely and indirectly necessary for salvation. His critics were exactly right to pounce on his position. There are other problems to be noted as well.

First, Wesley has misread the place of any doctrine of sin in the Christian tradition. A doctrine of sin, crucial though it is in a comprehensive theology, simply does not have the kind of definitional or creedal status that he gives it. The "analogy of faith" is not the general sense of Scripture, nor does the analogy of faith involve a doctrine of sin. The analogy of faith was the Trinitarian faith of the church that was hammered out over time and formally adopted in the Nicene Creed. Wesley has totally altered the inner content of Christianity in shifting to sin and salvation as the core of

Christian doctrine. Moreover, the Nicene Creed treats the topic of sin indirectly as subordinate to the deep truths of faith that are laid out in Trinitarian form. Wesley has replaced this canonical creed with his own minicreed; he has relocated the center of gravity of the faith in a foundational vision of sin and evil.

Second, while Wesley gives a secondary place to pride in his analysis of sin, he still overplays the place of pride in unpacking the idea of sin. Feminists and others have rightly pondered whether this move ignores other ways of rejecting our creaturely status. More particularly, they rightly insist that we can reject our creaturely status by accepting demeaning views of ourselves as doormats and victims who refuse to claim our dignity as made in the image of God. Pride is one way to reject the work of God in creation; cowering in the corner as victims is another. Clearly, if we focus on pride at the expense of the latter, we will only drive some people deeper into bondage. They will never get out of the corner, give up whining about being victims, and get to stand on their own feet as genuine agents. Pounding on about pride will destroy what little sense of agency they already possess. Hence, we need a much richer and better-rounded vision of sin than Wesley provides. Even then we all can benefit by retrieving the primary place he gives to understanding in sin and salvation.

Having lodged our worries, it is important to come back to the core of Wesley's vision. Wesley's general sense of the depth of human evil remains very attractive. Sin is a crucial theological concept, and we cannot dispense with it without shedding theological tears. We need to continue to ponder the Western tradition precisely because it challenges our reluctance to come to terms with human evil in all its pervasive intensity. Wesley calls into question the tendency to shy away from realistic conceptions of the human

situation and opt for generic, pious platitudes about the love of God that accepts us as we are. Equally, Wesley's robust vision of sin challenges all efforts to locate our problems in the social and the political. Moreover, there is something deeply insightful in Wesley's claim that sin has exposed the riches of God's love and mercy. Paradoxically, it is only as we deal with sin that we catch the full depths of God's grace and generosity toward us. More generally,

Wesley's descriptions of the human condition, his boldness in facing up to reality, and his conviction that God is at work from the outset of our lives to straighten us out are a breath of fresh air.

Of course, the real elephant in the room is whether Wesley's vision of salvation is so tied to his account of sin that flaws in the latter will undermine his proposals about the former. If Wesley is off the mark on the disease, will he not also be off the mark on the cure? We will keep this issue rumbling in the back of our minds as we turn now to his analysis of salvation.

CHAPTER FOUR

Starting All Over Again

Getting a Handle on the Language of Zion

In this chapter I want to unpack two critical concepts that governed the initial phase of the Christian journey, as Wesley saw it: justification and regeneration. In the next chapter I shall turn to the ideas of sanctification and assurance. Any serious engagement with Wesley must come to terms with these notions. In and around my expositions I shall touch on such themes as are essential to making sense of these pivotal doctrines.

Wesley is not always consistent in the exposition of his position. Sometimes he wants to make justification and regeneration his favorite notions; at other times he opts for justification and sanctification. In part this confusion is tied to his work as a preacher. He wants to drive home the topics of the day by marking them as the most important thing under the sun; sermonic hyperbole gets in the way of systematic clarity. However, both regeneration and sanctification occupy the same conceptual space. Both are concerned to draw attention to the real change that God works in the believer; they highlight what has been called "infused grace," that is, the energy of God that changes the sinner into a saint. So the central thrust of his thinking is clear. He is committed to a vision that embraces both forgiveness and radical personal transformation.

We might enter his map of the spiritual landscape in this way. In justifying us God pardons and forgives us our sins. Here the problem addressed is that of our guilt; in justification we are acquitted of the charges that are brought against us. In regeneration or new birth, we get to make a fresh start in life. Here the problem addressed is the power of sin in our life; God steps in and recreates us, making us into new people, moving us by spiritual birth from the kingdom of Satan to the kingdom of God. In sanctifying us, God gives us power to live a life of love toward God and neighbor. Here the problem addressed is our addiction to evil; in sanctification the ties of desire and affection toward evil are radically uprooted by an inflowing of the power and love of God. In giving us assurance, God builds within our hearts a robust subjective confidence in the gospel. Here the problem addressed is that of doubt and uncertainty; in giving us the witness of the Holy Spirit, God generates within us a deep sense of personal acceptance and deliverance from evil. Thus justification, regeneration, sanctification, and assurance address different dimensions of the human predicament as seen from a theological point of view.

In insisting on both justification and real spiritual change, Wesley was bringing together two great concerns of the Christian heritage that have often drifted apart. The Reformation traditions stressed justification; the Roman Catholic and Eastern Orthodox traditions stressed transformation. Wesley was sure that we needed both if we were to do justice to all that God could do for us here and now. It was as if we need two engines to run our spiritual life rather than one. Justification gets us out of despair and guilt and up into the air of gospel grace and love; regeneration, sanctification, and assurance bear us aloft and along in the journey from evil to goodness, from sin to holiness. Holding these twin concerns together was no mean achievement, not least because spelling them out took Wesley into the debate about the relation between faith and works, an issue that has haunted Christians for centuries. I shall take up this issue at the end of the chapter.

In the Dock

Given that we have all sinned against God, we human agents are in deep trouble. We appear before God in court without a leg to stand on. It is not just that we have sinned accidentally or haphazardly; we have sinned recklessly, voluntarily, and gladly. Confronted by the law of God we are guilty. The evidence is all in, our legal advocates have lost the case, and we stand naked and condemned before the Almighty.

Of course, at first we shun the truth. Initially it is as if we are fast asleep, so we have to be awakened by the Holy Spirit so that Christ may give us light, and so that we can begin to see how grim things really are. This is the situation of us as natural persons. We live in a dream world of self-congratulation and ignorance. Then we get mugged by

63

reality. We have a close shave with death, or we hear a sermon that really convinces us of our spiritual poverty. We become fearful of God, heading off to church as often as we can and striving to keep what we know of the commandments of God. We become legalistic persons. However, this treadmill of effort and good intentions, of success and failure, only serves to bring home that the real problem lies much deeper than was first thought. Hence, we find ourselves overwhelmed with guilt and moral despair.

It is at this stage that the preaching of the gospel begins to get our attention, and for the first time we begin wrestling with repentance and faith. Thus, we readily do all we can to find an answer to the spiritual dilemma that we are in. Hence, Wesley insisted that we need to use all the means of grace at our disposal rather than just sitting around waiting for God to zap us. At this point he broke ranks with others who believed that only God could bring us to faith. Wesley did not disagree with this. The issue was not whether we needed God to fix us; the issue was how God worked to fix us. For Wesley, the Spirit is already at work in our wills and hearts in the very initial turning to God, and we need to continue letting the Spirit work in all the means of grace available. The network of small groups he set up aided and abetted in this critical stretch of the journey to God.

Within the many means God had set in place, Wesley was adamant at this point about the importance of preaching. Good preaching at this stage focused on the law of God. Wesley had no patience for the kind of insipid lemonade that some preachers were tempted to ladle out in order to comfort the hearer:

> Why, this is the very thing I assert: That the gospel Preachers, so called, corrupt their hearers; they vitiate

their taste, so that they cannot relish sound doctrine; and spoil their appetite, so that they cannot turn it into nourishment; they, as it were, feed them with sweetmeats, till the genuine wine of the kingdom seems quite insipid to them. They give them cordial upon cordial, which make them all life and spirit for the present; but, meantime, their appetite is destroyed, so that they can neither retain nor digest the pure milk of the word.[1]

People need a good dose of realism so that they can face up to the truth about themselves. If they do not find their way to faith, they are on the road to hell itself. The law of God acts as a stark reality check; it provides an objective criterion that exposes the evil that we readily excuse. In addition, it shows how far human agents are in bondage to their pet sins and concealed vices. It is only when we have gotten the story about ourselves straight that we should be given access to the story of what God has done in Christ to save the world. If we move too fast, then the turn to God will be superficial and ephemeral. Wesley's basic pattern for preaching was simple: Open up with a little of the good news, then switch to the bad news, and then unload the gospel in all its beauty and fullness.

As folk start to come to terms with the truth, within this process they are to be invited to a living faith in Jesus Christ as the savior. Here precision is critical. All too often the seeker is left to flounder in evasion, half-truth, and confusion. Faith has a proper object. Vague faith in God as creator will not cut it. Nor will bare assent to the creed of the church be enough. Nor will even the kind of faith the disciples had in Jesus before the cross and resurrection be sufficient. Faith has to be directed to the atoning sacrifice of Jesus Christ for the sins of the world. God is rightly angry with us in a divine manner for our sins, but we have no resources in ourselves to propitiate the divine wrath. God himself has provided the remedy for our alienation in and through the death of Jesus Christ, his Son. It is faith in him, not some wishy-washy, sentimental thoughts about forgiveness and mercy that bring relief. It is only as we turn to God in Christ, preached to us objectively by sent messengers, that we are acquitted in the courts of God. We must see our plight, understand precisely what God has done in Christ, and turn explicitly to the savior whose name is Jesus. When we do so, aided and abetted all the time by the grace of God, we are immediately forgiven and pardoned by God.

Nobody else can undergo or undertake this process for us. Our conversion is inescapably personal. To be sure, we need all the help we can get from others in personal conversation, testimony, small-group interrogation, exhortation, reading, sermons, and the like. But these are external events in our biography. At some point the individual must see what is at stake and look to God for forgiveness, and God alone can supply the word of relief to the soul. Wesley was a quietist on this issue. He did not practice the kind of appeals and altar calls that became commonplace in modern forms of evangelism. There is no coming to the seeker, cap in hand, soft music in the background, imploring her to come to faith, as if we are somehow doing God a favor by repentance and faith. Faith is a gift from God; it is engendered within through the work of the Holy Spirit. So coming to faith in Christ is not first a matter of making a decision; it is more like waiting upon God in hearing his Word, until the penny drops and we see the gospel in the most personal terms possible.

It is vital not to rush this process. A proper foundation has to be laid wherein sin is acknowledged for the deadly reality it is, wherein the central truths of the gospel are

understood and received, and wherein the turning to God is activated by the inward working of the Holy Spirit in the human heart. Hence, there is both process and crisis. The seeker wrestles with the truth, coming to terms with it in depth, yet there is a specific moment when God delivers the verdict of acquittal, pardon, and forgiveness. The crucial metaphor at this point is forensic or legal: God justifies or acquits the sinner like the judge in the court acquits the criminal who is charged with breaking the law. The judge issues a pardon, and the sinner walks free from the court.

Wesley is clearly borrowing and yet breaking from the traditional practice of catholic Christianity. What he keeps intact is God giving a specific word of pardon and forgiveness to the individual in search of reconciliation. In the catholic tradition, one comes to receive forgiveness through those agents whom God has appointed to deliver the word of pardon and forgiveness. God designates and gives authority to duly recognized persons, bishops and priests, to make the pronouncement of forgiveness. For Wesley, the human agents of mediation have disappeared. The role of the human mediator in Wesley's vision is to preach the gospel and give the invitation; the Word of reconciliation must come from none other than God, acting through the agency of the Holy Spirit. Hence the laity, especially lay preachers, can play this role as much as an ordained priest can play it.

This strategy of eliminating authorized agents of the gospel clearly has a disadvantage. While the danger with having an official mediator is that the reception of forgiveness may be formal and perfunctory, the danger with Wesley's alternative is that the individual is left at the mercy of subjective feeling and discernment. The seeker can readily flounder around in a sea of uncertainty. To make the matter explicit: when a judge gives the verdict we know where we stand. In Wesley's vision, there is no judge other than God who can deliver the verdict. Who is to say what that verdict is? God has to speak. And who on earth knows what God has said? It is small wonder that Wesley had to wrestle with the whole problem of assurance in a way that is not as pressing for other versions of the Christian faith. We will come to that problem in the next chapter.

Life in the Maternity Ward

At the moment of acquittal in the divine court the sinner is simultaneously born again. Wesley took this shift of metaphors from the law court to the maternity ward in his stride. While justification is clearly a different idea from that of new birth or regeneration, the two happen at the same moment in time. The pardon is accompanied by a birth certificate. As the prisoner walks free, she gets to start all over again. We move from a legal state to an evangelical state, from the alleviation of guilt to the experience of the power of God giving initial victory over evil:

> Justification implies only a relative, the new birth a real, change. God in justifying us does something for us: in begetting us again he does the work in us. The former changes our outward relation to God, so that of enemies we become children; by the latter our inmost souls are changed, so that of sinners we become saints. The one restores us to the favour, the other to the image of God. The one is the taking away the guilt, the other the taking away the power, of sin. So that although they are joined together in point of time, yet are they of wholly distinct natures.[2]

Wesley mined the idea of new birth with gusto:

> Before a child is born into the world he has eyes, but sees not; he has ears, but does not hear. He has a very imperfect use of any other sense. He has no knowledge of any of the things of the world, nor any natural understanding. To that manner of existence which he then has we do not even give the name of life. It is then only when a man is born that we say, he begins to live. For as soon as he is born he begins to see the light and the various objects with which he is encompassed. His ears are then opened, and he hears the sounds which successively strike upon them. At the same time all the other organs of sense begin to be exercised upon their proper objects. He likewise breathes and lives in a manner wholly different from what he did before.[3]

There is a clear parallel with the new birth:

> While a man is in a mere natural state, before he is
> born of God, he has, in a spiritual sense, eyes and sees
> not; a thick impenetrable veil lies upon them. He has
> ears, but hears not; he is utterly deaf to what he is
> most of all concerned to hear. His other spiritual
> senses are all locked up; he is in the same condition as
> if he had them not. Hence he has no knowledge of
> God, no intercourse with him; he is not at all
> acquainted with him. He has no true knowledge of
> the things of God, either of spiritual or eternal things.
> Therefore, though he is a living man, he is a dead
> Christian.[4]

The new birth changes all this:

> But as soon as he is born of God there is a total
> change in all these particulars. The "eyes of his
> understanding are opened" (such is the language of
> the great Apostle). And he who of old "commanded
> light to shine out of darkness shining on his heart,"
> he sees "the light of the glory of God," his glorious
> love, "in the face of Jesus Christ." His ears being
> opened, he is now capable of hearing the inward
> voice of God, saying, "Be of good cheer, thy sins are
> forgiven thee": "Go and sin no more." This is the
> purport of what God speaks to his heart; although
> perhaps not in these very words. He is now ready to
> hear whatsoever "he that teacheth man knowledge"
> is pleased from time to time to reveal to him. He
> "feels in his heart" (to use the language of our
> Church) "the mighty working of the Spirit of God."
> Not in a gross, carnal sense, as the men of the world
> stupidly and wilfully misunderstand the expression,
> though they have been told again and again, we mean

thereby neither more nor less than this: he feels, is inwardly sensible of, the graces which the Spirit of God works in his heart. He feels, he is conscious of, a "peace which passeth all understanding." He many times feels such a joy in God as is "unspeakable and full of glory." He feels "the love of God shed abroad in his heart by the Holy Ghost which is given unto him." And all his spiritual senses are then "exercised to discern" spiritual "good and evil." By the use of these he is daily increasing in the knowledge of God, of Jesus Christ whom he hath sent, and of all the things pertaining to his inward kingdom. And now he may properly be said to live: God having quickened him by his Spirit, he is alive to God through Jesus Christ. He lives a life which the world knoweth not of, a "life" which "is hid with Christ in God."

God is continually breathing, as it were, upon his soul, and his soul is breathing unto God. Grace is descending into his heart, and prayer and praise ascending to heaven. And by this intercourse between God and man, this fellowship with the Father and the Son, as by a kind of spiritual respiration, the life of God in the soul is sustained: and the child of God grows up, till he comes to "the full measure of the stature of Christ."[5]

We might capture Wesley's central point again in this way. Imagine a baby in the womb. It has ears but cannot hear, eyes that cannot see, lungs that do not breathe, and so on. Then the great day arrives. The waters break, the birth canal opens, and out comes a new baby. There is now a living, breathing, shouting baby that sees and hears. It is likewise in coming to faith. Initially the conception and gestation are within and barely visible. Then one day one

73

comes to the point where one sees the mercy of God in the death of Jesus Christ for oneself. This is not just any old discovery; it is the beginning of whole new way of living. It is very apt therefore to speak of being born again or of being born from above.

Flies in the Doctrinal Ointment

It would appear at this stage that Wesley has simply given us the standard, stable fare of evangelical Christianity. We need to be forgiven and we must be born again. Is not this the vulgar, popular Protestantism of the Bible Belt? Appearances are deceptive here, however. In justification and regeneration, God is the agent who brings forgiveness and new life. Given Wesley's robust vision of sin and its consequences, the necessity of divine action is an obvious corollary of that vision. We naturally infer that Wesley is a standard Protestant who is committed to the doctrine of justification by faith alone. Sinners are surely justified by grace alone through faith alone. Yet this is not at all the whole story. Certainly there is no justification without faith; Wesley protested again and again that he was a staunch traditionalist on this score. However, given his concern about holiness and given the inseparable connection between justification and regeneration, he ends up developing a subtle doctrine of justification by faith and works. Let's unpack this as best we can. In the end we shall see that Wesley may offer a unique theological package that deserves our attention.

The problem Wesley is wrestling with is this: How do we fit repentance into the picture?

But does not God command us to repent also? Yea, and to "bring forth fruits meet for repentance?" To

"cease," for instance, "from doing evil," and "learn to do well"? And is not both the one and the other of the utmost necessity? Insomuch that if we willingly neglect either we cannot reasonably expect to be justified at all? But if this be so, how can it be said that faith is the only condition of justification?[6]

Clearly then, "both repentance, and fruits meet for repentance, are, in some sense, necessary to justification." How is this claim to be integrated into his vision of justification?

But they are not necessary in the same sense with faith, nor in the same degree. Not in the same degree; for those fruits are only necessary conditionally, if there be time and opportunity for them. Otherwise a man may be justified without them, as was the "thief" upon the cross (if we may call him so; for a late writer has discovered that he was no thief, but a very honest and respectable person!). But he cannot be justified without faith: this is impossible. Likewise let a man have ever so much repentance, or ever so many of the fruits meet for repentance, yet all this does not at all avail: he is not justified till he believes. But the moment he believes, with or without those fruits, yea, with more or less repentance, he is justified. Not in the same sense: for repentance and its fruits are only remotely necessary, necessary in order to faith; whereas faith is immediately and directly necessary to justification. It remains that faith is the only condition which is immediately and proximately necessary to justification.[7]

What are we to make of this kind of theological fancy footwork? The core claim is that we are truly justified by faith alone, but we quickly discover two critical qualifications in the small print. First, this really only applies to a very, very small number of people. After all, there are not very many thieves on crosses in the history of salvation! Yet it is the thief on the cross who is the model of justification by faith for Wesley. Second, we also quickly discover that works are essential for salvation even though they are only remotely necessary and necessary only in a secondary sense. The crucial point to observe, surely, is that Wesley has abandoned the traditional Protestant position on justification by faith alone. He keeps the verbal and technical form of the original doctrine of the Reformation, but he has radically abandoned the substance of the tradition. His protests and denials are precisely what we would expect from a hair-splitting, competent logician, such as Wesley clearly was. They do nothing to ease the theological shift he has made.

We see here the drive to holiness that animated Wesley's

theology as a whole. He is totally opposed to any vision of justification that will open a door to the denial or neglect of the moral law. Clearly, unwary doctrines of justification by faith alone have paved the way for views of the Christian life that downplay, if not reject completely, the quest for virtue and the struggle against vice. After all, if all I need is faith, then it does not ultimately matter what I do. Hence, Wesley is seeking to build in the indispensability of "works," that is, of repentance, of religious practice, of acts of mercy, of love to God and neighbor, and so on. If believers drop the ball at this point (assuming that they have time and opportunity), then they will cease to be justified, and they will regress in their spiritual journey. Wesley saw this in his ministry. There was no standing still; one either moved forward or backward. So his peculiar doctrine was in part fueled by spiritual observation.

Moreover, his doctrine of grace undermined any move to take any credit for "works" before or after justification. The very ability to do anything good was due to the grace of God working within, and the freedom to do good was a gift of the Holy Spirit. God is always at work in us both to will and to work for his good pleasure. Equally, faith without works is dead, so that faith is never an inert affair; faith is always the faith that works by love. Faith that fails to express itself in inward disposition and outward behavior is mere assent, mere dead orthodoxy dressed up as the faith of the church. Wesley took this line of thought to its ultimate expression in a doctrine of final justification by works. At the final judgment we would, as Jesus and Paul insisted, be judged on what we did. Given that works are remotely and secondarily essential to salvation, given that faith and works are inseparable, given that faith and works are the by-products of the presence of divine grace in our lives, it is fitting to insist that in the last judgment we are justified

by our works. The cat is now well and truly out of the theological bag.

Wesley's critics were right to be suspicious of his Protestant credentials at this point. At a minimum Wesley has a serious public relations problem, one that he did his best to address. More broadly, Wesley poses a challenge to two major shibboleths in contemporary thought that are worth noting.

First, Wesley would have no time for the common idea that grace is really a form of moral indulgence. Grace requires, it is often said, that we forgive and forget, that we set aside the whole idea of moral law as a snare, as an imposition, as a denial of freedom, as nasty legalism, and as a rejection of the love of God for the sinner. To believe in grace is to believe that God accepts us as we are, with all the crud that comes with us. God does not insist that we have to get dressed up in our Sunday best and show up on time for the appointment. God comes to us as we are, where we are, and when we are ready to receive him. Hence Wesley's vision, despite his best intentions, is really hopelessly out of tune with divine love and grace.

Wesley would surely see this as mistaken. The core problem with this line of thinking is that it sets grace over against moral renovation. Grace, for Wesley, is not some sort of syrupy, schmaltzy license to give up on the quest for virtue. It is an expression of a love that does indeed come to us as and where we are, but it is also a helping hand that enters into the deepest recesses of the human agent and redirects and re-engineers everything from top to bottom. For Wesley, any clash between divine grace and moral law, between divine love and human transformation, would be dismissed as bogus. The very giving of the moral law, the application of the law in bringing conviction of sin, and the ability to obey the law are themselves expressions of grace and generosity on the part of God. True freedom is not

freedom from law; it is freedom to be and become all that the moral law requires of us in the good purposes of God.

Mention of freedom takes us to the second shibboleth that Wesley's complex vision of faith and works challenges at its roots. To see what is at issue in this case we need to take a short tour through three centuries of cultural history. What Wesley is really after in his vision of faith and works is a quest for integrity. The twists and turns on this topic are surely fascinating.

For Wesley, integrity means bringing human agents into line with the original design that God put in place for them from the beginning of creation. Thus, human agents are meant to live as persons made in the image of God. His language and style here may be archaic, but the vision is a powerful one. Human beings are robust agents with real abilities, responsibilities, and moral capacities. They are intended to match a vision of what it is to be persons, and they are designed according to a divine plan that is objective and good. Essential to that plan is living a life in keeping with the moral law, a law that is itself a transcript of the divine nature. Hence, integrity means being aligned with this plan, fitting snugly, freely, and beautifully into what God has marked out for us. Of course, we have fallen from this plan, but God has acted in Jesus Christ through the Holy Spirit to bring us back into line with the original design. God has come to enable us to be and live as creatures made in the image of God. A healthy human person is not someone who rejects the law of God; on the contrary, she desires to bring her life into line with all that God intends for her. So God's laws, God's plan, God's objective design, are not a burden or a hindrance to true existence; they are essential to the objective order of things. Integrity means aligning one's life with this objective. This is exactly what divine grace makes possible and effects. In the end there is no clash between inner desire and the laws of God as worked out and practiced in the church. Discipline and healing walk hand in hand. On this score Wesley was at one with the fundamental sensibilities of the Christian tradition. These were still very much in operation in the England of his day.

Clearly, the match between inner direction or desire and the outward laws of God came apart for many in the nineteenth century. The laws of God and the conventions of church and society came to be seen as a burden, as inauthentic, as a hindrance to true freedom and personal subjectivity. Thus, in the Romantic tradition the primary stress was on being true to oneself over against the rigid and imposed traditions of morality and religion. Freedom was not freedom to be all that we were intended to be, but freedom to break with convention and law. Discipline was a hindrance to liberation. Hence, there was a radical shift from a positive conception of freedom to a negative conception of freedom, from freedom as a positive fulfillment of one's nature to freedom as liberation from the shackles of external constraints. Traditional religion was seen as inescapably oppressive and hypocritical. Nonconformity and interiority trumped law and grace. Integrity in this universe was thinned down to being true to oneself and to one's self-chosen vocation and form of life.

What has happened in the recent past is this: The sunny confidence that accompanied the Romantic revolution has been replaced by the disintegration of the self, by the aggressive assertion of rights, and by the antagonistic quest for power couched in terms of gender, ethnicity, race, class, and the like. The quest for a freedom disconnected from nature and discipline has collapsed. In the academy there is in many quarters an insipid nihilism that rejects all objective accounts of reality, including our human reality as persons.

Inside and outside the academy we are faced with persistent quests for power that are morally shrill and hollow. On the religious and political front we witness the revival of virulent forms of religion that flirt with terrorism and with the naked quest for political power. And in popular culture we find ourselves immersed in vulgar displays of greed, violence, consumerism, and sex that destroy human dignity at its roots. Integrity has disintegrated.

These descriptions are, of course, exaggerated and overdrawn. It would be silly to evade or deny the positive gifts that have come from the cultural and political developments of the last two centuries. Yet Wesley's robust vision of grace and works, of love and law, of energy and virtue, are a sorely needed corrective. His rich theism is at once both pessimistic and optimistic. His pessimism of sin is more than a match for the most hardheaded realist who wants to face the truth as it is today. His optimism of grace is surely an essential part of any spiritual medical kit that has any chance of making a real difference. We need justification and regeneration if we are ever to make it into the future that lies before us. We also need repentance, the moral law, works of piety, works of mercy, and the manifold means of grace. The theological and institutional packaging may be different, but the core requirements are all there in Wesley. Integrity can be born again.

CHAPTER FIVE

With God All Things Are Possible

Can We Really Achieve Victory over Evil?

Wesley's views on justification and regeneration do not sit well with many of our current cultural assumptions. His views on the quest for perfection and the possibility of certainty are even more difficult to swallow. Wesley believed that it was possible to achieve spiritual perfection and genuine certainty about God in this life. Indeed, these two ideas were connected like Siamese twins. It is precisely the awkwardness of Wesley's views that makes him such a stimulating conversation partner today.

"Be perfect, therefore, as your heavenly Father is perfect" (Matt. 5:48). If God has commanded perfection, then perfection must be possible. Every imperative of Scripture is a disguised promise. Clearly God knows what he is doing, so he would not command us to do something without at the same time providing the wherewithal to do it. Here is how Wesley puts the matter in his comment on this text:

> And how wise and gracious is this, to sum up, and as it were seal, all His commandments with a promise, even the proper promise of the gospel, that He will put those laws in our minds and write them in our hearts! He well knew how ready our unbelief would be to cry out, This is impossible! and therefore stakes upon it all the power, truth, and faithfulness of Him to whom all things are possible.[1]

Consider another difficult text of Scripture. "Those who have been born of God do not sin" (1 John 3:9). This is clearly an arresting declaration. Wesley insisted we take it straight. The true believer operates "by living faith, whereby God is continually breathing spiritual life into his soul, and his soul is continually breathing out love and prayer to God."[2] "For the divine seed of loving faith abideth in him; and so long as it doth, he cannot sin, because he is born of God—is inwardly and universally changed."[3]

How might we capture what Wesley is claiming in a plausible fashion? We need to approach our quarry by degrees and by analogy. We can then unpack Wesley's claim more fully in his own terms.

What Wesley is after is this: It really is possible to gain victory over specific, known, moral evils in our lives. Think of sin and evil initially as the voluntary transgression of a known law of God. Can God do more for us than merely forgive us our sins? Are we forever condemned to a life of

slavery where we simply fall and fall again into the pit and pick ourselves up as best we can? Do we just have to grin and bear it, knowing that moral failure is as sure as the morning sun? Can we really set limits to what God can do to eradicate sin this side of death? Wesley was convinced that this kind of pessimism fell short of what God had done when he inaugurated his kingdom in Jesus Christ. We really can have victory over moral evil in this life, not by our efforts but by divine grace.

Thus far we have kept the claim as minimal as possible. We have restricted our attention to particular evils. However, this is surely a low-level kind of moral victory. Consider now a more difficult question. Can human agents undergo a profound reorientation in their moral outlook and disposition? Think of an inveterate racist, whose life is poisoned by prejudice, hatred, falsehood, anger, and aggressive hostility. Everything such a person says and does is filtered through an orientation that is perverse. Is it never possible for someone to be rid of such an orientation? Are racist persons condemned to live forever as slaves to their misguided passions? Can they never gain freedom from their racism? We might say that this is very difficult, but it would surely be incorrect to say that it is impossible.

Consider now persons whose orientation is radically opposed to God. Their fundamental outlook is one of rebellion and hostility to God. Are we now to say that this fundamental orientation can never be changed? Can we claim that it is impossible in this life for them to be so transformed that they come to love God with all their heart, soul, strength, and mind? Can we dare to say that it is impossible for sinners to be changed into saints? Wesley was convinced that it was possible for believers to be so intoxicated and filled with the love of God that they were really changed to the core of their being. They could reach the point in their relationship with God where disobedience to God was no longer a live option for them. The orientation and energy for this kind of life came not from human effort but from divine grace; it was only the Holy Spirit poured ceaselessly within the human soul that could effect such a drastic change.

Improving on Excellence

In exploring the possibility of radical transformation, I have steered clear of the language that Wesley himself employed. In fact, Wesley was not sold on any one verbal formulation of his position. What mattered to him was the substance of the claim. Thus, he could speak of Christian perfection, entire sanctification, perfect love, circumcision of the heart, fulfilling the law of Christ, holiness of heart and life, union with God, being filled with the Holy Spirit, loving God with all our hearts and our neighbors as ourselves, and the like. His favorite rendering was the biblical phrase: having the mind of Christ and walking as he walked. He was equally happy to rely on poetry to make his point:

> O grant that nothing in my soul
> May dwell, but Thy pure love alone!
> O may Thy love possess me whole,
> My joy, my treasure, and my crown;
> Strange fires far from my heart remove;
> My every act, word, thought, be love!

Clearly what Wesley is in search of here is the idea of purity of intention, surely not an idea that is foreign to the Christian tradition.

In developing his doctrine of Christian perfection, Wesley was drawing on an important strand of Christian thought that had a ready home in the Eastern Christian tradition of the ancient church. A drive to conspicuous sanctity was also readily available in the Catholic West. The Protestant tradition as whole, however, had been much more cautious. The sense one has from much in the Lutheran tradition is that one is forever sinful and saintly. Hence, we should grin and bear it as best we can. In the Reformed tradition the basic message is that one simply has to fight the good fight from one day to the next until death itself. The best one can hope for is steady but radically incomplete progress in the battle against evil. Wesley never denied the need to fight against evil; nor did he deny that further progress was both essential and possible. His perfection was neither sinless nor absolute; it was in fact a

"Christian" perfection. At this point, his choice of language may have been unfortunate, but, as already noted, he cared more about the substance than the verbal expression.

In his solid, plain English Wesley states his case both negatively and positively. Negatively, he concedes that it is impossible to be free from ignorance, from mistakes, and from infirmities. Thus, Christians will always be lacking in all sorts of knowledge; they will make mistakes of fact and of judgment; and they can well show "weakness or slowness of understanding, dullness or confusedness of apprehension, incoherency of thought, irregular quickness or heaviness of imagination."[4] Such constraints clearly rule out the possibility of sinless or absolute perfection. If we are mistaken or dull in our understanding then we will inevitably be erroneous in our actions.

What then is really possible? It is possible to be free from outward sin, denoting "the ceasing from the outward act, from any outward transgression of the law."[5] More positively, it is possible to be free from evil or sinful thoughts and from evil tempers. On the first count (thoughts), Wesley appeals to the experience of Paul:

> "The weapons of our warfare," saith he, "are not carnal, but mighty through God to the pulling down of strongholds; casting down imaginations" (or "reasonings" rather, for so the word *logismo* signifies: all the reasonings of pride and unbelief against the declarations, promises, or gifts of God) "and every high thing that exalteth itself against the knowledge of God; and bringing into captivity every thought to the obedience of Christ."[6]

On the second count (tempers), he appeals to the word of Jesus. Freedom from evil tempers "is evident from the above-mentioned declaration of our Lord himself: 'The disciple is not above his master; but everyone that is perfect shall be as his master.'"[7]

In working through his ideas on perfection Wesley draws an interesting analogy between justification and sanctification. The person overwhelmed with guilt comes eventually to the point where he realizes that he cannot make any progress unless he is truly pardoned by God. Hence, there is an obvious process involved. First, one realizes the problem, then one hears about the possibility of divine forgiveness, then one comes to see that pardon is really possible personally (for me now), and in God's own time God speaks and sets the sinner free. Justification occurs there and then, in an instant. It can be likewise with entire sanctification. In this case the problem is not the guilt of sin but the power of sin. There is an analogous process. First, one realizes one's total inability to fix the problem of the power of sin, then one comes to hear that deliverance is really possible, then one begins to long for it, then one comes to have confidence that real change is possible, and so on.

> To this confidence, that God is both able and willing to sanctify us now, there needs to be added one thing more, a divine evidence and conviction that he doth it. In that hour it is done. God says to the inmost soul, "According to thy faith be it unto thee!" Then the soul is pure from every spot of sin; "it is clean from all unrighteousness." The believer then experiences the deep meaning of those solemn words, "If we walk in the light, as he is in the light, we have fellowship one with another, and the blood of Jesus Christ his Son cleanseth us from all sin."[8]

In the case of both justification and sanctification, faith is essential. While all sorts of human "works" are remotely and in a secondary sense essential, it is faith alone that is the only condition necessary. Moreover, God generally gives both justification and sanctification instantaneously. Speaking of the latter, Wesley writes:

> "But does God work this great work in the soul gradually or instantaneously?" Perhaps it may be gradually wrought in some. I mean in this sense—they do not advert to the particular moment wherein sin ceases to be. But it is infinitely desirable, were it the will of God, that it should be done instantaneously; that the Lord should destroy sin "by the breath of his mouth" [Job 15:30; Ps. 33:6] in a moment, in the twinkling of an eye. And so he generally does, a plain fact of

which there is evidence enough to satisfy any unprej-
udiced person.[9]

Even the most sympathetic reader is likely to have lost
patience with Wesley by now. It is hard enough to believe
that people can become saints in this life; it is harder still to
think that God creates them instantaneously; it is quite
impossible to believe that we can know that this has actually happened in any particular case. Surely, if there are any
saints, humility requires that their status as saints be a matter for divine discernment rather than human adjudication.
And surely the last person to know of any saintly status will
be the saint himself. How can Wesley think like this? In taking up this question we move to the issue of assurance and
certainty.

Can We Really Be Sure of God?

Wesley was convinced that human agents not only could achieve perfection, but that they could also have assurance that they had achieved perfection. More plausibly, Wesley was convinced that believers could have assurance that their sins were forgiven and that they were children of God. His claim about assurance of perfection is really an extension of this more basic claim, so it is best to begin at that point to secure what he means. The core claim is that the individual believer can really know that God loves him or her intimately and personally. Indeed, it is the awareness of this intimate, personal love of God that paves the way for the life of faith. We love God because he first loves us. Our love for God is an answering love; it is generated from the divine side by God's pouring his love into our hearts. It is also an expressive love; we love our neighbors because God also loves our neighbors, and we want to love the objects of God's love. Moreover, it is because the love of God is poured out in our hearts that we are enabled to love our neighbors. There is an intimate spiritual and psychological connection between personal transformation as developed in Wesley's vision of sanctification and our awareness of the love of God for ourselves.

It is important to grant the initial plausibility of Wesley's basic claim. Given the nature of God and the content of the Christian gospel, it is surely odd to think that God wants his children wandering around without any confidence about their spiritual identity or status. A loving God surely desires that the special creatures, whom he has created in his own image and redeemed at such cost, would know something of the deep love he has for them. There is an obvious link at this point to regeneration. To be born again is to become a child of God; it is to be adopted into

God's family. Imagine parents who leave their children to flounder around without any awareness of who they are or how much they are cherished and loved. To think of God as a Father is to envisage a God who cares intimately about his children, and who would therefore express his care intimately to his spiritual children. To think of God as a Mother who cannot forget her sucking child, a biblical image that Wesley picked up with ease, is to imagine a God who would make known her commitment in tangible, felt ways to her offspring.

Wesley's favorite text on assurance clearly deploys this parental image: "When we cry 'Abba! Father!' it is that very Spirit bearing witness with our spirit that we are children of God" (Rom. 8:15–16). The other metaphor that Wesley loved is also plainly visible in this text. It was drawn from the law courts, namely, the idea of the witness of the Holy Spirit. Here the basic idea is that of someone telling

the truth. You are struggling your way toward faith and you wonder if God really loves you. You know by now that God loves others; however, you are not sure this extends to you personally. Then God sends a witness, the witness of his Holy Spirit. It is as if God speaks within to you, to your heart, and you know inwardly that the love of God extends right up to you. The point of witness language is to bring out that you can rely on this inner voice. A good witness in court does not bring gossip or secondhand information; a good witness speaks reliably of what he or she knows. In this case we know that the witness is utterly reliable because it is none other than the witness of God, the Holy Spirit. Out of this experience you now perceive that God really does love you, just as you perceive that there are tables and chairs or good friends around you. You are able to relate to God in terms of intimacy and freedom, calling God "Father" without presumption or embarrassment. In turn this feeling of God's love for you engenders a change of heart and action, and you now have the additional witness of your own spirit that you are a child of God.

Many theologians before Wesley had written of the inner witness of the Holy Spirit. They used this idea in one of two ways. Some used it to ground the list of books in the canon of Scripture. On this theory, you know the current Bible is canonical because God witnesses to this in your heart. Wesley showed no interest in this notion. Wesley turned back to Paul who in Romans 8 was clearly thinking of a witness that had nothing to do with what books belong in the Bible. The other way to unpack the idea of witness was in terms of the fruit of the Spirit. You reached assurance about your status as a child of God by way of a syllogism or argument. Thus, you reckoned that every child of God exhibited such fruit of the Spirit as love, joy, peace, and the like. You then double-checked to see if you had this fruit. If you did, you then inferred that you were a child of God. Wesley refused to see this as the witness of the Holy Spirit. Perhaps he saw that on its own this argument was a rickety basis for assurance. After all, the closer we get to God, the more aware we are of our sin and of our failings. Thus, Wesley reached for a deeper analysis of the inner witness in our personal encounter and experience of God. It was this prior encounter that generated the fruit of the Holy Spirit, and that could of course then be seen as the witness of our own spirit, a witness confirmed by the more foundational witness of God's Spirit.

Wesley is in his own way adding up different kinds of evidence in this analysis. The witness of our own spirit is a form of inference where the data are supplied by Scripture and introspection. Thus, from Scripture we know the marks of the children of God, and by introspection we can discern whether we do or do not possess these marks.

> Now this is properly the "testimony of our own spirit," even the testimony of our conscience, that God hath given us to be holy of heart, and holy in outward conversation. It is a consciousness of our having received, in and by the Spirit of adoption, the tempers mentioned in the Word of God as belonging to his adopted children; even a loving heart toward God and toward all mankind, hanging with childlike confidence on God our Father, desiring nothing but him, casting all our care upon him, and embracing every child of man with earnest, tender affection, so as to be ready to lay down our life for our brother, as Christ laid down his life for us—a consciousness that we are inwardly conformed by the Spirit of God to the image of his Son, and that we walk before him in justice, mercy, and truth; doing the things which are pleasing in his sight.[10]

The witness of the Holy Spirit is logically distinct from this inference; it is superadded and conjoined to the witness of our own spirit. Wesley describes this additional evidence in this manner:

> There are none that will adequately express what the children of God experience. But perhaps one might say (desiring any who are taught of God to correct, to soften or strengthen the expression), the testimony of the Spirit is an inward impression on the soul, whereby the Spirit of God directly "witnesses to my spirit that I am a child of God"; that Jesus Christ hath loved me, and given himself for me; that all my sins are blotted out, and I, even I, am reconciled to God.[11]

Wesley is full aware of the skepticism that this kind of subjective claim is likely to engender. Might not the person be deluded and self-deceived? Is there not a real danger of spiritual presumption? Wesley takes a no-nonsense approach to these problems. The Scriptures are clear on the marks of the children of God. They provide in the plainest manner what is at stake in genuine spiritual experience and in genuine fruits of the Spirit, so the attentive reader can check out what is at stake for himself. Furthermore, the devil is not in the business of producing such experience or such fruit; he is resolutely opposed to this whole operation, hell-bent on producing sin rather than holiness. In the end, of course, there is an irreducible element of spiritual perception:

> How, I pray, do you distinguish day from night? How do you distinguish light from darkness? Or the light of a star, or glimmering taper, from the light of the noonday sun? Is there not an inherent, obvious,

essential difference between the one and the other?
And do you not immediately and directly perceive
that difference, provided your senses are rightly disposed? In like manner, there is an inherent, essential
difference between spiritual light and spiritual darkness; and between the light wherewith the sun of
righteousness shines upon our heart, and that glim-
mering light which arises only from "sparks of our
own kindling." And this difference also is immediately and directly perceived, if our spiritual senses are
rightly disposed.[12]

If the skeptic now requires further assurance about the
reliability of these spiritual senses, Wesley refuses to allow
the assumption behind this request. There is at this point a
basic capacity to perceive that we either allow or disallow.

At that point, as in the case of ordinary perception, either we trust our spiritual senses or we do not:

> To require a more minute and philosophical account of the manner whereby we distinguish these, and of the criteria or intrinsic marks whereby we know the voice of God, is to make a demand which can never be answered; no, not by one who has the deepest knowledge of God.[13]

In the case of the witness of the Spirit,

> he who hath that witness in himself cannot explain it to one who hath not. Nor indeed is it to be expected that he should. Were there any natural medium to prove, or natural method to explain the things of God to unexperienced men, then the natural man might discern and know the things of the Spirit of God. But this is utterly contrary to the assertion of the Apostle that "he cannot know them, because they are spiritually discerned"; even by spiritual senses which the natural man hath not.[14]

Note afresh that Wesley applies the doctrine of assurance both to justification and sanctification. We can see why, for Wesley was weaving together a complex network of evidence to undergird the claim that the believer can have intimate knowledge of God. In his own way he was developing a common Anglican form of argument, bringing together a network of evidence into a single cumulative case. Thus, he appeals to a hearing of the voice of God within the soul, to the witness of Scripture, and to the radical transformation that takes place in the life of the Christian convert. Hence, he cannot in the nature of the case limit himself merely to this or that episode of reli-

gious experience; with Scripture as a background assumption, he draws on the fullness of Christian experience as manifest both in moments of intense crisis and in the ongoing process of each person's spiritual journey from sin to sanctity.

The Personal and Social Challenge of Spiritual Experience

It took some time for Wesley to work through the experience of the inner witness of the Holy Spirit in his own life. In his early discovery of this idea in the theology of the Moravians in the late 1730s he initially believed that every Christian had to have this kind of assurance. He was an impatient hothead in pressing his claims on his hearers; not surprisingly, many solid Christian people were very offended, and leading theologians of his day attacked him. In time he mellowed, recognizing that not all Christians experienced the love of God in the terms he had worked out with such care. He even hit a really bad patch in his own journey, which he reported to his brother in June 1766, when he thought for a time that he never really was a Christian at all. He recovered from this and over time worked his way to a distinction between the faith of a servant and the faith of a son. To have the faith of a son was the ideal; it was good to be explicitly or consciously aware of God's love subjectively. However, one could have the faith of a servant and live a life pleasing to God; one could be accepted by God without full assurance of being accepted by God. Thus, Wesley developed a vision of degrees of faith in order to come to terms with the complexity of Christian experience of God.

Here we see the theology of Wesley wobbling somewhat. Or perhaps we should say that he grew wiser over time. Happily, he also came to see that people could know God without always agreeing on the precise verbal expressions by means of which they described their experience of God. He fought hard for a unity of faith that would provide diversity and latitude of expression, even though he failed in securing the unity he desired because many were deeply suspicious of his orthodoxy.

It is important to see that this subtle doctrine of the inner witness of the Holy Spirit had profound social consequences. For one thing, it acted as a leveler of social classes. The vulgar and the riffraff could know that they were children of God. This status outstripped any other designation we might care to name. It was better and higher to be a child of God than to be a princess, or to be a member of

the upper classes, or to be an intellectual, or to be a member of the in-crowd at work, and so on. One of the establishment ladies of the day clearly got the message:

> I thank your ladyship for the information concerning the Methodist preachers. Their doctrines are most repulsive, and strongly tinctured with impertinence and disrespect toward their superiors, in perpetually endeavoring to level all ranks, and do away with all distinctions. It is monstrous to be told that you have a heart as sinful as the common wretches that crawl on the earth. This is highly offensive and insulting, and I cannot but wonder that your ladyship should relish any sentiment so much at variance with high rank and good breeding.[15]

Thus, at the core of Wesley's vision of the Christian was an emancipation from the stereotypes and bonds of conventional society. It was small wonder that Wesley found a ready hearing among those who were at the bottom end of the food chain. Folk found a sense of dignity that was exhilarating and liberating. Another consequence came through in worship. Those who experienced God in this way were exuberant in their praise and joyful in their gathering together. Charles Wesley's hymns were a brilliant asset in this arena. In his lifetime he produced over seven thousand hymns and poems; these gave ordinary Christians both a body of concepts to describe their experience and a common way of thanking God together. In and around their praise the early Methodists loved to hear testimonies of the spiritual breakthroughs of others, and they gladly shared their own stories as a way of providing encouragement to those still seeking.

The Complexity and Simplicity
of the Christian Life

Looking back at the big picture, we can see that Wesley provided a unique vision of the Christian life that is worthy of admiration. He was Lutheran insofar as he insisted on justification as foundational; he was Reformed insofar as he believed that we shall be fighting sin to our dying day; he was Anglican in that he expected God to work objectively in the sacraments to mediate grace; he was Roman Catholic in that he held that conspicuous sanctity or goodness really is possible in this life; he was Pentecostal in that he stressed the pivotal role of explicit experience of the Holy Spirit in our lives; and he was Eastern Orthodox in that he saw human agents as genuinely acting through grace in the whole drama of salvation. This makes Wesley something of a theological oddball to everybody; he seems to be bouncing around all over the place.

It might be thought that the great virtue of this vision is precisely its complexity and its spiritual sensitivity. Yet we must be cautious in our judgments. We need to enrich this vision of the Christian life even further if we are to do justice to the mystery of God's action in our lives. This is what I mean. First, it is clearly possible that people are brought to the heights of holiness without having a clue about justification. Wesley would have been very puzzled by this because he liked to map out things very clearly and because Luther's vision of justification really spoke to him. However, there are many saints in the church who have come to faith through the door of sanctification and have yet to come to terms explicitly with justification and even assurance. Second, there is not enough room here for deep darkness and suffering in the journey of faith. We can appreciate the note of joy, of triumph, and of spiritual happiness, but we also need to come to terms with stretches of faith where we have nothing between God and us other than his Word in the gospel and in the sacraments. Without room for this kind of struggle, suffering, and darkness our vision will be impoverished and unrealistic. Wesley dealt with these concerns only partially and halfheartedly.

In making these objections of Wesley's vision of the Christian life, I expose myself to an obvious criticism. Wesley's language, while it may be biblical and hallowed by centuries of Christian usage, is really archaic. It worked well for him in the eighteenth century, but if we want to reach people today then this all sounds like religious twaddle. So surely we need to find a way to update Wesley's ideas so that they will speak in a credible way to our generation. Should we not reach out in contemporary terms in the language of today, rather than use this old hackneyed language of Zion?

Wesley has a very profound answer to this move. This evangelistic strategy of accommodation ignores the critical significance of sin. It assumes that folk are already aware of the problem the gospel addresses, when in reality they are thoroughly confused and even ignorant of their predicament. It is illusory to think that folk are always going to find the Christian message either intelligible or credible when they first encounter it. Often what is most effective in bringing people to faith is precisely the kind of humble sanctity and meek assurance that he was keen to see manifest among Christians. Saints are powerful evidence for the reality of God.

As we saw earlier, Wesley made this point about the difficulty of making sense to the world by deploying an old network of distinctions between the natural person, the legal person, and the evangelical person. Alternatively he speaks of a person being in a natural state, being under law,

and being under grace. Natural persons are the unawak-
ened sinners who have no idea of their predicament. They
think that all is well with themselves and the world. They
are in fact asleep, blind, and all too secure in their illusions.
They boast of their liberty and think that religious people
are addicted to superstition and bigotry. Then they get
mugged by reality. One way or another, they discover that
they are not the great moral heroes they are cracked up to
be. Perhaps a good friend is killed in an accident and the
funeral is a moment of illumination. They become aware of
the awesome reality of God and of the radical distance
between their sins and God's holiness. They are now under
law, wounded in spirit, despairing of ever being a better
person, and miserable to boot. Hearing the inner voice of

God's Spirit and attending to the gospel, they begin to dream of being accepted by God and of becoming what deep down they have always wanted to be. They are now under grace, and for the first time in their lives begin to understand the religious mumbo jumbo of the Christian tradition.

In these circumstances the strategy of translating the language of the faith into the jargon of the streets is superficial. The intention is good, and there is even a grain of truth on offer. It is wise to develop contemporary analogies that will capture in a vivid way the great truths of the gospel. Charles Wesley's poetic skills were a godsend to early Methodism in this arena. However, the mistake is to think that folk are ready to roll over and accept the Christian faith if only we could find a way to make it intelligible to them. This ignores the offense of the faith. To see what is at stake in salvation requires an intellectual revolution that shakes the foundations of one's standard conception of oneself. The darkness and cognitive malfunction are so great that the active grace of God is required to wake us from our dogmatic slumbers. We should permit the claims of the faith to call into question the common intellectual assumptions of our day rather than capitulating at the first sign of opposition. Moreover, it is not always easy to explain the deep things of God even to veteran believers. Thus, to rely on strategies of translation, or on cute analogies, or on church growth techniques, in order to relieve our anxieties is disastrous for the church in the long run. We need to keep our nerve, pray for divine assistance, and launch forth boldly in the teeth of opposition and ridicule. Cutting a deal with the world at this point and reworking the faith to accommodate its wishes is simply wrongheaded and ineffective.

CHAPTER SIX

Help Is in the Works

Give Me Jesus but not His Body

In the late 1730s John Wesley's older brother Samuel was not very impressed with the spiritual claims of his younger sibling. "As I told Jack, I am not afraid the church should excommunicate him, discipline is at too low an ebb; but that he should excommunicate the church."[1] Samuel died in the early days of Methodism, so he was not around to witness the possible fulfillment of his prophecy. Yet he had put his finger on a perennial problem for all renewalists in the history of the church, namely, their constant danger of underestimating the crucial place of the church in the life of faith. Young, enthusiastic converts and evangelists like

Wesley are prone to fall out with the church. They tend to look at the haggard old mother, complain about the state of her health, and forget that her own sons and daughters have caused the wrinkled and weather-beaten features of her face.

Wesley's complaints against the church were understandable. Here he was with lots of mouths to feed and souls to heal, but mother church was not helping to the degree desired. She was preoccupied with other business. Here he was going out into the highways and byways to round up the sick, the lame, and the wounded, but the general hospital staff was incompetent. The doctors had the medicines and resources for healing, but they no longer had the will or skills to use them properly. Wesley was sure that the Holy Spirit was at work in the church's ministry, but the Holy Spirit is not a labor-saving device. She depends on various means and instruments to ferret out sin and draw us to a life of holiness. Wesley himself was operating as a means of grace in his function as ordained priest of the Church of England, for God works through creaturely causes and not despite them. Hence, there were ineradicable institutional and instrumental dimensions to the work of the Holy Spirit.

So what was Wesley to do when the institutional church failed to work effectively? What was he to do with lazy, unbelieving bishops? Or with drunken colleagues in the priesthood who egged on the mobs against him? Or with regulations that prevented him from preaching in parishes across the nation? Or with highly placed intellectuals who attacked him without mercy? Or with vulgar opponents who went so far as to lock him out of his own father's parish church? Wesley never found a coherent way through these dilemmas either practically or theologically. Yet to watch him turn in the wind is a salutary experience for the

beginning theologian. In the end he settled for a pious pragmatism underwritten by his biblicism and his common sense.

On the one side, Wesley stood loyally with the Church of England as best he could. Thus, he kept in touch with friendly bishops, laid claim to the Anglican heritage for himself, urged his converts to go to services and sacraments, fought schism and separation to his dying day, held no truck for lay folk who served Communion on the sole authority of a sixpenny license, and so on. On the other side, he introduced a raft of supplementary spiritual practices that had all kinds of unforeseen effects, and he made at least two very embarrassing moves that are still skeletons in the closet. He hired an obscure Eastern Orthodox bishop to help out with ordinations, and in the end he himself ordained various preachers for the work in North America and Scotland. Wesley rationalized these moves with a show of history, practical wisdom, and logic. What they reveal is that he was torn between the institutional and the expedient in his thinking about the church. He simply wanted to keep open house for everybody, but the church did not know what to do with his smelly guests.

Not surprisingly, he framed the crucial issues that really mattered in terms of grace. He saw the church more as a means to an end than as intrinsically significant. This outlook explains many of his scattered comments on the church and the novelty of his practices. What mattered first was that people find God. Indeed, Wesley wobbled away from the traditional Protestant definition of the visible church as a congregation of the faithful in which the pure Word of God is preached and the sacraments are properly administered. Clearly the Roman Catholic Church did not meet these conditions; at times she taught error and was superstitious in her practices, yet within her bounds there

were those who possessed a living faith in God; hence, this definition needed to be revisited. On most days of the week Wesley comes across as a voluntarist in his doctrine of the church. The church simply is the gathered community of believers in any one location. He never really reconciled this with his high-church background or sensibilities.

I doubt if this bothered him very much. His first concern was the salvation of souls; God had supplied various means for the reception of grace, and most of these means were standard practices of the church. So the theological challenge was to describe the means of grace and persuade people to use them properly. Wesley left the wider background practices of the church to stay in place and do their work.

Sticking to Priorities and Proper Usage

Wesley's views on the means of grace are laid out in a sermon, "The Means of Grace," that falls toward the end of those dealing with how to become and be a real Christian but before Wesley's charting of the character and foundation of Christian morality. He begins with the simple observation that under the Christian dispensation, God has ordained certain means as the usual channels of his grace. Only a heathen would deny this fact; we can plainly see the practice of the early church as depicted in Acts 2. Two pressures, however, had led to problems. First, as love grew cold, folk began to mistake the means for the end, substituting outward forms for inward reality. Consequently, the means failed to function properly, and some inferred that they were obviously useless. Second, various holy and venerable leaders began to despise the means of grace in the name of inward religion, and in time others pressed this to the point where they rejected the claim that God had designed various channels for conveying grace. This conclusion was confirmed by the fact that some clearly have experienced grace without any outward form at all. The solution to this tragic development, as Wesley saw it, was to go back to the beginning and work through the necessity and proper functioning of the means of grace.

Means of grace are "outward signs, words, or actions ordained of God, and appointed for this end—to be the ordinary channels whereby he might convey to men preventing, justifying, or sanctifying grace."[2]

> The chief of these means are prayer, whether in secret or with the great congregation; searching the Scriptures (which implies reading, hearing, and meditating thereon) and receiving the Lord's Supper, eating bread and drinking wine in remembrance of him; and these we believe to be ordained of God as the ordinary channels of conveying his grace to the souls of men.[3]

As to be expected in a sermon, Wesley is not here covering all his bases. This list does not include baptism, for example. Nor does it include the distinctive Methodist practices that Wesley developed, such as class meetings, bands, love feasts, covenant services, watch-night services, and the General Rules he required be kept by those under his care. These were covered elsewhere, and they were implemented as needed in his ministry. His initial concern was to establish the principles at stake.

Elsewhere Wesley referred to the distinctive practices just mentioned as works of piety:

> But are they [works of piety] the only means of grace? Are there no other means than these whereby God is pleased, frequently, yea, ordinarily to convey his grace to them that either love or fear him? Surely there are works of mercy, as well as works of piety, which are real means of grace. They are more especially such to those that perform them with a single eye. And those that neglect them do not receive the grace which otherwise they might. Yea, and they lose, by a continued neglect, the grace which they had received. Is it not hence that many who were once strong in faith are now weak and feeble-minded? And yet they are not sensible whence that weakness comes, as they neglect none of the ordinances of God.[4]

The idea of works of mercy is a strange one, but it is easy to follow. We often find that we can make progress in the spiritual life by forgetting about our religious activity and ourselves and immersing ourselves in meeting the needs of others. Hence, feeding the hungry, relieving the stranger, and visiting those in prison are not just pressing duties; they are good for the soul as well. Wesley, in fact, develops the concept of works of mercy in a sermon, "On Visiting

the Sick." In this case he makes clear how grace is involved. Once we realize how demanding this work is, we will readily call upon God for help and get it. We will need to rely on God to give us humility, meekness, patience, and the like. Thus, by the exercise of virtue we will grow in understanding and virtue. To be sure, Wesley makes it clear that supplying the spiritual wants of others is more excellent than simply supplying their material wants. However, he is perceptive in noting how helping others rebounds in spiritual development for the agents of care.

More specifically, we might say that means of grace induce in us the knowledge and love of God. If we are to receive the grace of God we must wait for that grace in the means provided. Hence, we must use public and private prayer, we should constantly use the Scriptures (hearing, reading, and meditating), and we need to partake of the

Lord's Supper. Under no circumstances can we set aside the means of grace, for we are under the command of Christ to use them. Given that God ordains them, they must be used in the manner designed by God. They do not atone for sin, nor do they give any ground for merit. We approach them in a spirit of trust, believing that whatever God has promised to give us through them will be delivered to us. What God has promised is grace upon grace.

The critical role of these practices as means or instruments of grace is well brought out by Wesley's radical remarks about the nature of the means used:

> Before you use any means let it be deeply impressed on your soul: There is no power in this. It is in itself a poor, dead, empty thing: separate from God, it is a dry leaf, a shadow. . . . Settle this in your heart, that the *opus operatum*, the mere work done, profiteth nothing; that there is no power to save but in the Spirit of God, no merit but in the blood of Christ; that consequently even what God ordains conveys no grace to the soul if you trust not in him alone.[5]

Used in the wrong way, that is, for any aim other than the renewal of the soul in righteousness and true holiness, the means of grace are "dung and dross." With regard to the Lord's Supper, it is clear that Wesley rejected any notion of the real presence in the material creatures of bread and wine. In all likelihood he believed that Christ was spiritually but not materially present in the Eucharist. This does not mean that Wesley was lax in his attendance at the Eucharist. He probably had Communion every five days or so through most of his life. Moreover, he urged the duty of constant Communion on his converts.

Wesley also insisted that God was not limited in his use of means. God is above all means, so he can convey his grace either in or out of any of the means he has appointed. The point here is not to undercut the use of the means of grace, but to encourage the seeker of grace to look for grace anywhere at any time. God is always ready, always able, always willing to save. We must never set limits to the ingenuity or generosity of God.

Heeding the ingenuity of God also means that we should be open to any order that works in our use of the means of grace. God will meet us where we are, sensitive to the necessities of our particular situation. We can certainly expect there to be characteristic patterns of use, for surely one means will work better than another in serving a particular need:

> The means into which different men are led, and in which they find the blessing of God, are varied, transposed, and combined together a thousand different

ways. Yet still our wisdom is to follow the leadings of his providence and his Spirit; to be guided herein (more especially as to the means wherein we ourselves seek the grace of God) partly by his outward providence, giving us the opportunity of using sometimes one means, sometimes another; partly by our experience, which it is whereby his free Spirit is pleased most to work in our heart.[6]

Staying the Course

Wesley's doctrine of the church is inherently unstable. In his day he managed to keep his converts within the Church of England, but he was shrewd enough to know that the commitment to renewal inside the establishment might not last long after his death. There is a note of resignation in his tone of voice toward the end of his life. He was clearly cheered by the possibilities in North America, launching his spiritual children there to follow Scripture and primitive tradition to the promised land. In time the drive to restore primitive Christianity would become an obsession in North America; one suspects that Wesley played his part in inaugurating a trend to experiment that would eventually blow itself out in narrow, rationalistic exhaustion. It can be exciting to be part of a movement with the goal of restoring New Testament Christianity once and for all. However, when these restoration movements breed, cross-fertilize, and then breed again, the results can lead to disillusion and frustration in the search for the true church. Wesley said somewhere that he did not have the ability to start a new church. It was surely an astute moment of self-awareness and self-criticism.

Wesley's first instincts were toward both the renewal of the church and the unity of Christians at one and the same

117

time. While he wanted to restore primitive Christianity, he also wanted to keep continuity both with the ancient church and with his own Anglican heritage. While he was prepared to bend and even break the rules, he still desired to bring his converts back home to mother church. While he made up his own mind on the issues at hand, he still wanted to keep fellowship with his opponents and critics. Even when he was forced by circumstances to launch a new denomination, he was well aware that he needed to make provision for doctrine, liturgy, discipline, orderly succession of ministry, sacrament, and the like. From the outset he was convinced that there was no religion but social religion, so that the church was vital to the life of faith. At times he acted as if the church were merely a boat from which to go fishing for souls, but he also acted in ways that reveal a robust sense of the church as an institution that exists through space and time and that deserved his loyalty and affection.

Wesley certainly was no sentimentalist when it came to the need for comprehensive attention to the hard-drive of the church. When asked what was needed to keep Methodism alive when he was dead, he was reported as saying:

> The Methodists must take heed to their doctrine, their experience, their practice, and their discipline. If they attend to the doctrines *only*, they will make the people *antinomians* [lawless]; if to the experimental part of religion *only*, they will make them *enthusiasts* [pious fanatics]; if to the practical part *only*, they will make them *Pharisees*; and if they do not attend to their discipline, they will be like persons who bestow much pains in cultivating their garden, and put no fence around it, to save it from the wild boar of the forest.[7]

118

The tension between institution and effectiveness, between form and spirit, between maintenance and mission, between convention and innovation, between regulation and spontaneity, and between continuity and renewal, are still with us today in our ruminations on the nature of the church. In Wesley's vision of the church there are certain indispensable elements. Thus, he zeroed in on the church as the catholic or universal church, that is, all the Christians under heaven. He is right to look for nothing less than one body, one Spirit, one Lord, one hope, one faith, one baptism, one God and Father of all, as essential to the life of the church. He is also on the money when he notes that insisting on purity of preaching and sacramental practice will be exclusionary, for there is a clear gap between ideal and reality. Hence, there is realism as well as optimism in his thinking about the church. Yet we do not find in Wesley a fully rounded account of the church that will cope with all the issues that have to be addressed theologically.

One of the deepest challenges we face in this stretch of theology is the tension between pneumatology and ecclesiology, between the work of the Holy Spirit and the reality of the church. Catholic theologians start from the top and develop a strong vision of the church as an institution that exists across space and time, united by its bishops. Here the primacy of honor is given to ecclesiology, and the emphasis falls on the church as an institution. Thereafter Catholic theologians do what they can to cope with the work of the Holy Spirit outside their franchise. Wesley started from the bottom and developed a vision of the church as a body of believers whose faith unites them to Christ, who in turn unites them to every other believer. Here the primacy of honor is given to pneumatology, that is, to the Holy Spirit in creating a living faith in Christ. Yet Wesley then has to cope with the necessity of the church as an institution equipped by God with critical means of grace without which he will fail in his ministry. Thus, he has a bridge that connects him with the church as an institution.

Let us, for the moment, go with Wesley and give the primacy of honor in our thinking to pneumatology over ecclesiology. There are two simple notions from Wesley that can help us make progress. First, his idea of divine commands as disguised or covered promises can allow us to see the rich descriptions of the church as possibilities that are always available to the church in space and time. Thus, to say that the church is one, holy, catholic, apostolic, and the like is not just a vision from which we fall short; it is a summons to a reality made possible by the work of the Holy Spirit. Second, there is an obvious way of connecting the work of the Holy Spirit to the reality of the church as institution. The Holy Spirit does indeed work incessantly to bring folk to faith in Christ and connect them to each other in the body of Christ. However, does not the Holy Spirit also work to create the church as an institution that exists through space and time? So in following up on the comprehensive work of the Holy Spirit, we are drawn deeper into the life and work of the church as an institution. In practice Wesley was headed away from the institutional church. If we follow his best instincts we will do a U-turn and head in the opposite direction.

CHAPTER SEVEN

Making Moral Sense

Moral House Building

The heart of Wesley's theology is a quest for holiness. There is then a moral focus to his theology, for, like heroism, holiness is a form of conspicuous moral sanctity. In a famous summary of his theology, Wesley deployed the image of a building to bring out the critical place of holiness in his thinking.

> Our main doctrines, which include all the rest are three, that of repentance, of faith, and of holiness. The first of these we account, as it were, the porch of religion, then next the door; the third religion itself.[1]

It is good to be told there is a holiness house and how to get into it. But what if we are mistaken about the identity of the house? It is one thing to be told how we can become healthy moral agents; it something else entirely to know what it is to be truly moral. It is not enough for Wesley to walk us through the various stages of spiritual healing; we also need to find out what it is to be healed. Wesley is more concerned with the production of morality than with the meaning of morality; he is more interested in moral meat than in moral menus or moral cookbooks. He cannot evade, however, reflection on the nature and foundations of moral judgment. Nor does he try. In fact, he develops an extremely interesting vision of the nature and the content of morality.

The distinction between the means of becoming moral and the nature and content of morality reflects an ambiguity in the term *ethics*. *Ethics* can mean either the actual behavior of moral agents or theorizing about what constitutes ethical behavior. Both of these topics take us into a further underworld, where questions like these swirl in the wind:

What are the sources of moral virtue or character?

How do we move from moral ideal to actuality?

What is the basic content of morality?

What makes human action moral rather than, say, prudent?

What is the fundamental logic, if any, of moral reasoning?

The focus of Wesley's thinking is on the first two of these questions. He laces his account of the whole journey from original sin to eventual glory in heaven with a vision of grace that is meant to unpack how God moves people from sin to sanctity, from immorality to morality.

This concern with transformation is evident in the batch of sermons that Wesley devoted to the Sermon on the Mount in Matthew right in the middle of his canonical corpus and immediately after he had provided a meaty summary of how to become a real Christian. The very choice of text displays Wesley's obsession with holiness as the goal of the gospel. To see what holiness looks like, he turns eventually to the teaching of Jesus as summed up by Matthew. This is a very significant choice. It is hard to see how any theologian could challenge this way of identifying the moral center of gravity of the Christian faith. Wesley strikes us as having hit the bull's eye here. Even if he takes any and every excuse in the text to get back to his favored topics, his choice of text and the content of the text operate as a brake on his tendency to set us straight spiritually. The teaching of Jesus surely is the heart of Christian ethics where the content of morality is concerned.

So the drive to spell out the spiritual mechanics of moral transformation is not the whole story. Wesley provides a substantial account of the structure of the moral life that addresses the traditional concerns of his day and makes use of standard themes and concepts. Hence he has a vision of the place of law in the Christian life that he presses home systematically and aggressively. He also has a very interesting account of the relation between reason and revelation. This is filled out by an account of the person of Christ that speaks of the work of Christ as prophet, priest, and king.

If God Does Not Exist, Are We Free to Do Anything We Like?

There is an old conundrum that goes back to Plato. Is any command of God good because God commands it? Or does God command something because it is good? If we

take the first horn of this dilemma and say that the commands of God are good merely because God commands them, morality is logically dependent on theology in the strongest way possible. We only know the truth in morality if we have a true theology in hand. If God does not exist, everything is permitted. Atheists and nonbelievers should be moral skeptics and nihilists. If we take the second horn of the dilemma and say that God gives the commands he does because they are good, theology is totally irrelevant to morality. We can know right from wrong even if God does not exist. Theologians have no more to contribute to ethics than dustmen and barmaids. Calvinists have gravitated to the first option; Catholics and Anglicans have preferred the second.

The text of the sermon where Wesley touches on this topic shows his philosophical underwear: "So the law is holy, and the commandment is holy and just and good" (Rom. 7:12). The law of God would appear to be good not just because it is the law of God but precisely because it is in reality good. So it looks as if Wesley is choosing the second option. However, he is uneasy:

> "But is the will of God the cause of his law? Is his will the original of right and wrong? Is a thing therefore right because God wills it? Or does he will it because it is right?" I fear this celebrated question is more curious than useful. And perhaps in the manner it is usually treated of it does not so well consist with the regard that is due from a creature to the Creator and Governor of all things. 'Tis hardly decent for man to call the supreme God to give an account to him![2]

This comment is very perceptive. Wesley has realized that if we take the second option we are giving ourselves permission to stand in judgment over God and tell him how well he is doing on his moral sums. This is odd. God stands in judgment over us; we do not stand in judgment over God. Imagine you are sitting in the gallery at the Last Judgment and sending back a report to the *New York Times* on the divine court, giving God a grade for accuracy, fairness, knowledge of the moral law, and the like. This makes no sense when we realize who God is.

In working through the problem Wesley makes three claims. First, he insists that we should not think of God's will as distinct from God. The will of God is God himself. If we can causally connect morality and God, we have connected morality to the will of God. Second,

if the law, the immutable rule of right and wrong, depends on the nature and fitnesses of things, and on their essential relations to each other . . . then it must depend on God, or the will of God; because those things themselves, with all their relations, are the work of his hands. By his will, "for his pleasure" alone, they all "are and were created." And yet it may be granted . . . that in every particular case God wills this or this (suppose that men should honour their parents) because it is right, agreeable to the fitness of things, to the relation wherein they stand.[3]

Third, Wesley insists that God's goodness overflows into the whole of creation in every direction. Central to this operation is God making humans according to a certain pattern:

> The law then is right and just concerning all things. And it is good as well as just. This we may easily infer from the fountain whence it flowed. For what was this but the goodness of God? What but goodness alone inclined him to impart that divine copy of himself to the holy angels? To what else can we impute his bestowing upon man the same transcript of his own nature?[4]

What is happening here is that Wesley is adding an additional factor. He is suggesting that human agents, as made in the image of God, have the capacity to make moral judgments because of the way God creates them. This hint allows Wesley to forge a third way between the standard options laid down by Socrates. When forced to choose, he says that the law of God is good because it is indeed good. However, our ability to discern good and evil is a gift from God. Hence, we are in no way permitted to stand in judgment over God, because in discerning that God (or anything) is good, we are in fact dependent on the goodness of God to make such judgments. So the first option has a measure of merit. We cannot know the difference between right and wrong independently of God. Wesley even comes to "doubt whether the very words, 'right and wrong,' according to the Christian system, do not imply, in the very idea of them, agreement and disagreement to the will and word of God."[5] Presumably the point here is that factoring in the Christian theological tradition leads to a conceptual enrichment of our basic moral categories.

Don't Send Your Moral Brains on a Holiday

What lies below the surface here is a robust theory of conscience as the foundation of moral judgment. Human beings do not need theology to find out what is right and wrong

because theology is already hardwired into us from creation. We come equipped with the voice of God within. Or rather, the voice of God has been restored to us after the fall into sin by prevenient grace, by the grace that comes before justification and sanctification. Hence, it is not necessary to look to special revelation to see that it is wrong to roast babies alive for fun, nor to allow the principle that we should do to others as we would have them do to us. The rightness of these moral platitudes is given in our conscience, an intellectual faculty that discerns right from wrong. They are basic propositions that we see to be correct straight off. Wesley captures the logic of conscience in this way:

> First, it [conscience] is a witness, testifying what we have done, in thought, or word, or action. Secondly,

it is a judge, passing sentence on what we have done, that it is good or evil. And thirdly, it in some sort executes the sentence, by occasioning a degree of complacency in him that does well, and a degree of uneasiness in him that does evil.[6]

Wesley is subtle in his account of conscience. He allows for variation due to education and a thousand other circumstances. He also notes the possibility of a hypersensitive conscience. We can imagine things to be sinful that Scripture nowhere condemns, and we can suppose other things to be a duty that Scripture nowhere enjoins. Such a scrupulous conscience is a sore evil that can be removed by prayer and by conversation with a good friend. Wesley has no truck with any kind of infallibility or with any kind of irreversible, absolute certainty. And developing a good conscience is not automatic, for if we neglect to follow the moral truth available to us, we can become callous and hardened. Moreover, this theory of conscience allows Wesley to recognize that unbelievers have access to what is right and wrong independently of special divine revelation. Hence, we should pay attention to their intuitions and reasoning in moral matters. Yet he will not allow us to think of conscience as a natural endowment. Conscience always operates through the immediate activity of the Holy Spirit as one more manifestation of prevenient grace. Christian philosophers who deny this are atheists in drag.

Wesley also claims that conscience gives us knowledge of the rule whereby we are "to be directed in every particular, which is no other than the written Word of God."[7] Wesley has shifted to another level of analysis at this point. He is now proposing that conscience must be informed by divine revelation. He can make this transition with ease because he holds that such divine revelation is simply a clearer version of the revelation already available in conscience. To express the issue in terms of law, the law written initially on the heart is the same as the moral law of God, a law definitively revealed in Jesus Christ. Or, expressed in terms of more traditional theological categories, we can say that special revelation corrects and stands supreme over general revelation in conscience.

This layered vision fits also with other elements in Wesley's theological vision. It dovetails with his account of sin, in that sin clouds our moral perception so that we need the corrective of revelation to get things straight. It also complements his conviction that the Christian life is marked by joy and happiness, in that the law is meant to contribute to our God-designed welfare. In addition, this progressive process of enlightenment comports with his insistence that the revelation of God in the New Testament supersedes that

of the Old Testament. While the moral and ceremonial institutions of Israel do indeed express the moral law of God, they do not do so to the degree that occurs in the new covenant in Christ. In the end it is Jesus Christ who fully embodies and reveals the moral law. He alone is ultimately the true rule or norm of moral truth. In salvation the Holy Spirit writes this unsurpassable law of Christ on our hearts, so that as moral agents we possess the very mind of Christ in moral matters. Through faith, the Holy Spirit indwells us and, drawing on the objective revelation of the law of Christ, enriches our initial intuitions and capacities. The light originally given within every person by Christ in creation is now perfected in the work of redemption:

> To increase and perfect the light which we had before, let us now add the light of faith. Confirm we the former gift of God by a deeper sense of whatever he had then shown us, by a greater tenderness of conscience, and a more exquisite sensibility of sin. Walking now with joy and not with fear, in a clear, steady sight of things eternal, we shall look on pleasure, wealth, praise—all the things of earth—as on bubbles upon the water; counting nothing important, nothing desirable, nothing worth a deliberate thought, but only what is "within the veil," where "Jesus sitteth at the right hand of God."[8]

This progression toward enlightenment does not happen by accident. We have seen already that intellectual illumination depends on the work of the Holy Spirit. It also depends on the proper use of the law, a long-standing issue in theological discussions of ethics. In its first use the law convicts us of sin. It tears away the fig leaves of self-deception, and we see that we are blind and naked before God. In the second use, the law shows us how totally impotent

we are in ourselves and drives us by force to Christ that we may find life. In the third use, the law keeps us spiritually on our toes by constantly opening us up to further intimacy with God. The more we see of the law in all its depth, the more we desire grace to be all that the law calls us to be. This line of thinking is closer to Calvin than it is to Luther, for it expands the third use of the law to include not just its teaching function but its role in drawing us further into union with God. For Wesley there can be no setting aside of the law; law is a constant source of ethical enlightenment.

These uses of the law connect nicely, even though they do not correlate exactly, with Wesley's insistence that the church preach Christ in all his offices as prophet, priest, and king. As our great High Priest, Christ reconciles us to God through his death and through his present intercession for us. As our Prophet, he guides us by his Word and Spirit into all truth. As our King, he gives us laws by which to live, restores to us the image of God, and reigns within our hearts. By this point we can see that, while Wesley begins his account of ethics with creation, he moves step-by-step from creation to redemption, from general revelation to special revelation, and from the work of the Holy Spirit in conscience to the work of the Holy Spirit in writing the law of Christ on our hearts. By now ethics has been swallowed up in theology; the grace of God in creation has been flooded by the grace of God in redemption. Grace perfects rather than cancels nature.

Note the depth of Wesley's insight. It is easy to think of the relation between morality and religion as an all-or-nothing affair. We think that either theology has nothing to contribute to morality, or we think that theology totally determines the logic and content of morality. Wesley begins with conscience; hence, he can make contact with a notion available in general culture. Yet he moves immediately to redescribe this faculty of moral perception as operating under the direction of prevenient grace. His snapshot of morality is two-dimensional rather than one-dimensional. He has enriched our vision of our moral sense; he has introduced a thicker description of creation into the discussion; our moral sense is the voice of God speaking within us. More importantly, this theological move allows him to provide a video-vision of morality. He unfolds a narrative of development that shows how our thinking about morality matures over time. As we journey into the world of special revelation, we are given new vistas that open up a whole new world of thinking about ourselves and about morality that was not previously available to us. As we look back we naturally come to see the earlier phases of the journey in more robust theological terms. So below the surface in Wesley we catch a glimpse of a very rich vision of morality.

Getting to Love God and Neighbor

The final outcome to this intellectual and spiritual journey is that we get to love God with all our hearts, souls, and minds, and to love our neighbors as ourselves. Love, rather than justice, or rather than some particular virtue (like concern for the poor), is the core of Wesley's material vision in ethics. It is not that Wesley is uninterested in justice, or that he does not care about the poor. He has a passion for both. However, everything else in ethics is subservient to love. Love is the prior virtue to justice, mercy, and truth. The law of God is but a transcript of the reality of God, and God is love. Even faith itself is the handmaid of love. Faith in God is the spiritual perception of the love of God; hence, it is logically subordinate to the love of God. Such faith is never alone, for faith works by love. So love has the ultimate place of honor in Wesley's vision of reality: "Love is the end, the sole end, of every dispensation of God, from the beginning of the world to the consummation of all things."[9]

It is the love of God, made visible in Christ and shed abroad in our hearts by the Holy Spirit, that is the psychological ground for love of the neighbor:

> For there is no motive which so powerfully inclines us to love God as the sense of the love of God in Christ. Nothing enables us like a piercing conviction of this to give our hearts to him who was given for us. And from this principle of grateful love to God arises love

to our brother also. Neither can we avoid loving our neighbour, if we truly believe the love wherewith God hath loved us.[10]

There is nothing narrow or legalistic about this vision. The believer reaches up in love to God in faith and gratitude and simultaneously reaches out in love to the neighbor in starkly practical ways. This reaching out involves initially a right disposition to those in need. Love is as much a matter of right perception as it is a matter of right action.

The role of proper perception is beautifully illustrated in what Wesley has to say about courtesy. He insists that we have to get beyond the outward appearance and live into the deep truth about human agents:

See that you are courteous toward all men. It matters not, in this respect, whether they are high or low, rich or poor, superior or inferior to you. No, nor even whether good or bad, whether they fear God or not. Indeed, the mode of showing your courtesy may vary, as Christian prudence will direct; but the thing itself is due to all; the lowest and the worst have a claim to our courtesy. . . . Shall we endeavour to go a little deeper, to search the foundation of this matter? What is the source of that desire to please, which we term courtesy? Let us look attentively into our heart, and we shall soon find an answer. The same Apostle that teaches us to be courteous, teaches us to honour all men; and his Master teaches me to love all men. Join these together, and what will be the effect? A poor wretch cries to me for an alms: I look, and see him covered with dirt and rags. But through these I see one that has an immortal spirit, made to know, and love, and dwell with God to eternity. I honour him for his Creator's sake. I see, through all these rags,

that he is purpled over with the blood of Christ. I love him for the sake of his Redeemer. The courtesy, therefore, which I feel and show toward him is a mixture of the honour and love which I bear to the offspring of God; the purchase of his Son's blood, and the candidate for immortality. This courtesy let us feel and show toward all men; and we shall please all men to their edification.[11]

Wesley will not for one moment, however, allow us to stay content with mere accurate observation or pleasing disposition. Love is certainly not blind, nor is love anything but thoroughly intelligent, active, and practical. Thus, he moves far beyond the mere exercise of charitable giving. This is most powerfully illustrated in his response to the needs of the poor. He makes astute interpretations of the plight of the poor; he does his best to get to the causes behind their problems; he resolutely refuses to blame the poor for their predicament; he provides all sorts of services and self-help schemes; he harangues anyone in sight to lend a helping hand; he wanders the streets with his bullhorn and collecting box; and he beats the moral drum against the merchants, the distillers, the doctors, and the lawyers who exploit the poor in sundry ways.

It is important not to exaggerate the significance of either Wesley's thought or practice at this point. Wesley operates as a perceptive observer, as a moralist, as a fundraiser, as an inveterate organizer, and as a Christian philanthropist. He has no large-scale, causal theory of culture or society of the kind that was developed later by Karl Marx and modified in various ways in recent times by cultural theorists. Nor has he enough in place to provide us with some kind of evangelical economics that would take us very far into that murky science. Politically, Wesley was a High Tory who was resolutely committed to the political arrangements in England. He could appreciate the role of providence in allowing Deism to flourish in Europe and North America. He even says; "The total indifference of the government there [in North America], whether there be any religion or none, leaves room for the propagation of true, scriptural religion, without the least let or hinderance."[12] This observation does not amount to an endorsement of the separation of church and state, and it would be daft to think of Wesley proposing this for England, yet it is an interesting straw in the political wind.

To be sure, Wesley's ideas and practices unleashed little rivulets of radical thought that could be picked up and filled out to become rivers of radical endeavor and political fantasy, but these rivulets can just as easily be dammed up by other components of his scattered thought. It is no accident that his spiritual descendants have included both Senator Hillary Rodham Clinton and President George W. Bush.

Moreover, in no case will Wesley allow his ideas about politics to be cut loose from his fundamental convictions about sin, repentance, justification, sanctification, and the like. The root of all evil goes back to alienation from God; hence, any solution to problems of human behavior and society will have to take into account conversion and growth in grace.

We can capture this section of the bigger picture by noting that political activity or legislation cannot produce better people; only God can. Wesley's heart is set on being rather than simply doing. Being a certain kind of person is more fundamental than doing certain activities. Virtue is more important than action, for good moral actions may well spring from faulty motivation, as when people give to charity to make a name for themselves. Thus, inward moral purity and intention really matter in ethics. The weekly regime of self-examination Wesley set up for the Oxford Methodists in the 1730s consisted of love of God, love of humanity, humility, mortification and self-denial, resignation and meekness, and thankfulness. These were the themes that ran through the week from Sunday to Saturday; these exercises were an aid to genuine moral transformation. Hence, virtues are more basic than obligations, and both have to be ordered to truth. Thus, the truth of the gospel and the operation of grace were never far from the surface of Wesley's moral theology.

Making Room for the Paddy Factor

In small but significant ways Wesley can help us in sorting through the sticky domain of religion and politics today. There is a deep division in our culture at present on the role of religion in the public square. Some think that the world is on its way to deep trouble because of religion. Sec-

ularists are convinced that theology is more likely to confuse and corrupt than help when it is introduced into the public arena. This is especially the case in politics, where faith-based initiatives, for example, are greeted with deep suspicion if not hostility. Over against this, many Christian believers are convinced that theology is vital to ethics at every level and that the current plight of our culture stems from its absence from the public square. Thus, the opposition to, say, the role of Christian groups in politics is seen as crass discrimination and prejudice.

Clearly Wesley lived in another world. For him religion was a vital part of the public square. He lived in a confessional state that took the positive role of religion in politics for granted. God governs all of life; God is as much present in the White House or in Buckingham Palace as in the bedroom or the boardroom; to pretend otherwise would be rank atheism. If some people deny this, that is their problem. As an ambassador of heaven who must one day give an account, his job was to ensure that God's will be known and enacted everywhere. Wesley's theism was a robust, public theism that made a difference at every level of existence. Moreover, he was an inveterate fixer. Give him a problem, ethical or otherwise, leave him alone for a couple of weeks, and he will come up with a solution and print it the next day. If initially he finds that someone else has solved the problem he will steal it, repair it, and publish it. Critics no doubt would see him today as an arrogant meddler; he saw himself as a faithful servant of God with a mission to heal the nation.

Wesley can have a rich conversation with his critics, no matter what they think of him, because of his commitment to civility, courtesy, and rational deliberation. His vision of morality not only makes this possible but mandates a frank exchange of views. Hence, he occupies a place between two extremes. On the one hand, he avoids any kind of theocracy where the church dominates the world of education, law, the media, cultural expression, politics, and the like. God is already present in the world in prevenient grace. The world of human and ethical deliberation has its own measure of autonomy that must be respected. To be sure, one has to keep a critical eye on such deliberation because our reason is fallen and corrupted. However, there is critical space for honest conversation and debate. On the other hand, Wesley avoids the opposite extreme of retreating into a private world of subjective religious experience that refuses to step out into the public order and work for the common good. The Christian community cares about the whole of creaturely existence and takes whatever steps are necessary to express that care personally and corporately. Within this arena, a life devoted to politics is an entirely honorable vocation. To be sure, deep differences are bound to arise, because Christians will ultimately see the world through the eyes of faith. However, even when radical differences arise, there is no place for coercion or intellectual intimidation.

This kind of vision may initially appear muddled and indecisive. It is better understood as sophisticated and discerning. It harbors no illusions about the depths of human evil, and it creates space for everybody to come to the table and say their piece. From beginning to end, politics is a moral enterprise. For Wesley morality is enriched and deepened by faith, so there is no severing the link between theology and politics. Therefore, we should resist the move toward a secularist vision of politics.

Given the secularization of the state over the last century in the West, it has been tempting for one group within this new swirling universe to lay claim to the title deeds of this exhilarating new political and cultural arrangement. Hence secularists, liberals, pluralists, agnostics, and atheists have tried to develop a new confessional state that privileges their particular moral, epistemological, and metaphysical commitments. We can only admire the intellectual efforts they deploy to work through their vision of the state, democracy, the relation between faith and politics, and the like.

Not surprisingly, many Christians outside those who take on the role of fawning chaplains to the new political aristocracy feel locked out and alienated. Poor Paddy can be let in, but he can only stay if the new secular confessionalists suitably housetrain him. Some of the latter really demand intellectual sterilization or castration as the entry price to their political forums. Moreover, the new confessionalists cannot understand why Paddy keeps dragging in his particular religious commitments; he should have left

his religion at the door and burst out in a chorus of gratitude to his secular sponsors for all they had done to make room for him. Clearly, the Paddy factor is a serious nuisance. Happily, Wesley makes room for the Paddies of the world both in theory and in practice.

CHAPTER EIGHT

Spiritual Hiccups and Measles

Virtue Turned to Vice

The Irish are religious, and it is impossible to make them moral. The English are moral, and it is impossible to make them religious. Different people sin differently. The same applies to religious traditions. Lutherans sin, and then they ask for forgiveness afterward. Roman Catholics sin, and then they find a learned Jesuit to excuse it. Presbyterians sin, and then they vow to try harder the next time. Southern Baptists sin, and then they find a place for it as temporary backsliding. Methodists sin, and then they plead infirmity and divine grace. There are predictable false trails in our spiritual visions once we see the basic direction of their logic.

Much of the theology of Wesley is devoted to addressing this dilemma. Perhaps he unwittingly realized that his spiritual agenda had its peculiar temptations and liabilities. More likely, he was an astute observer of his converts and sought from time to time to address the very particular vices to which they were all too prone. He was often at his best in identifying and addressing a standard set of problems that kept recurring among his people. Certainly this is the kind of theological endeavor that can readily be done on horseback. Wesley was an itinerant wet nurse in clerical garb.

His early converts were more likely to be bigoted than lukewarm, more likely to be judgmental than lenient, more likely to be smug than self-critical, more likely to be workaholic than indolent, and more likely to be puritanical than relaxed. Those later shaped by his theology are more likely to have a low-grade sense of inferiority than be snobbish, more likely to be mediocre than brilliant, more likely to be pragmatic than attentive, more likely to be hypocritical than transparent, more likely to be rich than poor, and more likely to be control freaks than disorganized. Indeed, those schooled in Wesley's form of the faith can be so organized that they can readily spread corruption across a nation.

Yet there is a characteristic optimism of grace that runs through the lives of those shaped by his spirituality that is deeply attractive. Realistic to the core, given their vision of sin, they never give up on anyone. Tolerant to a fault, given the personal nature of faith, they expect disagreement yet strive for consensus. Fully equipped with a policy handbook, given their obsession with planning, they can be wonderfully spontaneous. Prudent on most occasions, given their commitment to reason, they can be remarkably imaginative. Conservative in disposition, given their respect for the past, they can be startlingly innovative. God is with us, so all things are possible, and a small group will sprout into existence to fix any problem that crops up.

Given the characteristic kinds of temptations that inevitably befell his converts, it is no surprise that Wesley gave serious attention to providing the appropriate medicine to heal them. Sometimes he comes across as a scolding father. If only they would have done what he had already told them, if only they would pray more, if only they would be more disciplined, then all would be well. At other times, it is clear that the problem he faces is of his own making. His own medicine of salvation has been doled out without proper precaution and without the appropriate dosage. In some cases his medicine cannot but make the patient sick; the cure did not match the diagnosis. At his best, however, Wesley was insightful and effective in both the choice and administration of his medicine. We shall briefly explore five problems Wesley confronted that are still pertinent today: spiritual fanaticism, bigotry, sectarianism, spiritual depression, and money. The last batch of sermons in his canonical corpus deals with a ragbag of issues like these, interspersed by reminders of the depth of sin and of how one becomes and remains a true Christian.

How Not to Be over the Top and in Your Face

Lukewarm Christians do not become fanatical; evangelical or gospel Christians do. I suspect that Wesley was acutely aware of this. Critics early fastened on his claim to possess direct inspiration of the Holy Spirit and readily boxed his ears with it. In defense he both hit back and set a guard.

One favored term of abuse deployed against Wesley was that of his being an "enthusiast," that is, of setting aside reason and following direct divine inspiration. Obviously,

they thought, madness must now be in the wings. In response Wesley exploited the ambiguity of the term and cleverly turned it against his critics. He agreed that enthusiasm is a form of cognitive malfunction; it is a disorder of the mind. Where a fool draws wrong conclusions from false premises, the madman suffering from enthusiasm draws right conclusions from wrong premises. With these observations in place he could now deal with the problem.

True enthusiasm is not a matter of being open to the intimate operation of the Holy Spirit; it is a form of cognitive malfunction all too visible in the lives of Wesley's critics. So they imagine that they have grace when they have none; they suppose they are Christians when they are not. They envision they have special gifts from God when they do not; they think they are inspired by the Holy Spirit, when they are really only following strong impressions and impulses. They ignore the clear teaching of Scripture and set aside reason and experience. Their most common error is to think that they can attain the end without using the means. They read Scripture on their own without help, or they get up to speak without any preparation. Practices like these in turn lead to pride, stubbornness, unteachability, and rigidity of thought and action. All the while, as Wesley is defending himself, he is indirectly schooling his converts in spiritual discernment and the right use of reason.

The same strategy is manifest in his treatment of bigotry. This time, while Wesley is inculcating tolerance, he is hitting back at those who are hindering the work of God in the Methodist movement by challenging the practice of lay preaching. In this instance he takes as his text the incident in the gospels (Mark 9:38–39) where the disciples stop outsiders doing exorcisms in the name of Jesus. After making it clear that there is more than enough evil to keep every Christian worker busy, he insists we need all hands on deck. We cannot afford to let differences in opinion or even radical differences in the essentials of faith get in the way of running the devil out of town on the first bus available. To ignore this advice is to be a bigot, no more and no less. Indirectly, this is as good a defense for unauthorized lay preaching as one could desire. All the while, the new convert is learning to appreciate the work of God outside the Methodist franchise.

Underneath this call for collegiality lies Wesley's unswerving commitment to love God and neighbor. Bigotry in the end is a moral as much as a cognitive fault; bigotry is an intolerance that rests on error of judgment. The ultimate antidote to this is the cultivation of a catholic spirit, that is, true, universal love. Yet the execution of love is a tall order even among Christians because they differ in deep ways in theology and practice. Wesley supplies a formula at this point derived from an obscure text in 2 Kings that has

nothing to do with the topic in hand: "If your heart is with my heart, give me your hand" (10:15, paraphrased).

We might identify the problem Wesley addresses here as sectarianism. Sectarianism essentially is a bigoted attachment to the tenets, practices, and interests of a denomination. It arises for Christians because we cannot avoid coming to different convictions on our beliefs and practices. Hence, we will disagree on core beliefs, on modes of worship, on sacramental practices, on ethical convictions, and so on. In other words, given our fallibility and given genuine freedom of conscience, Christians will come up with competing visions. Given differences of opinion, we will join different congregations or churches; we cannot at this point impose our ideas on other believers. So how are we to relate to each other in these circumstances? How are we to avoid falling into thinking that we, and we alone, are God's agents of truth and grace? Wesley's solution was to seek agreement on a core set of theological beliefs and moral commitments and then urge tolerance in matters of opinion. Beyond this, Christians must love each other in word and deed, pray for each other, and provoke one another to love and good works.

This solution is easier to implement than to state. Thus, we need to know what constitutes the core beliefs that all have to sign off on. Here Wesley supplies a list of essentials that is daunting in the extreme. The fine print runs the gamut from beliefs about God through beliefs about Jesus Christ and justification by faith to such practices as loving God, having purity of intention, and loving the neighbor in body and soul. At one level Wesley is cheating by smuggling in his own favorite doctrines. At another level he is plainly wrong because he has left out, for example, the person and work of the Holy Spirit. Elsewhere Wesley supplies different lists of essentials beliefs, so he adds to his troubles the vice of inconsistency.

Yet there is wisdom too. Wesley makes it clear that there is no merit in wishy-washy Christianity. There can be no

> indifference to all opinions. This is the spawn of hell, not the offspring of heaven. This unsettledness of thought, this being "driven to and fro, and tossed about with every wind of doctrine," is a great curse, not a blessing; an irreconcilable enemy, not a friend, to true catholicism. A man of a truly catholic spirit has not now his religion to seek. He is fixed as the sun in his judgment concerning the main branches of Christian doctrine. 'Tis true he is always ready to hear and weigh whatsoever can be offered against his principles. But as this does not show any wavering in his own mind, so neither does it occasion any. He does not halt between two opinions, nor vainly endeavour to blend them into one.[1]

But having settled for oneself the big issues of doctrine and practice, and having given to others the same moral and theological space, love must rule supreme. The Christian's heart must be enlarged toward all; he or she "embraces with strong and cordial affection neighbors and strangers, friends and enemies."

Under the Weather with Money in the Bank

The last two problems addressed above arise because Christians schooled in Wesley's version of Christianity live in the world and in the church. Bigotry and sectarianism are essentially social sins; they arise because we have to relate to others. Yet there are some sins that arise more purely from within. As with the case of spiritual fanaticism, this is true for two other problems Wesley tackled: spiritual depression and the inability to handle money spiritually.

We can track the etiology of these two spiritual diseases in this fashion. Spiritual depression was a serious problem in early Methodism because Wesley set the holiness bar so high for the convert. Hence, failure was highly likely for the ordinary Christian. Handling money became a problem because, given the discipline inculcated by Wesley, many of the new converts inevitably became rich. Let us explore these issues further and see how Wesley dealt with them.

Imagine some persons who are already converts and who have started pondering Wesley's views on Christian perfection. They are struck by Wesley's claim that it is possible to be free from evil thoughts; they turn this idea over in their minds. Suddenly it hits them that their thought life is chaotic. They cannot control what they think; their mind simply wanders all over the place. So how can they ever be

153

perfect? How can they ever bring every thought they have to be captive to Jesus Christ? Not surprisingly, as they ponder these questions, they develop a bad case of spiritual blues. They cannot see how they can attain Christian perfection and become spiritually depressed. Wesley's solution to this was to make a distinction. There are two kinds of wandering thoughts. There are those thoughts where we wander from God in our thinking, and there are those thoughts where we simply wander from the particular point that we have in hand. These latter thoughts are not under our control. They change with the state of the weather, the condition of our bodies, our mental health, and the present state of spiritual warfare with the enemy of our souls. They are constitutive of human nature; hence, having them is not a form of sin. To have this second kind of wandering thought is not at all inconsistent with perfect love. So we need to readjust our sense of what it means to have our lives brought under the will of God. Properly understood we can, through the grace of God, have a thought life where our fundamental orientation is to have every thought governed by our love for God and neighbor.

Consider a slightly different problem. We are attracted to Wesley's robust and optimistic vision of the Christian life. However, we are hedged in by setbacks on every side. We cannot believe that God loves us as specified in the gospel. We get over this, make it through justification and regeneration, and gain a measure of assurance. But then we hit a roadblock. We lose our joy and peace; we get sick, and we naturally worry about the judgment up ahead; we look at the progress we have made, and it seems so meager; we begin to listen to critics and skeptics; we become envious and jealous of those who have been zapped by God and immersed in his grace. In short, we give up on going on to perfection because we have been hammered by the devil

into despair. Wesley's solution in this instance is to walk us
back over the course and to insist that we let God work as
he sees fit. We must stop tormenting ourselves, stop taking
our spiritual temperature, remember how far we have
come, stay focused on the goal set for us in the gospel, and
stir up the gift of God within us. Sufficient unto the day is
the grace given to us. So take one day at a time and leave
God to work as and when he sees fit.

It is clear by now what Wesley has been doing in this last
set of sermons within the canonical corpus. He is answering obvious problems that will naturally emerge for those
on the journey of faith as he has taught it to them. He is
going back over first principles again so that folk really

understand sin, Christian perfection, and new birth. And he is working through conventional spiritual challenges (e.g., periods of spiritual darkness, spiritual grief and sorrow, self-denial, inability to control one's tongue).

Within this network of issues Wesley was especially concerned with the effect of money on the spiritual life. We can readily understand why. Most of Wesley's converts came from the lower end of the social scale. In coming into Methodism not only did they find a fresh start in life and a whole new purpose in living, but they were also initiated into a set of dispositions and skills that readily took them up the social ladder. They became trustworthy and disciplined; they learned how to speak for themselves in private and in public; they started reading and were introduced to a whole new world of learning; they stopped drinking and indulging their lusts; they became thrifty and businesslike. Consequently, they became rich and moved up in the world. In the process they were enticed afresh by the world of money and all it made available.

Wesley was deeply frustrated by this development. In some of his last sermons he came close to despair. On one occasion he lamented that he had not imposed a dress code on his converts and had not required that they bring all surplus money to him for dispersal to the needy. On another occasion he tried to make the case that those who had voluntarily come under his spiritual care had a clear duty to obey him in all things indifferent in the Christian life. In these instances we see Wesley flirting with an alternative vision of Methodism; without knowing it, he has envisaged his movement as a lay order within the larger church. However, he knew that the die was cast and that there was no going back to the beginning and starting all over again.

He could still do what he could, however. Wesley's very last canonical sermon is his best shot at addressing the problem of money. He works through three rules, and they can be put on a postcard: Gain all you can, save all you can, and give all you can. In typical fashion he drives it home in the climax:

> Heathen custom is nothing to us. We follow no men any farther than they are followers of Christ. Hear ye him. Yea, today, while it is called today, hear and obey his voice. At this hour and from this hour, do his will; fulfil his word in this and in all things. I entreat you, in the name of the Lord Jesus, act up to the dignity of your calling. No more sloth! Whatsoever your hand findeth to do, do it with your might. No more waste! Cut off every expense which fashion, caprice, or flesh and blood demand. No more covetousness! But employ whatever God has entrusted you with in doing good, all possible good, in every possible kind and degree, to the household of faith, to all men.[2]

Wesley's theology is a theology that reaches all the way into our wallets.

CHAPTER NINE

Providence and Predestination: Double or Nothing

On the Balancing Beam

By this stage the perceptive reader may well begin to wonder if Wesley's theology is not hopelessly off-key. He comes across as obsessed with the central doctrines of the Christian life, with the work of God in the innermost depths of the human person. To be sure, in and through his doctrines of justification, regeneration, sanctification, and assurance we still hear the sound of the classical doctrines of the faith. Yet we are still not satisfied. Is God's action confined to the soul? Is God not at work in creation and history? More positively, given the acute attention that God lavishes on believers, does this not suggest a set of choices on the part of God that takes us into the neighborhood of divine predestination?

The material we shall cover in this chapter is not formally covered in the canonical sermons. It does not therefore fall inside the boundaries of what Wesley considered to be the essentials of true religion. In fact, what follows is something of a shock, given the conventional picture of Wesley that flits around in the history of theology. There is merit in giving it attention, however. We can round off our account of Wesley's theology by noting again how dependent Wesley is on wider background assumptions that are usually taken as the marrow of Christian theology. By the time we are finished we will also see that the doctrine of the Christian life is never far from Wesley's angle of vision. He takes up the topics of providence and predestination on various occasions precisely because they have a bearing on his vision of faith.

The tendency to move rather quickly to the practical import of doctrine is fostered by two striking features of Wesley's thinking that apply across the board in his theology. First, he was reserved and cautious in his vision of the place of human reason in theology. He was convinced that theology had to be based on divine revelation. Of course, once revelation was available in Scripture, reason was essential for understanding it, but Wesley affirmed that we have to stick to what God has revealed and not stray beyond this boundary. In the case of providence and predestination, Wesley stays close to the text of Scripture, the oracles of God.

Second, Wesley was cautious about how far we can really understand God; we rightly rely on analogy, but we must recognize the limits that the concept of God imposes on our thinking. In thinking of providence and predestination we are thinking of certain types of divine action. The danger is that we will conceive of divine action in crassly literal terms:

The works of providence and redemption are vast and stupendous, and therefore we are apt to conceive of God as deliberating and consulting on them, and then decreeing to act according to the "counsel of His own will"; as if, long before the world was made, He had been concerting measures both as to the making and as to the governing of it, and had then writ down His decrees, which altered not, any more than the laws of the Medes and Persians. Whereas, to take this consulting and decreeing in a literal sense, would be the same absurdity as to ascribe a real human body and human passions to the ever-blessed God.[1]

In the case of God the effects of the divine action, say, of consultation and decrees, are the same as in the human case, but there is clearly no "need of a moment's consultation in Him who sees all things at one view." In reaching

out to us God happily condescends to our level of thinking and speaking. One suspects that this kind of reserve left Wesley more at ease in discussing the action of God in the human soul, even though he insisted that "human words cannot fully describe the motions of the soul that are full of God."[2]

Taking Care of the Universe

Despite these qualifications, Wesley developed a very robust doctrine of divine providence. He was convinced by divine revelation that God was intimately at work in every event that occurred in space and time. There could be inklings of this truth outside of special revelation, but only God could give a clear, consistent, perfect account of his manner of governing the world. "Even the hairs of your head are all counted" (Luke 12:7). To be sure, this text should not be read literally, but its implication is clear: "Nothing is so small or insignificant in the sight of men as not to be an object of the care and providence of God, before whom nothing is small that concerns the happiness of any of his creatures."[3]

The presuppositions of this claim to intimate divine presence were, for Wesley, the standard classical doctrines of the creation and preservation of the universe. God called the world in its teeming complexity out of nothing into being. God preserves this world moment by moment. He is omnipresent within it and thus sees everything that happens through the whole extent of creation. In God we all live and move and have our being. The manner of God's presence is incomprehensible; not even the angels are likely to comprehend it, but the fact is certain. Given that God is present everywhere, God sees and knows all the properties of all the beings he has made:

162

He knows all the connections, dependencies, and relations, and all the ways wherein one of them can affect another. In particular he sees all the inanimate parts of the creation, whether in heaven above or in the earth beneath. He knows how the stars, comets, or planets above influence the inhabitants of the earth beneath; what influence the lower heavens, with their magazines of fire, hail, snow, and vapours, winds and storms, have on our planet. And what effects may be produced in the bowels of the earth by fire, air, or water; what exhalations may be raised therefrom, and what changes wrought thereby; what effects every mineral or vegetable may have upon the children of men: all these lie naked and open to the eye of the Creator and Preserver of the universe.[4]

God's knowledge extends beyond this to embrace the animal and human world.

God's knowledge of the creation is matched by his care for it: "He is infinite in wisdom as well as in power; and all his wisdom is continually employed in managing all the affairs of his creation for the good of all his creatures." The only constraint on God's action at this point is that he cannot overturn his own work. He cannot consistently deprive human agents of genuine freedom:

> For he created man in his own image: a spirit, like himself; a spirit endued with understanding, with will, or affections, and liberty—without which neither his understanding nor his affections could have been of any use, neither would he have been capable either of vice or virtue. He could not be a moral agent, any more than a tree or a stone. If therefore God were thus to exert his power there would certainly be no more vice; but it is equally certain, neither could there be any virtue in the world. Were human liberty taken away men would be as incapable of virtue as stones. . . . All the manifold wisdom of God (as well as all his power and goodness) is displayed in governing man as man; not as a stock or a stone, but as an intelligent and free spirit, capable of choosing either good or evil.[5]

God governs the world without overruling human freedom:

> An attentive inquirer may easily discern, the whole frame of divine providence is so constituted as to afford man every possible help, in order to his doing good and eschewing evil, which can be done without turning man into a machine; without making him incapable of virtue or vice, reward or punishment.[6]

Yet within the human world there are three circles of providence that represent three different degrees of care. In the outer circle we have all human agents scattered across the face of the earth; in the second circle there are all those that profess to be Christian; in the innermost circle, there are real Christians,

> those that worship God, not in form only, but in spirit and in truth. . . . It is to these in particular that he says, "Even the very hairs of your head are all

numbered." He sees their souls and their bodies: he takes particular notice of all their tempers, desires, and thoughts, all their words and actions. He marks all their sufferings, inward and outward, and the source whence they arise. . . . Nothing relative to these is too great, nothing too little, for his attention. He has his eye continually, as upon every individual person that is a member of this his family, so upon every circumstance that relates either to their souls or bodies, either to their inward or outward state, wherein either their present or eternal happiness is in any degree concerned.[7]

What Wesley insists on then is a doctrine of both general and particular providence. Providence is double or nothing. On the general front God works by general laws. However, he is perfectly at liberty to work through exceptions to those laws, that is, by miracle. Moreover, there is no general providence without particular providence. To work through the whole of nature requires, as a matter of logic, that God work through the parts. Equally, to deny God working through the parts is to deny God's omnipresence. Is God keeping an eye on the Arctic Circle but not on Texas? Clearly omnipresence requires us to believe that God works everywhere.

As to the details, Wesley leaves that to God. He stays clear of explaining how God might set limits to evil or how God might work to bring good out of human evil. His ultimate concern is pastoral. The doctrine of providence should drive us to walk humbly with God and to be grateful for such good news. Above all, it should teach us to trust God in everything:

What is there either in heaven or in earth that can harm you while you are under the care of the Creator

166

and Governor of heaven and earth? Let all earth and all hell combine against you—yea, the whole animate and inanimate creation—they cannot harm while God is on your side; his favourable kindness covers you "as a shield."[8]

This deep trust in God did not always come easily to Wesley. Yet it is magnificently visible in his own life, especially in and around the loss of the love of his life. When his brother Charles stupidly intervened and had Grace Murray married off to a rival suitor, he was devastated. After the marriage was enacted, he arrived on the scene a half-hour late. As he tried to come to terms with what had happened, he found some relief in working on a sermon. In the end he did not flinch from chalking the disaster up to divine providence. He captured the matter in a poem laced with suppressed anger, agony, and faith:

> O Lord, I bow my sinful head!
> Righteous are all Thy Ways with Man.
> Yet suffer me with Thee to plead,
> With lowly Reverence to complain:
> With deep, unutter'd Grief to groan,
> O what is this that Thou hast done?
>
> Teach me from every pleasing Snare
> To keep the Issues of my Heart:
> Be Thou my Love, my Joy, my Fear!
> Thou my eternal Portion art!
> Be Thou my never-failing Friend,
> And love, O love me, to the End!

Particular Plans and Policies

The issue of trust in God also surfaces in Wesley's vision of predestination. The popular picture of Wesley is that of a

great foe of the doctrine of predestination. His various and vigorous blasts against predestination are taken as clear proof that he totally rejected the whole idea and saw nothing of value in it. This is a mistaken reading of Wesley and one that misses the spiritual and intellectual sustenance he derived from his vision of double predestination.

I think this false reading and this tacit approval of Wesley's opposition to predestination is a fatal error for theology that ignores the great value of a robust vision of predestination for today. We need to recover our nerve at this point and find a way to retrieve Wesley's vision. The challenge facing us is daunting.

The standard view of predestination is very simple. In eternity God has decreed that certain people (the elect) will be saved and certain people (the rest) will be damned. In time God implements this decree by giving prevenient, justifying, and sanctifying grace to the elect. The rest are left in their sins to be damned forever because of their wrongdoing. Despite the deep unease about this vision of predestination, it dies hard in the corridors of the church. We can readily see why. This vision can easily be read off certain familiar passages of Scripture. It engenders a sense of intellectual humility before the divine mystery. It is developed in weaker and strong versions by some of the greatest minds of the church, not least the great Augustine. It helps to explain why some conversions are so dramatic. (In

some cases folk are swept off their feet by God; it is not as if they sat down and made some sort of decision about salvation.) It gives all the credit to God for salvation. And it provides deep security to the believer. On the one hand, if salvation depends on our weak, feeble wills, the chances of damnation are pretty high. If we have a choice between total divine determinism and damnation, then surely we should opt for divine determinism. On the other, if God determines the whole course of salvation from beginning to end, we know that once we are saved, we are always saved. Once we get on the salvation train, there is no getting off, and the train will make it to journey's end come hell or high water.

Wesley was well aware of some such vision of predestination, yet he did not at all shrink back from the language of decrees or of predestination. It is worth pausing to hear him at some length:

> Yea, the decree is past; and so it was before the foundation of the world. But what decree? Even this: "I will set before the sons of men 'life and death, blessing and cursing.' And the soul that chooseth life shall live, as the soul that chooseth death shall die." This decree, whereby "whom God did foreknow, he did predestinate," was indeed from everlasting; this, whereby all who suffer Christ to make them alive are "elect according to the foreknowledge of God," now standeth fast, even as the moon, and as the faithful witnesses in heaven; and when heaven and earth shall pass away, yet this shall not pass away; for it is as unchangeable and eternal as is the being of God that gave it. *This decree yields the strongest encouragement to abound in all good works, and in all holiness; and it is a well-spring of joy, of happiness also, to our great and endless comfort.*[9]

170

I will tell you, in all plainness and simplicity. I believe it [election] commonly means one of these two things: First, a divine appointment of some particular men, to do some particular work in the world. And this election I believe to be not only personal, but absolute and unconditional. Thus Cyrus was elected to rebuild the temple, and St. Paul, with the twelve, to preach the gospel. But I do not find this to have any necessary connexion with eternal happiness. Nay, it is plain it has not; for one who is elected in this sense may yet be lost eternally. "Have I not chosen" (elected) "you twelve?" saith our Lord; "yet one of you hath a devil." Judas, you see, was elected as well as the rest; yet is his lot with the devil and his angels? I believe election means, Secondly, a divine appointment of some men to eternal happiness. But I believe

this election to be conditional, as well as the reproba-
tion opposite thereto. I believe the eternal decree con-
cerning both is expressed in those words: "He that
believeth shall be saved; he that believeth not shall be
damned." And this decree, without doubt, God will
not change, and man cannot resist. According to this,
all true believers are in Scripture termed elect, as all
who continue in unbelief are so long properly repro-
bates, that is, unapproved of God, and without discernment touching the things of the Spirit.[10]

The sovereignty of God appears, (1.) In fixing from
eternity that decree touching the sons of men, "He
that believeth shall be saved: He that believeth not
shall be damned." (2.) In all the general circumstances of creation; in the time, the place, the manner
of creating all things; in appointing the number and
kinds of creatures, visible and invisible. (3.) In allot-
ting the natural endowments of men, these to one,
and those to another. (4.) In disposing the time,
place, and other outward circumstances (as parents,
relations) attending the birth of every one. (5.) In
dispensing the various gifts of his Spirit, for the edification of his Church. (6.) In ordering all temporal
things, as health, fortune, friends, every thing short
of eternity. But in disposing the eternal states of men,
(allowing only what was observed under the first article,) it is clear, that not sovereignty alone, but justice,
mercy, and truth hold the reins. The Governor of
heaven and earth, the I AM, over all, God blessed for
ever, takes no step here but as these direct, and prepare the way before his face. This is his eternal and
irresistible will, as he hath revealed unto us by his
Spirit; declaring in the strongest terms, adding his
oath to his word, and, because he could swear by no
greater, swearing by himself, "As I live, saith the Lord
God, I have no pleasure in the death of him that

dieth." The death of him that dieth can never be resolved into my pleasure or sovereign will. No; it is impossible. We challenge all mankind, to bring one clear, scriptural proof to the contrary. You can bring no scripture proof that God ever did, or assertion that he ever will, act as mere sovereign in eternally condemning any soul that ever was or will be born into the world.[11]

The core of Wesley's convictions about predestination is rooted in his profound sense of the reality and superintending providence of God. For Wesley, God really is an

agent who has made the world and who knows from the outset what is going to happen within it. Thus, from "before the foundation of the world" God can design a way out of the sin that has befallen us. There is here a deep backbone in Wesley's vision of God. This God is no wimp; this is not a deity who is making up the rules as he goes along; this is not a hand-wringing deity who is caught napping by the recalcitrance and ingenuity of human agents; this is not a God who is guessing as best he can as to what human agents will do, and then adjusting the game plan. This is a God who stands behind the whole universe: omnipresent, omniscient, and totally loving toward all his creation. God has made a good world that has gone astray, he is totally committed to its healing, he has a plan that has been set in place, and he is not going back on that plan for anything.

Within this plan, God has critically decreed two unalterable policies. First, God has decreed that one group will be saved and another will not; there is a heaven and a hell and God decides who goes where. There is thus a vision of *double* predestination. Wesley cuts through all attempts to dodge this disjunctive decision. For God to choose one group and just pass over the rest is an intellectual fudge. In practice, to pass over one group of people and just let them remain in their sin is to decide that they will be damned. Second, the distinction between these two groups, while known in advance by God, is determined by their decision whether to accept or reject the mercy of God in Christ. Thus, the predestination involved is *conditional.* God has decreed that those who believe will be saved; those who do not believe will not be saved. For Wesley this was simple and clear. God makes the decree, but the decree does not exclude genuine human agency and freedom; indeed, it builds the exercise of such freedom into the very content of the decree.

These two elements of Wesley's proposal are set in the context of a powerful vision of God's timelessness, so that the "foreknowing," "decreeing," "designing," "deciding," and the like that we attribute to God are spoken of with appropriate qualification and reserve. As we noted earlier, Wesley brackets everything at this level very carefully, but once the brackets are acknowledged, he is relentless in pressing his case. His deepest worry is that the competing Calvinist account (that of *unconditional* election and *unconditional* double predestination) is morally outrageous, making God into a nasty tyrant. He is so sure of his theological ground at this point that he is even prepared to insist that any interpretation of Scripture that backs the Calvinist vision must be wrong; it is nothing short of blasphemy.

Much of Wesley's writing on predestination is negative and polemical. He is at pains to show the oddity of the Calvinist position, how it undermines church practice and holiness, how it tends to sow seeds of doubt and unease, how the texts used to support it do not really do so, and the like. Perhaps this is why so many modern Christians have abandoned all talk of predestination or of decrees. Sharing Wesley's moral outrage, they sense that all talk of predestination makes one's skin creep. As Wesley says, "Such blasphemy this, as one would think might make the ears of a Christian to tingle!"[12] His spiritual grandchildren have generally thought that any and every doctrine of predestination must be set aside forever. It surely comes as a surprise, then, to see Wesley write, "This decree yields the strongest encouragement to abound in all good works, and in all holiness; and it is a well-spring of joy, of happiness also, to our great and endless comfort." This comes as a bolt from the blue. How might we unpack this amazing claim?

Divine Backing for the Riffraff

We might think of it this way. Wesley's vision of predestination is one way to give backbone to his doctrine of justification by grace through faith. If persons come to God through Christ, then Wesley insists that in doing so they really will be saved; they should have no doubts about their standing and their destiny. They really do have access to the mercy of God. Why? Not just because of some vague and general vision of God as merciful and loving, but because God has designed things to work this way, and he has no intention of operating any other way. Thus, suppose the riffraff Gentiles show up and get baptized; they are then attacked by their good Jewish brethren as needing to add circumcision or law-keeping as an extra condition for the healing of their lives. How can they respond? By insisting that it is God who has planned to save by grace and mercy through faith, and that God is sticking to his plan. It is God who is running the universe and setting the policies of healing for the world. So if folk have a problem with God saving the riffraff through the gospel, let them take the problem up with God. Suppose someone complains that this policy or decree of God is unfair; that the riffraff are coming in at the tail end of the day and getting the same deal as those who started early. How is this to be handled? By insisting that what we think is fair/unfair, just/unjust is totally beside the point. We are not running the universe, God is; so if God decides to have mercy on those who believe in Jesus, there is not a thing anyone can do about it. Hence, we can well imagine believers under this kind of pressure finding in the doctrine of predestination "a well-spring of joy, of happiness also, to our great and endless comfort."

But what can we say with regard to the other half of Wesley's comment? Can we also say that, "this decree yields the strongest encouragement to abound in all good works, and in all holiness"? I think the logic works in a similar but not identical manner here. The core idea is this: When tempted to dismiss the struggle against evil and for good as useless, as just too difficult, then we can take heart from this, that abounding in good works and holiness is exactly what God has designed us to do and be. Just as dolphins are designed to frolic in the ocean and eagles are designed to soar in the sky, human agents are designed to revel in goodness and holiness. Like it or not, be it difficult or not, this is the kind of life that God has designed for us in Christ. God has designed the world and his work of renewal and restoration in such a way that the intention in Christ is not just that we are forgiven but that we should now abound in good works. Thus, there is no point in giving up; this is the very shape of the universe as designed in

Christ. The plan remains in place no matter what happens; God has decreed things this way. Sooner or later, this is what we shall be in Christ, so we might as well lean fully into our destiny and take heart. Teenagers are designed to grow up and act responsibly, so we urge them to grow up and be what they are supposed to be. All human beings are designed to be intoxicated with love for God and neighbor, so we should stop fooling around and get with the program. In going with the grain of this destiny in Christ, we shall find true happiness and fulfillment.

These observations dovetail with those scholars who have made Wesley's sense of time and eternity pivotal in their understanding of his theology. Wesley's eternal vision was that of a workaholic: Even when we die we get to help out in the battle between good and evil. Just when we were hoping for a rest, we are given a new work assignment. Moreover, Wesley was exceptionally confident in himself, standing up to mobs, to criticism, and to hostility with amazing calmness and even surefootedness. His relentless pursuit of renewal in the church and nation of his day is astonishing in its persistence and intensity. It is hard to believe that these features of his character and behavior are unrelated to his deep sense of the very specific God he adored and served.

God was part of the air he breathed. Wesley's God was not the generic God of mere theism, or the teddy bear God of so much popular liberal sentiment, or the activist God of contemporary academic orthodoxy. There is not a hint of passivity, or sentimentality, or aggression in Wesley's vision of God. For Wesley, God is perfect, loving, omnipresent, omniscient, manifest in history as triune, and so on. He could rattle off the attributes of God, the redemptive acts of God in history, and the action of God in the human agent with ease and flexibility of expression. Yet this was

the fruit of something much deeper, namely, his enduring sense of the sovereign purposes of God, carried out on God's part with total commitment in the arena of time and eternity. It was this very particular God of time and eternity who had designed the universe and who had set about fixing it when it lost its way and descended into evil, suffering, and death. It was wonderful to know personally that one was really forgiven, accepted, and turned around toward health and happiness by this God; Wesley was relentless in pressing home this theme in season and out. However, it was even greater to live each day, knowing that this God was no fool and knowing that absolutely nothing would stop the march toward the final realization of the decrees and plans that had been resolved before the foundation of the world. Wesley did not need to explain the decrees of God to himself and others at great length; he felt them in his bones and lived them to his fingertips.

It is a surprise to us that a doctrine of predestination can work like this, but I think that Wesley is profoundly correct in his assessment. Predestination in any shape or form is strong medicine. It is a medicine whose prescription we should seriously consider reordering for our own day.

Notes

1. On the Road Again

1. Quoted in Stanley Ayling, *John Wesley* (Nashville: Abingdon, 1979), 16.
2. Quoted in Albert Outler, ed., *John Wesley* (New York: Oxford University Press, 1964), 66.
3. Frank Baker, ed., *The Bicentennial Edition of the Works of John Wesley* (Nashville: Abingdon Press, 1990), vol. 19, 46 CD-ROM. In future this work will be cited as *Works*.
4. Thomas Jackson, ed., *The Works of John Wesley,* 3rd ed., vol. 13 (London: Wesleyan Methodist Bookroom, 1872; repr., Grand Rapids, MI: Baker, 1979), 143. In future this work will be cited as *Works* (Jackson).

3. Life Is Nearly As Bad as You Thought It Was

1. *Works,* 2:188.
2. Ibid.
3. Ibid., 1:586.
4. Ibid., 1:226–27.
5. Ibid., 1:427.

4. Starting All Over Again

1. *Works* (Jackson), vol. 11, 491.
2. *Works,* 1:431–32.
3. Ibid., 2:192.
4. Ibid.
5. Ibid.
6. Ibid., 2:162.
7. Ibid.

5. With God All Things Are Possible

1. John Wesley, *Explanatory Notes upon the New Testament* (London: Epworth Press, 1944), 35.
2. Ibid., 911.
3. Ibid.
4. *Works*, 2:103.
5. Ibid., 2:106.
6. Ibid., 2:117.
7. Ibid.
8. Ibid., 2:168.
9. Ibid.
10. Ibid., 1:273–74.
11. Ibid.
12. Ibid., 282.
13. Ibid.
14. Ibid.
15. This quotation is from a letter from the Duchess of Buckingham to Lady Huntingdon. It is cited in Donald Dayton, "'Good News to the Poor': The Methodist Experience after Wesley," in *The Portion of the Poor*, ed. M. Douglas Meeks (Nashville: Abingdon Press, 1995), 69.

6. Help Is in the Works

1. Quoted in Ronald Knox, *Enthusiasm* (Oxford: Clarendon Press, 1950), 506.
2. *Works*, 1:381.
3. Ibid.
4. Ibid., 3:385.
5. Ibid., 1:396.
6. Ibid., 1:395.
7. Quoted in Rupert E. Davies, Raymond George, Gordon Rupp, eds., *A History of the Methodist Church in Great Britain*, vol. 3 (London: Epworth Press, 1983), 194.

7. Making Moral Sense

1. *Works*, 9:227.

2. *Works*, 2:13.
3. Ibid.
4. Ibid.
5. Ibid., 3:485.
6. Ibid., 3:483.
7. Ibid., 3:485.
8. Ibid., 2:40.
9. Ibid., 2:38.
10. Ibid., 2:42.
11. Ibid., 3:425.
12. Ibid., 3:452.

8. Spiritual Hiccups and Measles

1. *Works*, 2:93.
2. Ibid., 2:279.

9. Providence and Predestination

1. John Wesley, *Explanatory Notes upon the New Testament* (London: Epworth Press, 1944), 551.
2. Ibid., 555.
3. *Works*, 2:537.
4. Ibid., 2:539.
5. Ibid., 2:541.
6. Ibid.
7. Ibid., 2:543.
8. Ibid., 2:548.
9. Ibid., 3:558 (emphasis added).
10. Quoted in Albert Outler, ed., *John Wesley* (New York: Oxford University Press, 1964), 433.
11. Ibid., 453.
12. *Works*, 3:555.

For Further Reading

Wesley's Own Writings

Sermons on Several Occasions. London: Epworth Press, 1944. These constitute the canonical sermons for Irish and British Methodism. Unfortunately, they are not available in the United States.

Explanatory Notes upon the New Testament. London: Epworth Press, 1944.

John Wesley's Sermons: An Anthology. Edited by Albert C. Outler and Richard P. Heitzenrater. Nashville: Abingdon Press, 1991. This is a fine collection of sermons organized in chronological order.

John Wesley. Edited by Albert C. Outler. New York: Oxford University Press, 1964. This remains one of the best selections of material from Wesley, with provocative introductions by a scholar who gave a lifetime of effort to the study of Wesley.

The Bicentennial Edition of the Works of John Wesley. 35 vols. Editor-in-chief, Frank Baker. Nashville: Abingdon Press, 1984–. CD-Rom.

The Works of John Wesley. 3rd ed. 14 vols. Edited by Thomas Jackson. London: Wesleyan Methodist Book Room, 1872; repr. Grand Rapids, MI: Baker, 1979.

The Works of John Wesley on Compact Disc. Franklin, TN: Providence House Publishers, 1995.

The Standard Sermons in Modern English. Edited by Kenneth Cain Kinghorn. Vol. 1, *John Wesley on Christian Beliefs*. Vol. 2, *John Wesley on the Sermon on the Mount*. Vol. 3, *John Wesley on Christian Practice*. Nashville: Abingdon Press, 2002–2003. This is a slightly longer set of sermons than the

Sermons on Several Occasions and is useful for those who find Wesley's language dated.

Materials about Wesley

Ayling, Stanley Edward. *John Wesley*. Nashville: Abingdon Press, 1979. A fine study of Wesley's life by a distinguished English historian who specializes on the eighteenth century in England.

Baker, Frank. *John Wesley and the Church of England*. Nashville: Abingdon Press, 1970. A classic study by an outstanding scholar of Wesley.

Collins, Kenneth J. *A Real Christian: The Life of John Wesley*. Nashville: Abingdon Press, 1999. A thoroughly competent overview of Wesley's life and developing thought.

———. *The Scripture Way of Salvation*. Nashville: Abingdon Press, 1997. A fine overview of Wesley's theology that concentrates on the core of Wesley's theology as Wesley himself identified that core.

Heitzenrater, Richard P. *The Elusive Mr. Wesley*. 2nd rev. ed. Nashville: Abingdon Press, 2003. A wonderful introduction to Wesley as seen by contemporaries and biographers.

———. *Mirror and Memory: Reflections on Early Methodism*. Nashville: Abingdon Press, 1989. An invaluable set of essays covering various aspects of Wesley's work. The essay on Wesley's famous Aldersgate experience is a jewel.

———. *Wesley and the People Called Methodists*. Nashville: Abingdon Press, 1995. A brilliant study of Wesley in his context by the foremost contemporary historian of Wesley's life and work.

Maddox, Randy L. *Responsible Grace: John Wesley's Practical Theology*. Nashville: Abingdon Press, 1994. This has become the standard work that seeks to cover all of Wesley's theology, written by a systematic theologian aiming to connect Wesley's views with the concerns of contemporary theology. The bibliographical material is a treasure.

Rack, Henry D. *Reasonable Enthusiast: John Wesley and the Rise of Methodism*. Nashville: Abingdon Press, 1993. The best full-length biography of Wesley available.

Runyon, Theodore. *The New Creation: John Wesley's Theology Today*. Nashville: Abingdon Press, 1998. An important attempt to bring Wesley into conversation with contemporary theology.

Weber, Theodore R. *Politics in the Order of Salvation: Transforming Wesleyan Political Ethics*. Nashville: Abingdon Press, 2001. A splendid study of Wesley's political language that avoids the common tendency to reproduce Wesley in our image.

Wesleyan Theological Journal. This journal regularly provides a wealth of discussion on the meaning and significance of Wesley's theology.

Index

accommodation, 104
acquittal, 67–69
agnostics, 143
Aldersgate experi-
ence, 8–9, 34
altar calls, 67
analogy of faith, the,
50, 57
Analogy of Religion,
31
Anglican Tradition,
4, 9, 29–31, 98,
103, 109, 118,
127
annual conferences,
15
anti-Trinitarian
thinkers, 31
*Appeals to Men of
Reason and Reli-
gion*, 14
Aristotle, 42
Arminian Magazine,
20
Asbury, Francis, 20,
22
assertion of rights, 81
assistants, 15
assurance, 7–9, 61,
62–63, 69,
91–92, 97–100,
154, 159
atheism, 32, 141

atheists, 143
authority, 69

basic perception
capacity, 97
being versus doing,
140
Bell, George, 17
Bernard of Clairvaux,
St., 42
biblicism, 109
bigotry, 147,
149–50, 152
bishops, 69, 108–9
blood of Christ, the,
138
Boardman, Richard,
20
Böhler, Peter, 6, 8, 9
*Book of Common
Prayer*, 22
born again, 69–74,
92
Bush, George W.,
139
Butler, Bishop
Joseph, 14, 31,
32
Bristol, 10

Calvin, John, 134
Calvinism, 14, 19,
20, 38–39,

126–27, 175. *See
also* Reformed
Cambridge, 31
Chestnut College,
18
canon of Scripture,
94
canonical writings,
Wesley's, 35–37,
160
casting lots, 10, 28
catholic Christian tra-
dition, 87
catholic spirit,
149–52
causation, 56
certainty, 8, 83,
91–92. *See also*
assurance
*Christian Library:
Extracts and
Abridgements, A*,
15
church, Wesley's doc-
trine of the,
117–21
indispensible ele-
ments, 119–
20
as institution
deserving loy-
alty, 118–19,
121

Index

Church *(continued)*
  as a means to an
    end, 110,
    118–19
  tension between
    institution and
    effectiveness,
    119
  tension between
    pneumatology
    and ecclesiol-
    ogy, 120–21
church growth tech-
  niques, 106
Church of England,
  30, 32, 33, 39.
  See also Anglican
  Tradition
circuits, 15
circumcision of the
  heart, 87. *See also*
  perfection
City Road Chapel,
  London, 23
civility, 142
Clinton, Hillary Rod-
  ham, 139
cognitive malfunc-
  tion, 106, 148
Coke, Thomas, 22
comfort, 170, 175,
  177
common good, the,
  142
common sense, 109
Communion, 9, 19,
  109, 112, 114–15
Conference Minutes
  of 1770, 20,
  37–39
conscience, 129–32,
  135, 150
consumerism, 82
conversion, 140

courtesy, 137–38,
  142
creation, doctrine of,
  41, 46–48, 50,
  162
creation, grace in,
  135. *See also* pre-
  venient grace
critics, 13, 14, 17,
  57, 78, 100, 118,
  142, 147–48
Crosby, Sarah, 19

death, 179
decree, 169–70,
  172–74, 180. *See
  also* predestination
Deed of Declaration,
  22
deism, 31, 139
democracy, 143
devil, 96, 149, 154
direct divine revela-
  tion, 147
discipline, 81, 118
dissenters, 4
doctrine, 118

Eastern Orthodox,
  19, 63, 87, 103,
  109
Edwards, Jonathan, 9
election, 171. *See also*
  predestination
English, 145
enlightenment,
  26–29
enthusiast, 147–48.
  See also fanaticism;
  spiritual fanati-
  cism
entire sanctification,
  87, 89
  as instantaneously

wrought by
  God, 90–91
  See also perfection
Epworth, 3
Erasmus (Eastern
  Orthodox
  Bishop), 19, 109
ethics, 124, 135,
  140, 150
evangelical econom-
  ics, 139
evangelism, 11,
evil, 140, 178–79
excommunication,
  107
exhorter, 19
experience, 27, 29,
  98–99, 103, 148
*Explanatory Notes
  upon the New Tes-
  tament*, 17, 19,
  35, 39

faith, 35, 37, 64, 66,
  104, 111, 133
  alone, 74, 76–77
  degrees of, 100
  as directed toward
    atoning sacri-
    fice of Christ,
    66
  as divine seed, 84
  as the door of
    religion, 123
  as a Gift from
    God, 67
  as the handmaid
    of love, 136
  and politics, 143
  and works,
    74–77, 80, 82
  works by love, 136
faith-based initiatives,
  141

faith of a servant versus faith of a son, 100
fall, 41, 48, 50, 130
fanaticism, 147. *See also* spiritual fanaticism
feminists, 58
Fetter Lane Society, 8
filled with the Holy Spirit, 87. *See also* perfection
final justification by works, doctrine of, 77
Fletcher, John, 20
forgiveness, 34, 67–68, 74, 92, 177, 179
Francis of Assisi, St., 42
freedom, 79–81, 86
    shift from positive to negative conceptions of, 81
free will, 37
fruit of the Spirit, 94–95
fulfilling the law of Christ, 87. *See also* perfection

Georgia, 4, 6
ghosts, 28
God
    as agent, 46, 74, 173–74
    analogical understanding of, 160–62
    commands something because it is good versus something is good because God commands it, 125–29, 135
    as holy, 46, 105
    is love, 47, 136
    as judge, 69
    as mother, 93
    as omnipotent, 46
    as omnipresent, 166, 178
    as omniscient, 46, 162–64, 178
    as sovereign, 46
    as timeless, 175
    as triune, 178
    univeral love of, 20
good works. *See* works
gospel, 104, 140
grace, 77–82, 85–86, 103, 106, 110–16, 124, 135, 140, 146, 150, 155
    perfects nature, 135
grace and freedom, 39, 54
gratitude, 137, 144
Great Awakening, 9
greed, 82
guilt, 70

happiness, 132, 170, 175, 177, 179
Harris, Howel, 10
having the mind of Christ, 87. *See also* perfection
healing, spiritual, 124

history, 110
holiness, 20, 33, 37, 74, 76–77, 103, 108, 123–25, 153, 170, 175, 177
holiness of heart and life, 87. *See also* perfection
Holy Spirit, 43–44, 51, 62, 65, 69, 71–72, 77, 80, 86–87, 93–100, 103–5, 108, 115, 117, 120–21, 131, 133, 135–36, 147–48, 151
Homilies, 9
Hopkey, Sophia, 6
humans
    as agents, 46, 80, 137, 174, 178
    as children of God, 92–96
    conformed to the image of Christ, 95
    made in the image of God, 47, 58, 129, 164
    possessing genuine God-given freedom, 164–65, 174
    restored to the image of God, 70, 80, 135. *See also* integrity
    transformed by love of God, 86

Index

humility, 114, 140

incarnation, 31
infused grace, 62
inner witness of the
    Holy Spirit,
    62, 93–100,
    103–5
    as leveler of social
        classses,
        100–101
    expressed in exu-
        berant wor-
        ship, 102
integrity, 80–82
Ireland, 12
Irish, 145

Jesuit, 145
Jesus Christ, 9, 35,
    41, 43–44, 56,
    71–74, 77, 80,
    132–33, 149,
    151, 154, 157,
    174, 178
    as King, 125, 135
    as Priest, 125,
        135
    as Prophet,125,
        135
    the teaching of,
        89, 125
    the work of, 35,
        37, 66–67,
        95–96, 125,
        135
joy, 72, 103, 132,
    154, 170, 175,
    177
justice, 95, 136
justification, 9,
    34–35, 37,
    61–63, 67,
    69–70, 74–77,

82, 83, 89–90,
    98, 103, 130,
    140, 151, 154,
    159

kingdom of God, 43,
    45, 62, 72, 85
Kingswood School,
    15

language of Zion,
    104
Law, William, 33
law and gospel, 37
law of Christ. See law
    of God
law of God, 65–66,
    68, 79–82,
    104–5, 125,
    132–34
    as written on our
        hearts, 84,
        132, 135
law court metaphor,
    68–69
lay preachers, 69,
    149
Legal Hundred, 22
Lincoln College,
    Oxford, 4
life of God in the
    soul, 72–73
liturgy, 118
Locke, John, 28, 31,
    42
logic, 110
Lord's Supper. See
    Communion
love, 136–38,
    151–52
    as right percep-
        tion, 137
love of God for us,
    79, 82

assurance of, 92
    sense of the, 72
    poured out in our
        hearts, 92,
        136
loving God, 87, 136–
    37, 140, 149,
    151, 154, 178
loving our neighbor,
    87, 92, 136, 140,
    149, 151, 154,
    178
Luther, Martin, 8,
    42, 103, 134
Lutheran, 87, 103,
    145

Mallet, Sarah, 23
marks of the children
    of God, 96
Marx, Karl, 139
maternity ward
    metaphor, 69–74
Maxfield, Thomas,
    17
means of grace, 65,
    82, 108, 111–16
"Means of Grace,
    The," 111
mediation, 69
meekness, 114, 140
mercy, 95, 136
Methodism, 20, 106,
    149, 156–57
Methodists, 11,
    145–47
Methodist Societies,
    4, 12
miracles, 28, 166
money, 147, 152–53,
    156–57
moral despair, 64
moral law. See law of
    God.

morality, 124–29, 135, 142
Moravians, 6, 9, 35, 99
mortification, 140
Murray, Grace, 15, 167

natural person, 104–5
nature, 81
new birth, 69–74, 156. *See also* regeneration
new life. *See* new birth
Newman, John Henry, 30
New Testament versus Old Testament, 132–33
Newton, Sir Isaac, 31
New York Times, 127
Nicene Creed, 57–58
nihilism, 81
North America, 109, 117, 139
nonconformity, 81

obligations, 140
offense of the faith, 106
"On Visiting the Sick", 113–14
open-air preaching, 10
opus operatum, 115
ordination, 22, 109
original sin. *See* sin
orthodoxy, 32, 40
Oxford, 4, 5, 9, 10, 30, 31
Oxford fellowship, 4–5, 15

Oxford Methodists, 140

Paddy, 140, 143–44
pardon,34, 69–70, 89
parish jurisdiction, 14
Parliament, 30
patience, 114
Paul, the apostle, 77, 89
peace, sense of, 72, 154
Pentecostal, 103
perfect love, 87, 154. *See also* perfection
perfection, 83, 87–88, 92, 154, 156
   negatively understood, 88–89
   as neither sinless nor absolute, 87–89
   positively understood, 88–89
Philadelphia, 20
Pilmore, Joseph, 20
Plain Account of Christian Perfection, A, 18
Plain Account of the People Called Methodist, A, 14
Plato, 125
pluralists, 143
political insights, 139–40
politics, 140–43
politics, English, 29, 139, 141
poor, the, 136, 138–39
practical wisdom, 110

pragmatism, 109
prayer, 112, 114
preaching, 65–66, 69
predestination, 14, 37–39, 159–60, 167–76, 180
   conditional versus unconditional, 174–75
Presbyterians, 145
preservation, 162
prevenient grace, 51–56, 65, 130, 135, 142
pride, 48–49, 58
priest(s), 69, 108
primitive Christianity, 117
Principles of a Methodist Further Explained, The, 14
process of salvation, 89–90
providence, 117, 139, 160–67, 173
   three circles of, 165–66
   general and particular, 166
public square, 140–41
public theism, 142
puritans, 29
purity of intentio, 87. *See also* perfection

radical transformation, 86. *See also* perfection
real presence, 115

Index

reason, 27, 29, 31, 142, 147, 149, 160
and revelation, 125, 160
Reasons Against Separation from the Church of England, 16
rebellion, 86
reconciliation, 68, 69, 96
redemption, 41, 135, 161
Reformed, 87, 103. *See also* Calvinism
regeneration, 61–63, 69, 74, 82, 83, 92, 154, 159
as occuring at the same time as justification, 69–70
renewal, 107, 118
repentance, 64, 74–77, 82, 140
as necessary to justification, 75
as the porch of religion, 123
resignation, 140
Roman Catholic, 29, 30, 103, 110, 127, 145
romantic tradition, 81

sacraments, 21, 103–4, 109, 118, 150

saints, 70, 86, 91, 103–4
sanctification, 37, 61, 62, 63, 89–90, 92, 98, 103, 130, 140, 159
Savannah. *See* Georgia
schism, 16, 109
science, 27–28, 31
Scotland, 12, 109
scriptural imperatives as disguised promises, 84, 120–21
scriptures, 112, 114, 148–49, 160, 175
sectarianism, 147, 150, 152
secular confessionalists, 143
secularists, 141, 143
secularization, 143
self-denial, 140
self-examination, 140
Sermon on the Mount, 125
Sermons on Several Occasions, 17, 19, 35, 39, 41
sex, 82
sin, 48–51, 57–60, 66–67, 74, 79, 82, 84, 90, 95, 103–4, 108, 130, 132–33, 140, 145–46, 154, 156, 174
as disposition, 85–86
as power rather than guilt, 90

as voluntary transgression, 84–85
skepticism, 96–97
slavery, 23
Socrates, 129
Southern Baptists, 145
special revelation, 130–32, 135
spiritual depression, 147, 152–54
spiritual direction, 11
spiritual discernment, 149
spiritual fanaticism, 147
spiritual perception, 96. *See also* spiritual sense(s)
spiritual sense(s), 71–72, 97–98
St. Paul's Cathedral, London, 8
Strangers' Friend Society, 23
subjective religious experience, 142
subjectivism, 69, 96, succession of ministry, 118

Taylor, Jeremy, 33
thankfulness, 140
theocracy, 142
Theresa of Avila, St., 42
thief on the cross, 75–76
Thirty-Nine Articles, 22, 30, 39
time and eternity, 178–79

194

tolerance, 146, 149–50
Tory, 139
transformation. *See* sanctification
Trevecka College, Wales, 18
Trinity, 29, 30, 31, 41, 45, 57, 58
truth, 95, 136, 140, 150
Twenty-Four Articles, 39

uncertainty, 69
under law versus under grace, 105–6
union with God, 87. *See also* perfection
unity, 118

Vazeille, Molly, 15, 23
violence, 82
virtue, 114, 140, 164
visible church, 110
voice of God, 130, 135. *See also* conscience
voluntarist view of church, 111

Wales, 10, 18
Wesley, Charles, 5, 7, 15, 22, 23, 102, 106, 167
Wesley, Samuel (John's brother), 107
Wesley, Samuel (John's father), 3, 4, 6

Wesley, Susanna, 3, 4
Westminster College, Cambridge, 19
Whitefield, George, 10, 14, 19–20
Wilberforce, William, 23
William III, 3
William of Orange, 29
women preachers, 19, 23
works, 20, 37–38, 57, 63, 74, 77, 82, 151, 170, 175, 177
works of mercy, 113
works of piety. 113. *See also* means of grace

AFALCONGUIDE®

Best Bass Tips
Secrets of Successful Lure Fishing

Steve Price

FALCON®

GUILFORD, CONNECTICUT
AN IMPRINT OF THE GLOBE PEQUOT PRESS

Cover photo and interior photos by Steve Price

Illustrations by Chris Armstrong, Smackwater Studio

Library of Congress Cataloging-in-Publication Data is available.

ISBN 1-58592-081-9

♻ Text pages printed on recycled paper
Manufactured in the United States of America
First Edition/First Printing

CONTENTS

Dedication v

Acknowledgments v

Introduction vii

Chapter 1 How to Locate Bass 1

    Bass by the Numbers 1

    Choosing a Tributary 3

    Locating Bass with Water Color 6

Chapter 2 Improving Your Crankbait Fishing 11

    Speed Reeling 11

    Ten Tips for Deep Cranking 13

    Why You Need Lipless Crankbaits 17

    Power Cranking through Shallow Brush 20

    Crankbaiting in Winter 23

    Advanced Jerkbait Tactics 26

    Cranking Those Endless Flats 29

    Cranking Those Huge California Swim Baits 32

Chapter 3 Using Spinnerbaits and Buzz Baits 37

    How to Choose a Spinnerbait 37

    How to Slow-roll a Spinnerbait 40

    Fast-Rolling in Deep Water 43

    Ripping Deep Water for Big Bass 45

    Fishing Spinnerbaits after Dark 47

    Understanding Buzz Bait Versatility .51

    Buzzing Bluffs 53

    Don't Overlook the In-Line Spinners 56

Chapter 4 Using Soft Plastics 61

    Finding Bass with Soft Plastics 61

    How to Finesse a Boat Dock 64

Gaining Confidence in the Carolina Rig 67

Split-Shotting, Drop-Shotting, and Dead-Sticking 71

Weird, Wonderful Wacky Worms 75

More Versatile Grub Fishing 77

Fishing Floating Worms and Rats 80

Using Monster Worms and Plastic Jerkbaits 84

Power Tubes 87

Chapter 5 Having Fun with Topwaters 91

Ten Tips for Better Topwater Success 91

Should You Be Noisy or Quiet? 96

How to Wobble up a Bass 99

Fishing Shallow in Summer 101

Twitching Tactics 105

Old Reliables: Zara Spooks and Jitterbugs 107

Chapter 6 Learning to Use Jigs 111

Developing Jig Awareness 111

Fishing Jigs in Heavy Grass 115

Ultra-Deep Jigging 118

Fishing the Fly 'N Rind 121

Jigging in Current 123

How and When to Swim a Jig 126

Index 131

About the Author 135

DEDICATION

To my longtime friend Bill Stephens of Alabama, who loves bass fishing for all the right reasons.

ACKNOWLEDGMENTS

For more than twenty-five years I have had the distinct pleasure of bass fishing with many of the most skilled and knowledgeable anglers in America, on trips that have taken me from one end of the United States to another, as well as to several foreign countries. Every excursion has been a learning experience, and this book is really a result of all of those trips and all those years. To everyone involved with them, I owe a deep debt of gratitude for their time, patience, and willingness to teach.

As this particular project began to take its final form, a number of fishermen, close friends all, consented still again for additional interview time, and to them I am especially appreciative. Lee Bailey, Terry Baksay, Cody Bird, Brent Chapman, Rick Clunn, Alton Jones, Larry Nixon, Mike O'Shea, Skeet Reese, Dean Rojas, Zell Rowland, Bernie Schultz, Mark Stephenson, Byron Velvick, and Clark Wendlandt all added valuable insight and experience on a number of topics and techniques.

Behind the scenes, a special note of thanks must also go to Peggy O'Neill-McLeod, my editor at Falcon, who so patiently waited for each chapter to arrive, even though my deadline had long since passed. I'm sure my excuse of being on the water to gather more information wore thin many times over.

The fun and the challenge of bass fishing comes from the unpredictablity of the quarry. Much of what we think we know about largemouth bass is actually based on theory.

INTRODUCTION

Anyone who has spent more than a few casual hours fishing specifically for large-mouth, smallmouth, or spotted bass usually realizes very quickly how complex the sport can become as his level of participation increases. That's because of the quarry itself; even though bass fishing has been practiced as a sport for well over half a century, beyond a few generalities not a great deal is known specifically about why a bass acts the way it does.

That is precisely what makes bass fishing so much fun. So much of what we think we know—which is concentrated primarily on how to catch the bass—is based on theory. True, many of these theories derive from repeated experiences by anglers throughout the country, and once in awhile we actually get to observe first-hand a certain behavior trait. For the most part, however, the simple act of repeatedly casting a lure into dark water and hoping a bass we can't see and don't know for certain is even present will strike it is frequently frustrating and hum-bling to even the most skilled anglers.

Again, that's what makes bass fishing so much fun and such a challenge, and over the years American fishermen have responded to that challenge by develop-ing new techniques and presentations that attempt to answer some of the unan-swered questions. This book describes a number of those fishing techniques.

Throughout, readers may become aware of one recurring theme, which in itself is not based on a theory of bass behavior. That theme emphasizes the impor-tance of changing lure presentations repeatedly until a bass finally does strike. We don't know why a bass often hits a lure retrieved one way but not another way (there are lots of theories) but it happens often enough to realize that something does trigger the fish to react.

This is precisely why so many different techniques have developed in bass fishing during the past three decades. Every new lure and technique represents another way to try to trigger that reaction. For instance, for many years the accept-ed way to fish crankbaits has been to use a fairly slow retrieve, but in recent years a few fishermen have been extremely successful reeling them in as fast as possible. Thus, a new technique has been recognized and anglers now have a choice of which retrieve to use.

Most of what this book attempts to do, then, is encourage fishermen to try some of these techniques. There is absolutely no substitute for spending time on the water and learning to become efficient with the ones that suit your own style of fishing. Hopefully, that time on the water will also result in a few more bass fishing theories of your own, which is exactly how the sport has evolved over the years.

One of the methods anglers use to locate bass is to divide a lake and its tributaries into sections and then fish those sections according to a broad seasonal pattern based on the time of year. The idea is to narrow a big lake down to manageable size.

1

How to Locate Bass

BASS BY THE NUMBERS

The idea of locating bass on a huge impoundment can be a daunting one for any angler, regardless of his level of experience. Professional tournament fishermen who face this problem often have developed several different ways to solve it, and one of the simplest and most efficient is a system often described as "bass by the numbers."

While this system relies heavily on an angler's understanding of broad seasonal habits and movements of bass between shallow and deep water and does not specifically pinpoint bass, it is very effective at eliminating water that is likely to be non-productive. In so doing, the bass-by-the-numbers technique allows you to concentrate more fully on a small section of a lake and thus make your casts more efficiently and hopefully, with more confidence. While this technique is used in various forms by numerous top-ranked pros, it has probably been refined the most by four-time world champion Rick Clunn.

Here's how it works: A lake and its tributaries are simply divided into three or perhaps four different sections. If you spread a lake map before you and have a pencil, you can see how bass-by-the-numbers will work. Section one will be the deepest water, so on your map draw a line across the lake approximately one-third of the way up from the dam on the lower end.

Draw another line across the lake approximately one-third of the way down from the upper end of the lake where it begins to turn into a river. The area above this line is section three, and the area below it down to the first line you drew is section two. After you become familiar with this system, you may decide to create section four, at the far, far upper end of a lake (essentially all river), and the very back reaches of tributaries.

It's important to mark each major tributary the same way, with section three being the back of the creek, section two the middle, and section one the mouth.

What you have just done is divide the lake according to water depth, and arbitrarily, by water temperature and also water clarity. Bass tend to be in shallow, warmer water in spring, and again in autumn, so your basic starting point in these two seasons of the year should generally be wherever you have marked section three. Conversely, because bass are deeper in summer and winter, you can concentrate on section two or possibly section one (maybe even section three), depending on current lake and weather conditions.

Simply by marking your map in this manner, you can begin to see how this system can immediately help you organize your fishing. By studying the various areas that you've marked as section three, for instance, you can prepare very specifically for the type of fishing you'll be doing, and when you're actually at the lake you can go directly to the area you've chosen.

Here is a quick guideline to which sections tend to be the most productive, according to the months of the year. Bear in mind that this timetable varies according to latitude in the United States, and that a severe winter or an unusually wet autumn may change the timetable and alter your choice of sections. Like every fish-finding system ever developed, this bass-by-the-numbers technique is only designed to serve as a broad outline for your planning.

January: Consider sections two and three in tributary creek channels. Much depends on the severity of the winter, but bass may be on the bottom so think of using a jig or jigging spoon.

February: In many areas the same patterns for January will continue in February, although some bass will begin moving toward shallow water on certain lakes. If the weather has been particularly warm, section three of large tributary creeks may be worth exploring, and spinnerbaits could be effective.

March/April: This is spawning time on many lakes, which makes section three in tributaries (in section three of your lake) a primary choice. These creeks will usually warm faster so bass will spawn here first. Jigs, spinnerbaits, minnow-type twitch baits, and soft plastics can all be used.

May: This is a good time to fish main lake points in section three if the fish have spawned. Look for water depths down to about 15 feet, such as flats that edge major channels. These areas can be fished with crankbaits, plastic worms, and possibly even topwaters.

June: You might find bass in section three of a lake, especially if heavy vegetation is present. Action here would normally indicate resident, rather than migratory fish. Without vegetation, concentrate along the edges of channels in section three, with plastic worms or deep crankbaits.

July/August: If your lake has weeds and vegetation, then this is often a good time to consider section one. Without vegetation, however, many bass will suspend in the deeper waters of both sections one and two and be difficult to catch. The main river channel of section three may be workable if water movement (which means cooler temperature and more oxygen) is present. Even section three of a large tributary may be fishable if current is flowing. Depending on the conditions, many different lures might be used at this time of year, including jigs, crankbaits, soft plastics, and topwaters.

September/October: Baitfish and bass begin moving to the backs of tributary creeks (section three) at this season. The best tributaries are nearly always those with moving water, but the hard part can be determining which section of the creek to fish. Begin at section one around the mouth initially, then gradually work through section two to section three. Cover usually dictates lure choice, so keep rods rigged with crankbaits, spinnerbaits, buzz baits, and plastic worms.

November/December: Bass are usually moving back to deeper water, so section two in the tributaries is a good place to start. If the weather has already turned very cold, concentrate more on the deeper water of section one. Section one of the main lake, which may have steeper bluffs, banks or definitive ledges, is also a possible option, depending on weather conditions. Spoons, jigs, and possibly crankbaits can be used.

This, in a broad overview, is how to use the concept of bass-by-the-numbers. There are many variables that have to be considered on every lake that can affect this timetable, but, as stated earlier, this technique is not designed to pinpoint bass specifically. Instead, it is a quick and relatively simple method of whittling any large body of water down to manageable size in a very short period of time.

The more you use it, the more you will probably refine it to suit your own particular fishing style, or to more closely match the conditions of the lake you fish most often. The important thing to realize with bass-by-the-numbers is that it can be used anywhere, anytime, to at least put you close to the fish.

CHOOSING A TRIBUTARY

Perhaps the most common method of locating bass on any of today's large reservoirs and river systems is the tactic of choosing a particular tributary creek and concentrating all your fishing efforts in that single area. The advantages of such a tactic far out-weigh any disadvantages, and it's a technique that practically any bass fisherman can use.

The primary reason for choosing one tributary rather than trying to cover an entire lake is that a good tributary will offer the same fishing choices as the main lake, but in a much smaller area. Naturally, this smaller area can be fished faster, so you should be able to locate bass much quicker.

The problem, of course, is making the right tributary choice, since not all feeder creeks and rivers are alike and offer the same things to the fish. Among the criteria the pros use in making their choices are tributary size, water depth, the availability of cover, and the presence of baitfish.

The size of a tributary is important because the larger it is the more likely it will have a greater variety of the depth and cover options. In essence, it will

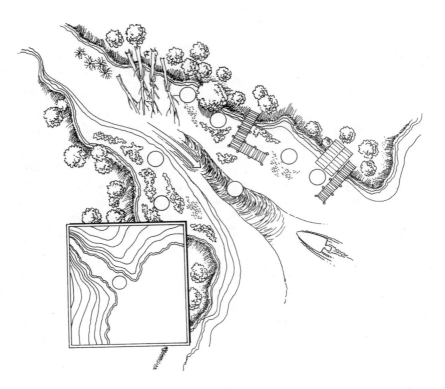

A large tributary will often duplicate the types of cover and structure found throughout the majority of a lake and is more likely to keep bass present throughout the year.

contain the same habitat and conditions as the main lake itself. Smaller tributary creeks, for example, may have abundant cover but lack sufficient deep water. Basically, the idea is to choose a tributary that will keep bass present throughout the entire year, not just for several weeks.

If you've never before visited the lake you're fishing, the quickest way to see the size of any tributary is by studying a good lake map. The best maps will show not only the size of the tributary but also depth changes as well as possible cover options, including standing timber, vegetation, or even boat docks. Look for a map that has the smallest contour interval you can find, such as 5 to 10 feet, because these are the types of changes most important to bass.

In the spring, you're generally looking for a tributary in the upper part of the lake. These tend to be more shallow and will warm faster than the deeper tributaries on the lower end of the lake. Upper lake tributaries should also be consid-

The best tributaries are those that include a large variety of cover and structure options. Vegetation can be extremely important, because it frequently holds bass throughout the year.

ered first in the autumn, because they also cool earliest and thus attract migrating baitfish and bass first.

In contrast, lower lake tributaries often produce better results in the summer and again in the winter because they're deeper. That means water temperatures tend to be more agreeable to bass.

Still, the other factors of depth, cover, and baitfish must also be considered, regardless of the season. Depth is particularly important because it provides bass with increased freedom to move within the tributary, such as from a shallow spring spawning flat to a deeper summer channel. Depth also means more agreeable oxygen levels in summer, as well as more stable temperature zones in winter.

Normally, you should look for a fairly steep, well-defined channel with a depth range of 15 to 25 feet. The tributary will be even more attractive to bass if it is winding rather than straight (increased shoreline means more cover), and if somewhere in the tributary there are shallow flats that can be used for spawning. Again, a good lake map will show these features.

Ideally, a tributary will have both vegetation and woody cover, since bass use both at different times of the year. In spring, for instance, bass and baitfish both relate very strongly to vegetation. This is when young bass are hatched and the greenery provides shelter as well as a source of food.

Later in summer when water temperatures are higher, bass often use wood cover more than vegetation. Look for fallen trees, stumps, standing timber, boat docks, and even overhanging tree limbs when you're searching for a tributary. Shade becomes extremely important during the hot weather months, especially when high temperatures may make vegetation unsuitable due to lower oxygen levels.

Because oxygen is an important consideration, many anglers look for tributaries that have flowing water. This can be an important consideration, and is one reason the far upper ends of a reservoir—where it is literally a river—are favorite fishing spots.

The presence of baitfish in a tributary will immediately tell you two very important facts about your search for bass. The first is that baitfish indicate that the cover, the depth, and the oxygen content of the water are satisfactory to support fish life. The second is that you're close to bass, because wherever you find baitfish, bass are always fairly close.

You don't necessarily have to see shad minnows flick across the surface in front of your boat—but it's nice if you do—all you need to see are a sunfish or two hiding in the shadows under an overhanging willow or minnows nibbling at the algae on a dock piling. Small but subtle indicators like this definitely tell you the water also holds bass.

At this point, it's probably time to start actual fishing, and here several options are open. You can fish one particular type of cover, such as boatdocks, exclusively and try to determine if that's the best option, or you can simply find a good shoreline that contains a variety of cover, such as laydown trees, patches of vegetation or weedbeds, and boatdocks, and fish all of them carefully with a variety of lures.

Professional anglers do both. Some prefer to try to completely eliminate one type of cover before moving to another, while others try to eliminate areas or sections of a creek.

One additional consideration often makes this particular choice a little easier, which is choosing where you actually start fishing in a tributary. In summer and winter, consider starting your fishing closer to the mouth of the tributary because of the deeper water, and gradually fishing your way further back into the tributary. In the autumn, because bass migrate to the backs of creeks, think about starting in the middle of the creek and fishing toward the back. In spring, head to any flats near the back of the creek.

Many of these decisions depend on your own particular style of fishing, daily weather conditions, and experience as an angler. The most important thing to remember is that by choosing a single tributary you have basically eliminated all of the rest of the lake and thus can fish longer and more thoroughly.

LOCATING BASS WITH WATER COLOR

Although water color is probably the first thing any bass angler notices when he heads across a lake, not many use it as a primary tool for actually locating fish. In truth, studying water clarity and correlating that color to the season of the year can be a reliable way to find bass.

Water color can provide valuable clues about the depth bass may be in, which in turn can help you choose the proper lure and presentation technique to use. Because water color often varies in different parts of a lake, it is often possible to locate the type of water you want to fish.

"Water clarity can tell you the basic depth bass will be using, or which type of structure the fish are likely to be holding on, and that, in turn, tells you which lure to use," explains veteran tournament angler Larry Nixon, who has used water color to help him find bass ever since his guiding days on Toledo Bend in the 1970s.

"There are no specific rules that define water clarity, but it will certainly give you a starting point on any lake, anywhere," Nixon says.

The basic rule of thumb to remember is that the clearer the water, the deeper bass normally tend to be, while the muddier the water the more shallow they usually move. Most fishermen use several categories of clarity to describe water conditions between extremely clear and extremely muddy, but here are some basic guidelines:

Extremely Clear Water: Here visibility ranges from 8 or 10 feet to possibly more than 20 feet. Visibility like this most often occurs on the lower end of a lake, and is best fished in spring and in winter, although either season can be difficult since the fish are usually in deep water. Because bass can see your lure clearly, consider using a small profile, shad-colored crankbait or a small, natural-hued plastic worm

Clear Water: Anglers often define water as clear when visibility ranges between 4 and 8 feet. This can be an excellent water color to fish in winter, but may be fishable in warmer weather, especially with fast-moving spinnerbaits. The mouths of lower lake tributaries often have this type of water.

Moderate Water: This type of water usually has the familiar greenish tint caused by algae, and has a visibility of 2 to 4 feet. It is preferred by many fishermen because it allows the use of many different types of lures; often, the best place to find this condition is in tributary creeks in the upper half of a lake.

Stained Water: With visibility of 1 to 2 feet, this is an excellent time to fish spinnerbaits and crankbaits. Upper lake creeks tend to have this type of water most often.

Dingy Water: Here visibility ranges from just a few inches to perhaps 1 foot. This may be the most preferred type of water in bass fishing, since it can be worked with crankbaits, plastic worms, jigs, spinnerbaits, and even buzz baits. Bass will normally be in water less than 10 feet deep under these conditions, and holding close to cover.

Muddy Water: With visibility no more than 3 inches in these conditions, bass will be holding very close to shallow cover, generally less than 3 feet deep. Although this is probably the worst type of water to fish in winter, it is fishable at other seasons with jigs, spinnerbaits and plastic worms.

With these definitions in mind, then, try to match them with the different seasons:

Summer: The easiest bass will be in moderate to muddy water less than 4 feet deep, normally in the backs of creeks or perhaps in the upper end of a reservoir. Bass will likely be holding on visible cover or on shallow breaklines. Buzz baits, crankbaits, and jigs can all be productive lure choices.

Autumn: The classic autumn pattern is to look for moderate to dingy water where visibility is 4 feet or less in the backs of tributary creeks. Both baitfish as well as bass are migrating to the backs of tributaries this time of year, and spinnerbaits, crankbaits, and topwater lures fished around shallow, visible cover are excellent lure choices.

Winter: One pattern to consider this time of year is fishing steep, bluff-type shorelines where water clarity ranges from clear to moderate (2 to 8 feet of visibility) and the depth may be 15 to perhaps 35 feet deep. Drop-shot rigs with small plastic worms work well on many lakes under these conditions.

Spring: If you're after a big bass in early spring, abandon the shoreline and look instead for clear to ultra-clear water (visibility 4 to more than 20 feet) and consider fishing a deep-diving jerkbait over channels leading into spawning flats, around steep-sided points, and over submerged roadbeds. These are potential staging areas where big bass hold before moving shallow. The key depth range is usually 8 to 12 feet.

Later in spring when many bass have moved shallow, look for moderate to clear water with visibility to about 8 feet. This is still a good time to use a floating jerkbait, but tube jigs and plastic lizards fished over hard bottom flats and points in 5 to 8 feet of water are also effective.

Using water color to help you find bass should simply be considered another tool in solving the puzzle of bass location. The water types and lure selections described above are those often used by Larry Nixon and other pros, but they are not the only options available. At any given time, most lakes will have a variety of water clarity conditions present, so it is frequently possible to find everything from clear to dingy water only a few miles apart.

The most important rule to realize about water clarity is, of course, that there are no specific rules that govern exactly how bass will behave under the conditions. Sometimes, they really are shallow in ultra-clear water, for example.

For the most part, however, these guidelines can be used as part of a broader framework that includes consideration of current weather conditions, water temperature, fishing pressure, and other factors. More often than not, too, water clarity is the key piece of the puzzle.

Missouri angler Rick Clunn learned many years ago that a fast retrieve with a crankbait generally produces better results than a slow one. His professional tournament record, including four world championships, proves that such a retrieve should be considered.

2

Improving Your Crankbait Fishing

SPEED REELING

One of the most misunderstood aspects of fishing crankbaits involves speed of retrieve; a majority of anglers generally believe these diving lures need to be reeled back slow to only moderately fast, in order to reach their maximum depth and produce their most effective vibrations.

Most of the time, this is a false assumption, and any bass fisherman who limits himself to a slow retrieve with a crankbait is severely limiting the lure's potential to attract strikes. By far, the most effective retrieve with a crankbait is absolutely as fast as you can turn your reel handle.

No less authority than four-time world bass fishing champion Rick Clunn learned this lesson some twenty-five years ago, and has used it more successfully than any other fisherman. The man who taught Clunn the lesson was none other than Fred Young, the legendary creator of the first modern crankbait, the Big O, whom Clunn drew as a partner one day in a professional tournament.

"He gave me one of his crankbaits to use," Clunn remembers, "then sat in the back of the boat and watched me fish it unsuccessfully for a couple of hours. Finally, he asked me for my rod, and when I gave it to him, I never believed anyone could crank a lure back so fast. He told me I would catch 75 to 80 percent more bass by retrieving a crankbait as fast as possible, and over the years I have realized he was absolutely right."

The reason a fast retrieve works is because it changes the appeal of the lure. Instead of a slow-moving bait plodding along the bottom that bass have a chance to study, it becomes a fast-moving object that bass hit purely on reflex, even when they're not necessarily hungry or actively feeding. Fast reeling causes your crankbait to dive faster and thus reach the bottom—where bass are located—and stay there longer, too.

Another basic rule of crankbait fishing also applies when you're reeling fast, which is hitting rocks, stumps, and other cover as much as possible. In fact, the practice of bouncing your lure off a stump becomes even more effective when you're reeling fast, because the lure ricochets off much more erratically and causes more commotion—which simply helps get the attention of a fish.

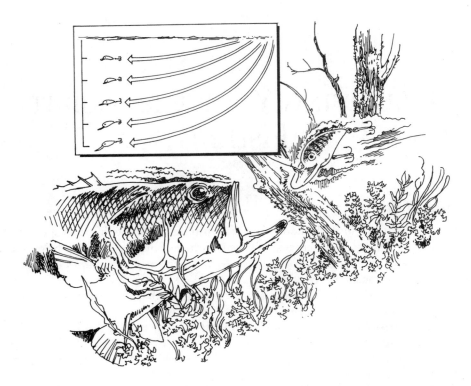

Crankbaits are designed to cover specific depth zones, so it's important to choose a variety of lures that cover the water from the surface down to about 15 feet.

Speed reeling crankbaits does make your lure selection more critical. When you're buying crankbaits, don't simply purchase a few of different sizes, thinking that the larger the lure the deeper it dives. Read the manufacturers' labels carefully and purchase a number of crankbaits that that are designed to reach specific depth zones.

The importance of this cannot be overstated. Don't purchase one crankbait designed to dive 12 to 14 feet, for example, and think it will perform just as well in three feet of water, because it won't—at least not with a fast retrieve. While deep diving lures are fished successfully in shallow water, they cannot be retrieved as quickly because all they want to do is dig into the bottom and bass can't get them.

Instead, purchase lures designed to reach certain depths, such as 0 to 3 feet, 3 to 5 feet, 5 to 8 feet, and so on until you can thoroughly cover water down to about 15 feet. Even after you purchase these lures, you're still going to have to test and evaluate them yourself with your own rod and line combination to see how they do perform.

Clunn, considered by many to be the best crankbait fisherman in America, can vividly remember how important this was during the Bass Masters Classic world championships in 1989 and 1990 on the James River in Virginia. Just prior to 1989, Clunn had designed his own diving crankbait, the RC-3, but it did not perform that well during the 1989 Classic; it dived too deep into the bottom mud and while bass hit it, they couldn't completely engulf it.

After learning the Classic would be held on the same river the following year, Clunn designed the RC-1, which did not dive quite as deep. The bass loved it, and the Missouri pro won his fourth world title—fishing the very same spot on the river where he'd used his deeper diving crankbait unsuccessfully the previous year.

Another secret to this fast reeling technique is that by studying your lures carefully and understanding how deep they will run is that it will allow you to use a heavier line. Most fishermen use lines as light as 10-pound test and some even drop as low as 8-pound test with crankbaits, but if you know and understand how your crankbaits perform at speed, you can certainly use stronger lines. Heavier lines obviously mean more security when you're fishing in and around heavy cover, or for big bass.

The key to using heavier line is also using a long 7- or 7½-foot casting rod that will increase your casting distances. The further you cast, the longer you can keep a crankbait near the bottom. With a long rod, consider using one of the fast retrieve reels now available, too, such as one with a 6.3:1 gear ratio. Even normal reeling with a reel of this type moves the lure quickly through the water, and when you increase your cranking speed, the lure absolutely races.

If you're having trouble accepting the idea of speed cranking, consider for a moment the favorite retrieve used by bass fishermen working lipless crankbaits. These lures are almost universally fished as fast as possible, even in the cold water of early spring. The idea is to tip the top of submerged vegetation (see "Why You Need Lipless Crankbaits," page 17) and draw fish out of that vegetation for a strike. These rattling, vibrating lures are getting pure reflex-type strikes, and there is no reason to think a crankbait with a diving lip can't accomplish the same thing.

There are two primary exceptions when speed reeling is not necessarily the best choice for crankbaits. These occur at either extreme end of the temperature scale, when the water is either too cold or too hot. The reason is simply that in such conditions bass do not move as fast and won't go after a fast-moving lure.

TEN TIPS FOR DEEP CRANKING

Of all the crankbait techniques used by today's bass fishermen, "deep cranking" presents the most problems. Although the depth to be covered ranges roughly from 12 to 20 feet (and occasionally deeper), fishing crankbaits in deeper water is not really about depth so much as it is about choosing a potentially good area and then being persistent and fishing that spot thoroughly—even though you have no visible, above-water references to use.

When it works, deep cranking can produce spectacular results in a very short time, but conversely, it may take you hours to determine that it isn't the right tactic or that you're not in the right spot. Today's crankbaits, rods, and electronic

Most crankbaits produce better results if they are either deflecting off cover on the bottom or hitting the bottom itself. The erratic action seems to trigger reflex-type strikes.

depthfinders make the task easier than ever before, but many anglers still refuse to master deep cranking because of the time factor involved.

Here are 10 tips that can shortcut the learning process for you:

1) Pick the Right Place

The first consideration for deep cranking is locating cover, such as bushes, trees, rocks, or vegetation, and structure, primarily a depth change in the 12- to 20-foot range. Ideal locations are creek channel bends, particularly channels with well-defined breaks, which are even more attractive if there is any type of brush near that edge. In nearly every instance, deep cranking keys on a change in depth.

2) Think Tributaries

Large tributaries (typically on the lower end of an impoundment) hold fish year-round and often provide excellent deep cranking opportunities. Study a map and find a creek with a lot of twists and turns, good variations in depth, and abundant shallow water with cover. Sunken roadbeds are excellent deep cranking areas, and they're usually marked on good lake maps. Most of the consistently successful bass tournament pros pick a tributary and then dissect it completely during a tournament—without worrying about any of the rest of the lake.

3) Consider the Time of Year

Deep cranking produces best in the summer but it works from late spring into the autumn. Thus, the time of year generally determines where bass will be in their various migrations. In early summer, look for sharp depth changes around the first major bends close to shallow points and spawning flats. As summer progresses, concentrate on the underwater points at the mouths of the major tributaries (the bass have migrated from the backs of the creeks to the mouths), as well as on underwater humps and ridges. In the fall, gradually work back into the creeks, concentrating on bends leading up into shallow water. In winter, key in on the outside edges of grasslines or around rock riprap.

4) Don't Forget Cover

Although deep cranking basically revolves around depth changes, the presence of some type of cover makes a depth change that much more attractive. Bushes, trees, rocks, and stumps first attract baitfish, and where baitfish are present, so are bass. Sometimes you'll see a channel outlined by standing timber, but many times you have no idea of its presence unless you see it with a depthfinder or hit it with your crankbait. The outside

15

bends of creek channels frequently have limbs and logs that have washed in, which is one reason they're such excellent spots for deep cranking.

5) Use Your Depthfinder

When you first start looking for a potential area, watch your depthfinder and look for either a depth change or cover, or both. Don't just back off then and start casting; idle over the spot several times to form a mental picture of what is down there on the bottom and also to determine just how large an area it may be. Don't hesitate to throw out marker buoys when you see anything interesting.

If you locate a long ridge, try to find one end and mark it with a buoy, and if you find an underwater hump or island, drop one or two markers on top and several around its edge; when you back off to start casting, you'll have specific reference points.

6) Pick the Right Lure

Ideally, you want to use a big-billed crankbait that gets to the bottom quickly and then digs along that bottom as long as possible. The lure needs to be hitting and bouncing off something as much as possible, so if you don't feel the bottom after a few casts, change to a deeper running lure. Chartreuse is a favorite color for deep cranking lures, and both silent and rattling crankbaits are used. If you've been catching bass consistently on a rattling crankbait but the bites stop, sometimes changing to a silent one (and vice versa) can trigger the fish into hitting again.

7) Use Different Retrieves

In some instances, a slow retrieve produces better results than a fast one. Reel fast only to get the lure to the bottom, then slow down. It is much easier to keep a crankbait on or near the bottom by reeling slow than it is by reeling fast. When you feel the lure's bill hit something, stop reeling so the lure will rise slightly, then jerk it suddenly forward to make it look as if the lure is trying to escape something; this is when most strikes happen.

Of course, there will be times when fast reeling will be the only thing that draws strikes, so if you firmly believe you're fishing a good area but aren't getting any strikes with a slow retrieve, crank a little faster before moving to a different spot.

8) Don't Forget Casting Angles

No matter how small the area you're fishing, make your casts at various angles. The easiest deep cranking is by casting shallow and retrieving your lure down the incline, as this eliminates many of the hang-ups and snags you'll get by casting deep and trying to retrieve up the grade. If you're fishing a long breakline, try casting at an angle that brings your crankbait down the slope diagonally, and if you're fishing a submerged hump or island, work your way completely around it as you cast. Large areas will generally have a smaller spot within them that holds the most fish and the only way you'll find it is by casting at different angles.

9) Use the Proper Equipment

All experienced deep cranking pros use rods of 7 feet or 7½ feet because of the greater casting distance these rods provide. Longer casts mean your crankbait will be on the bottom longer, and the longer the lure is on the bottom, the more opportunities a bass has to hit it. Because most crankbaits are relatively light, the rod should have a limber tip, but it must still be strong enough overall to handle big bass.

Many anglers prefer reels with slower gear ratios, such as 4.4:1, as opposed to 5:1 and higher. With these reels you don't have to conscientiously slow down your retrieve because the lower gears do it automatically. They're also much less tiring to use during a full day on the water, too.

Favorite line sizes range from 10- to about 17-pound test, depending on the depth, type of cover, and size of fish anticipated. Lighter, smaller diameter lines can increase the depth a crankbait runs by a foot or more.

10) Be Persistent

Deep cranking can be hard and discouraging fishing, so it's important not to give up too quickly. The bass you're looking for in summer tend to be schooling bass, so when you find one, you'll usually find more. The trouble is, it may take you awhile to find the first one, so keep fishing and trying to learn more about the spot you've chosen on every cast.

WHY YOU NEED LIPLESS CRANKBAITS

In February 1996, angler Bud Pruitt won a national bass tournament on Sam Rayburn Reservoir in Texas, weighing in a total of 53 pounds of bass. Almost exactly four years later to the day, Pruitt won again at Rayburn, this time with 54 pounds.

Most interesting of Pruitt's two wins was the fact he used the same lure and fished it the same way in both events. That lure was a ½-ounce lipless crankbait, a flat-sided, shad-shaped, rattling lure that Pruitt retrieved over the top of submerged hydrilla beds.

These amazing lures have been in production for many years, and today several different manufacturers offer them in a variety of colors. The most well-known of these lures is probably the one named the Rat-L-Trap, produced by the Bill Lewis

Lipless crankbaits are among the easiest lures to use, and also among the most productive, especially when fished over the top of submerged vegetation in early spring. These lures can be retrieved many different ways, however, including being jigged vertically like spoons.

Company of Alexandria, Louisiana; thus, "Rat-L-Trap" and "Trap" have become generic names for this entire class of lures. The most popular bass fishing sizes range from ¼ to ¾ ounce, although both lighter and heavier models are made.

Lipless crankbaits are important in bass fishing because they can be fished many different ways. Because of their noise and tight vibration pattern, they attract bass, which makes them good "search" baits when you're looking for fish, and because they can be presented in such a variety of ways, they're excellent lures to use after you've located bass.

Perhaps the most significant way to use lipless crankbaits is the way Pruitt did it, by working them over the top of submerged vegetation, especially hydrilla or milfoil. In essence, these are simple cast-and-wind lures that you throw out and retrieve at whatever speed seems to produce the most strikes.

What sets them apart from other lures is that you can easily control a lipless crankbait's depth by your retrieve speed and the angle of your rod tip. Because most of these crankbaits sink at rest, all you have to do is raise or lower your rod tip to change the depth at which the bait is running. This is critical, because not all submerged vegetation grows to a uniform height; the moment you feel the lure hitting grass, you can raise your rod tip and guide it a little higher. Likewise, reeling faster or slower will also cause the lure to run at a different depth.

No matter how careful you are, your crankbait is going to collect some grass eventually, or probably even get completely snagged in it. When this occurs, rip it out by yanking your rod to the side—but be prepared for a strike when you do. Very often, just as the lure breaks free of the vegetation, bass will hit it. When you reel in and the lure has a few strands of vegetation on it, a quick, light slap of the lure and rod tip on the water usually clears it.

Vegetation is not the only place to fish lipless crankbaits, however. In the spring and again in the fall, these are excellent lure choices to fish around long points and the adjoining coves and pockets behind them. The best retrieve is perhaps the one for which lipless crankbaits are best-known: a long cast, followed by reeling as fast as you can crank your reel handle, keeping the lure within a foot or so of the surface.

You can fish lipless crankbaits much slower, too, and even bump bottom cover with them. All you do is slow down your retrieve. These lures are not weedless, and you're going to snag your share of them. But when you do reel very slow and stop whenever you feel it hit a stump or log, you can lift the lure over the obstacle by raising your rod tip. Some will argue that these are the types of places a spinnerbait is much more efficient, but the vibrations produced by a lipless crankbait are completely different from those of a spinnerbait, and at times the bass do want something different.

In fact, lipless crankbaits are excellent lures to use when you're fishing in a crowd and everyone else is throwing spinnerbaits or some other type of lure. If you're fishing water just two or three feet deep, for example, all you have to do is hold your rod tip higher to keep the lure from snagging cover.

In the summer, lipless crankbaits can be fished vertically on submerged humps and ridges like jigging spoons. Simply cast and let the lure sink completely to the bottom, then just raise your rod tip and lower it again just as you would fish a plastic worm or jig. You'll feel the lure's tight vibration as you pull it up, then feel a completely different vibration as it falls.

Of course, lipless crankbaits can be fished at mid-depth ranges, too. All you have to do is count it down to a desired depth, and then start reeling steadily. This is a technique that produces well when bass are suspended, or when they're schooling. One variation of this retrieve for schooling bass in deeper water is letting the lure sink, then ripping it forward and upward by rapidly raising your rod tip, then quickly lowering it again to let the bait fall.

These lures can also be fished around visible cover like boatdocks, riprap walls, duck blinds, and even standing timber. Often, it takes repeated casts to these targets to generate a strike, but sooner or later the fish just can't seem to resist any longer.

That's why lipless crankbaits are a near-universal lure choice among the bass pros when they have to resort to what they call "junk fishing." This is when all their other patterns and techniques have failed and they simply start running a shoreline casting to anything and everything as fast as they can. They're just looking for active bass that will hit the crankbait on reflex.

Pruitt's two tournament wins only tell a small part of this lure's long history of success in the bass fishing world. The fact lipless crankbaits have survived virtually unchanged as long as they have, plus the fact every crankbait manufacturer has one in its lineup, tell a more complete story, which is that this is one of the most universal bass lures any angler can use.

POWER CRANKING THROUGH SHALLOW BRUSH

Serious bass anglers know one of the real keys to successful crankbait fishing is bouncing and deflecting the lure off cover so it richochets off at a different angle and draws reflex strikes. When it comes to deliberately retrieving a crankbait through thick brush, however, even the most experienced fishermen hesitate.

This technique, basically described as power cranking shallow brush, can be one of the most successful of all shallow water techniques during the spring, summer, and autumn months. The keys are using the proper crankbait and retrieving it right through shoreline bushes, laydowns, and standing timber.

How effective is power cranking like this? Extremely effective! Consider, for example, the experience of professional angler Cody Bird of Granbury, Texas, who boated 18 pounds of bass in just an hour of cranking shoreline brush—after he had just spent two hours fishing the very same brush with both a spinnerbait and a jig without a single strike. Other well-known tournament pros, including former world champions Rick Clunn and George Cochran, have also used the technique to win national events.

The most popular crankbait for this is the Bagley Balsa B-3, a 3-inch lure with a square bill. The bill gives the lure a wide wobble but more importantly, keeps the

Certain types of crankbaits, particularly small ones with a square lip design, can often be retrieved through brush without snagging. Knowing how to use this presentation can be extremely important when bass are in shallow water.

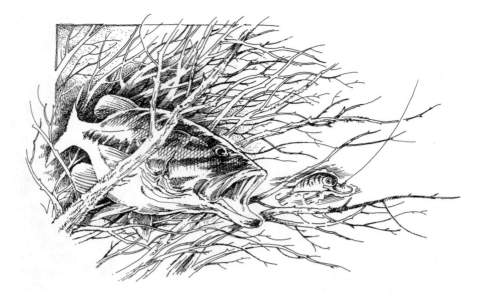

Small, square-lipped crankbaits can be worked carefully through brush and laydown timber; the lip design helps deflect the lure and keep it from snagging.

crankbait moving at an angle to prevent it from snagging. Other lures can be used, but the square bill design is extremely important. A larger overall body size is also part of the key, since the lure represents a baitfish.

What you're looking for primarily are laydowns, those trees that have fallen into the water along the shoreline and whose tips are rarely more than six or eight feet deep. Aim your casts so the crankbait will track right down the tree trunk—and right through the limbs. When the lure does hit a limb, don't stop reeling. Just keep cranking, or jerk your rod tip to rip the lure free; because of the angle at which the crankbait moves, rarely will it snag a limb very hard.

This technique also works around stumps, standing timber, and other forms of shallow brush (not vegetation) in depths down to about 10 feet. Don't be concerned that the crankbait doesn't hit the bottom because with this technique you're not trying to imitate a crayfish and cover the bottom. You're fishing through the brush because that's where shad are located.

Because you're fishing heavy cover, consider using slightly heavier line, ranging from 14- to 20-pound test. A medium/heavy action rod can also be used; most presentations will be short, and a moderate retrieve speed can be used.

Power cranking the shallows can produce big bass as early as the pre-spawn in early spring, but is usually better after bass have spawned. At this time of year you can fish either the upper or lower end of a lake, backwater sloughs, or any big tributaries, as long as you're targeting heavy cover. Later in the summer, the pattern produces much better in the upper ends of lakes where you may have more of a river-type condition, and in the fall you can concentrate again in either the large tributaries or in the main lake.

This is also an excellent technique to use during low water conditions, because falling water pulls bass away from the immediate shoreline; those fish tend to hold along the ends of laydowns and other thick cover. Falling water also seems to make bass somewhat less aggressive in chasing lures, which is why running your crankbait right through the heart of the brush is important.

"I also think the wide wobble is critical," adds Bird, who, after his 18-pound catch with one of the square-billed lures immediately ordered 100 more just so he wouldn't be caught short in future competitions. "A wide wobble is much more erratic, because the lure actually tracks as much as 6 or 8 inches from side to side, depending on how fast you reel it. That, in itself, is an erratic movement that immediately attracts bass, and when you start hitting limbs, the crankbait really looks like an injured shad.

"Of course, you can stop the crankbait and leave it beside a piece of cover, but that isn't really what this presentation is about. When you feel the lure hit a limb, you want to keep reeling, and if it snags, just jerk it free. You don't stop to let the lure float up and then continue reeling with with your rod tip high. You just keep plowing right into the brush," Bird says.

Bird isn't sure why power cranking shallow brush works so well in the upper ends of lakes where the conditions are more riverine, except possibly because there is generally less shallow water available to both the baitfish and the bass. Shallow shorelines give way immediately to the deeper channel, thus making any shoreline cover prime habitat.

This is not a new technique by any means. Anglers have been raking diving lures through shoreline cover for years, but rarely with the success they're getting by using the shallow-running, square-billed crankbaits. Many prefer to slow-roll a spinnerbait down the same laydown, and others like to pitch a jig or plastic lizard into the cover. Crankbaits work because they offer a different type of presentation and perhaps also appeal to the bass in a different way.

For the angler, power cranking is also faster than fishing with either a spinnerbait or a jig, and it also seems to attract larger bass.

CRANKBAITING IN WINTER

"Most anglers think of crankbaits as fast-moving lures for summer, but I use the lures all year, especially in December and January when the water is cooler. Crankbaits are fun to fish in the winter, and they're certainly easier to use than jigs."

The speaker was Alabama bass fisherman Bill Stephens, who at the time of these comments had just put an 8-pound largemouth in the boat—his sixth fish over 6 pounds on six consecutive January fishing trips. All had come on a crankbait retrieved slowly around boat docks and piers in less than 10 feet of water.

Crankbaits are made to resemble small shad, but because bass are more sluggish in winter, it's important to choose a lure with a smaller body but with a larger bill so it dives deeper. Using a suspending crankbait will allow you to reel even slower without losing depth.

There is no question these diving plugs can be some of winter's most effective lures. Cold weather bass generally want their lures presented slowly, which is easy to control with a crankbait; and the fish frequently suspend around cover and structure at mid-depth ranges, which is where crankbaits truly out-shine other lures. With a slow retrieve, these lures can also be worked through brush and limbs without snagging, and they can be retrieved right over the top of grassbeds, too.

Probably the most important aspect of winter crankbaiting is choosing the proper lure. Winter bass are not interested in speed, nor are they often attracted to big, bulky baits. Colder water has made them sluggish so they are more inclined to eat smaller, slower-moving items. This means using the shorter, smaller crankbaits, but choosing one with a long bill that will allow you to fish slightly deeper water and also help keep the lure from snagging. On a slow retrieve, the long bill will deflect the crankbait around objects.

Suspending crankbaits work especially well in the winter because you can reel them down to a certain depth or to a particular object (such as a brush pile) and they'll remain suspended there even after you stop reeling. This neutral buoyancy design is built into many crankbaits and is always advertised on the package, but you can create your own suspending crankbaits by adding a product named SuspenDots to the belly of the lure. These small, stick-on tabs were developed by Storm Manufacturing Co. (now owned by Rapala) and have proven to be extremely popular among bass anglers. Normally, several Dots are needed to achieve neutral buoyancy on a crankbait.

Because winter bass are often around brush, a favorite retrieve technique utilizes a rod pumping action rather than simply turning the reel handle. You can cast, reel quickly to take the lure down, then when you feel the crankbait hit a limb, stop reeling. By raising your rod tip and using it as a type of lever you can pull the crankbait up and through the branches. Often, this slight change in direction, speed, and action will be enough to generate a strike, too.

One retrieve trick certainly worth trying around scattered winter cover is known as stand-still crankbaiting, and for it you'll need a suspending model lure. Crank the bait down to the brush and stop reeling. Very slowly the lure will begin to rise, and when it does, just pop your rod tip downward slightly to make the lure dive back down several inches. When it starts to rise again, pop it once more—you can do this as long as you want to, without moving the crankbait forward at all.

The only time you should consider using a crankbait with a shorter bill is when you're fishing over winter moss, hydrilla, or other submerged vegetation. The ideal situation is to find this vegetation with one to two feet of open water above it; you want to swim your crankbait through this open zone just above the vegetation. Don't be surprised if you catch big bass just a few feet deep doing this, because hydrilla and milfoil will definitely keep bass shallow in even the coldest weather.

Even if the vegetation grows to the surface, you can still fish it with a crankbait. Instead of casting over it, you should fish along the edges, retrieving your crankbait parallel to the edge. Normally in winter, the outside edge will be more productive, and irregularities in that edge like points and channels will be the most productive of all.

You can also crankbait the backs of creeks in winter, just as you did in the autumn. Key ingredients are locating cover like stumps and standing timber, and finding deep water near this shallow cover. Several days of bright, sunny conditions will frequently pull bass out of deeper water to hold around this cover where they actually become more active than normal. A crankbait works so well in these places because it not only looks like a small baitfish, it can also be cast around the cover and retrieved slowly all the way out to the edge of the deeper water to effectively probe the entire zone.

Two other types of winter conditions are well worth exploring with crankbaits. These are rocky riprap walls and long sloping points. Riprap can be very effective on sunny afternoons because even in winter the rocks under the surface will grow moss that attracts minnows that in turn bring in bass. The slightly warmer water also tends to bring bass closer to the surface.

You can fish riprap several different ways, but probably the best way to start is by casting to the rocks at a 45-degree angle, making sure some of your casts actually put the crankbait into just two or three inches of water. This will allow you to cover different depths but with the angle of your retrieve, your crankbait will progress down them slower. You want your lure to actually bounce off the rocks, too. If the bass are using the riprap (afternoon fishing is often better than morning fishing) you'll soon determine what depth they're holding in and can then adjust your casts to keep your lure in that particular zone longer.

Long points are reliable in winter because many of them offer the magical combination of deep and shallow water in close proximity. One favorite tactic is to hold your boat in deeper water and fan-cast up the point toward the shallow water until you contact bass. Many anglers like to use the deepest running crankbaits they can, reeling them down so they bounce off the bottom like a crayfish. Even though you'll have to retrieve slowly to satisfy the bass, you'll still be able to cover more water more quickly with a crankbait than with any other lure.

Bill Stephens discovered this several winters ago, and his results certainly show that cold weather bass can be caught on crankbaits. In fact, he extended his streak of catching a 6-pounder-per-trip twice more before it ended, and it only stopped then because spring arrived.

ADVANCED JERKBAIT TACTICS

California angler Skeet Reese likes to remember a cool February day he spent fishing on the southern end of Clear Lake not far from his home in Cotati. Actually, what he remembers most is a single hour when he fished a jerkbait over a submerged rock pile; during a wild sixty-minute spree he caught about thirty bass weighing between 4 and 11 pounds.

Those are the types of results a jerkbait can bring. These long, thin, lipped lures with two or three treble hooks are designed to dive several feet below the surface where they mimic a dying shad. They are fished by twitching or jerking your rod tip downward with quick, short movements, and as Reese proved, there are times when bass simply can't resist them.

"The presentation of short, quick jerks and pauses triggers strikes from quality bass that may come from 10 to 15 feet away," explains Reese. "Jerkbaits are lures you fish around cover but not in cover, so you can target suspended bass if you need to, which are some of the most difficult of all fish to catch.

"Probably the best overall time of year to fish jerkbaits is when bass are in their pre-spawn cycle, which can be from as early as January in some parts of the United States, to as late as June in other areas. I personally prefer water temperatures ranging from 48 to about 56 degrees, but you can fish a jerkbait anytime between early spring and late fall and catch fish."

The key to jerkbait fishing is in the presentation, but it is the pauses between jerks, rather than the jerks themselves, that are the most important. The most effective jerkbaits are those that suspend at whatever depth they're in when you stop reeling, so if you can jerk one of these lures down right beside a bush or rock pile, you can pause and the jerkbait will stay right there in the strike zone. This capability to suspend is the major advantage jerkbaits have over spinnerbaits, Carolina rigs, and other popular fish-finding lures.

Jerkbaits are designed to dive several feet below the surface where they can be retrieved with short twitches that cause the lure to dart erratically. Fish may come from 10 or 15 feet away to hit the lures.

How long you let a jerkbait suspend at a particular depth depends on several factors, not the least of which is the mood of the bass themselves. Reese often employs a two-one cadence of jerk-jerk-pause, jerk-stop. This gets the lure to its maximum depth quickly, and once there he may let the jerkbait stay motionless for as long as thirty seconds. More often than not, he never has to wait that long to jerk it again, for the line simply starts moving away as a bass takes the lure.

Retrieve speeds and cadences are something you simply experiment with as the day progresses. You can begin by jerking the lure rapidly and using only brief pauses, but if this doesn't produce any strikes, you certainly don't have to keep doing it. You can make short jerks or long sweeping ones, and you can vary your speeds, the number of times you jerk the bait, and of course, the length of time you pause it.

Jerkbaits, like regular crankbaits, are made in a variety of sizes to reach different depths. Generally speaking, during the early spring pre-spawn season you'll need a lure that reaches only 4 to 5 feet deep. Later in summer, however, you'll probably achieve better results with a jerkbait you can get down between 7 and 10 feet. In the autumn when bass begin moving shallow, you can use the shallow runners again.

Many anglers try to match jerkbait size with the size of the forage bass are feeding on. Often in summer this may mean downsizing to a jerkbait measuring only 2 inches in length. Don't hesitate to pack such small lures in your tackle box, for when bass are schooling, this may be the only size they'll hit.

Most of the time, you do best by fishing a jerkbait over cover. This can include practically anything from bushes and fallen trees to rocks and vegetation, which may be at depths of 20 feet or more. Even when bass will not strike a jig or crankbait, you can frequently bring them up to hit a suspending jerkbait.

When you're fishing over shallow, submerged hydrilla or other vegetation, a floating jerkbait is nearly always more effective than a suspending one. You still jerk the lure down until you feel it touch the vegetation, but when you pause, the lure will begin rising toward the surface. This allows you to jerk it again so that it dives downward and forward at the same time, moving in a type of sawtooth pattern. Were you to use a suspending jerkbait over vegetation, each time you jerked it the lure would dive down into the grass where the hooks would get fouled.

The majority of anglers who use jerkbaits limit them to clear water conditions, but in truth, this is a lure you can also use in dingy, off-colored water. If bass are not willing to chase a spinnerbait, you can sometimes tempt them with a jerkbait, again primarily because you can suspend it. In off-colored water, however, you probably will want to change from silver and gray shad-colored patterns to brighter chartreuse or firetiger colors.

"Jerkbaits are excellent search baits for bass," adds Reese, "because you can work them rapidly to cover a lot of water. At the same time, they are excellent big bass lures, because you can fish them over offshore structure like humps, points, and ridges.

Suspending jerkbaits can be kept near a target for an extended length of time, thereby increasing the chances for a strike. Matching lure size of the forage can also be important.

"You can also fish them effectively in shallow water around boat docks, bridge pilings, and other visible structure. In fact, you can fish a jerkbait practically anywhere, and catch bass with it."

Naturally, after his experience at Clear Lake, some of Reese's favorite spots are submerged rock piles.

CRANKING THOSE ENDLESS FLATS

If there is anything at all discouraging about bass fishing, it is looking out over hundreds of acres of open, fairly shallow water without a tree, stump, or stickup in sight, and knowing that somewhere out in that nearly endless expanse is a school of bass. The next most discouraging thing is fishing that water for hours without a strike, and then seeing someone else who did find the fish and caught a limit in minutes.

In all honesty, fishing wide, shallow flats is not easy. Even some of the best crankbait anglers in the world go hours and even days without catching a bass in such places. Perhaps the very first ingredient for flats fishing, then, is patience. After all, it's not a lot different than looking for a needle in a haystack; well-known North Carolina bass fisherman David Fritts once caught 26 pounds of bass from

Finding a ditch, channel, or some type of cover on a wide, shallow flat and then fishing it carefully and thoroughly with a crankbait can sometimes lead to results like this. Bass often position themselves where shallow and deep water meet.

a spot no larger than a suitcase, but only after he'd been crankbaiting the general area for hours.

Still, flats are always worth exploring. There are bass on them somewhere throughout the year, and no lure covers the water as well as a crankbait. There are very few shortcuts in crankbaiting the wide open spaces of flats, but there are a few.

As in other forms of bass fishing, one of the first shortcuts is to study a good lake map to try to locate something different on a flat. Specifically, you're looking for a nearby channel, ditch, or some other form of depth change that might attract the fish. This is true universally wherever you're fishing—some type of change in the bottom contour draws bass to it, and it need not be a major depth break, either. Just a couple of feet of difference is all that's necessary.

Whenever possible, try to match a depth change to the time of year, since bass migrate from shallow to deeper water and back to shallow water during different seasons. As a general guideline, for example, most springtime bass will be in water less than five feet deep; late in spring and through most of the summer the fish will move down to between 10 and about 15 feet; in the autumn bass move back up to 8- to 10-foot depths; and in winter they migrate back to 15 feet and possibly deeper.

With these basic depths in mind, the next step is criss-crossing the flat by boat, studying a depthfinder to actually locate any such depth changes along the bottom. Don't rush through this process, even though it may be taking away from your actual casting time. If you see anything at all that looks promising, mark it with a buoy and cross over it several times until you understand what's down below.

Frequently, bass will be located where the deepest water meets the shallowest water, so once you do locate what appears to be a depth change, start working it with a crankbait. Cast shallow and work the lure to deeper water, making certain you're using a crankbait that runs deep enough to hit the bottom. Don't speed through this process; remember, you're usually looking for a fairly small area— possibly just a single stump, small pile of rocks, or a slight bend in the ditch or contour break that will hold the fish. Place your casts close together so you can cover the area as thoroughly as possible.

One reason it's important to use a crankbait that hits the bottom is because it will bounce off any type of cover or structure like rocks or stumps rising above the bottom. Another reason is that the crankbait can tell you the bottom composition. You want to know if the bottom is hard (which bass prefer) or soft (which they dislike) to learn if you're fishing the correct area. Sometimes small spots of hard bottom will hold bass, even though those spots may be surrounded by a softer, muddier bottom.

Baitfish are another thing to look for on flats while you're cranking. In spring and autumn, baitfish tend to school horizontally, which can give you an indication of how deep bass will be; at these times of the year, try to locate the bottom at the same depth at which you found the baitfish. In summer and winter, baitfish school vertically and the bass are generally deeper and often below the baitfish.

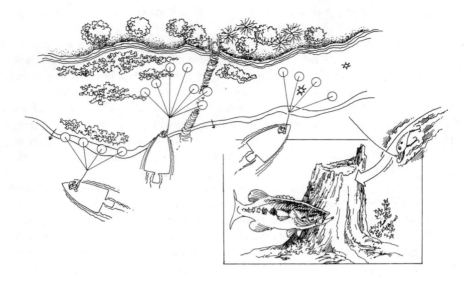

When exploring large flats with a crankbait, pay close attention to ditches, channels, and any underwater cover. Deflecting the lure off cover often generates strikes.

You can really start looking for a baitfish "activity zone" as you leave the launching ramp on your way to the flats. In fact, this is a popular fish-finding technique employed by many of the tournament pros. The presence of baitfish does not always necessarily indicate the immediate presence of bass, but if you see a lot of baitfish activity at a certain depth, that depth is usually a good place to start looking for bass, and the easiest way to do that is to find a place on the flat where the bottom corresponds to that same activity zone depth.

Throughout the process of fishing a flat, boat control is extremely important. You want to be able to follow right along any depth change contour you locate, which means keeping a close watch on your depthfinder. Don't be in a hurry to cover the area, because if you do, you'll invariably miss some of the important features.

Just remember to be patient and to keep casting. No matter what season you're on the water, flats are good places to fish because they hold bass somewhere on them all 12 months of the year.

CRANKING THOSE HUGE CALIFORNIA SWIM BAITS

For more than two decades, the bass fishing world has waited for a new world record largemouth bass to be caught in California; after all, the state has produced more fish over 20 pounds (the world record is 22 pounds, 4 ounces) than any other state. Most of these bass have come in recent years as biologists have stocked larger-growing Florida-strain largemouths into lakes where smaller rainbow trout are also stocked. Feeding on these hapless trout, the bass have grown huge.

Thus, it probably should surprise no one that California has also produced its own category of artificial lures to use in catching some of these big bass. They're typically known as "swim baits," and the earliest models were actually developed for saltwater use. Two basic designs dominate: one style features a solid plastic body measuring up to 10 or 12 inches in length and fashioned to look like—you guessed it—a rainbow trout or other type of natural bass food. The second type of swim bait features a hard plastic head with an attached (and replaceable) large soft plastic body, which together can measure 8 to 10 inches in length.

Today a number of different manufacturers offer swim baits like these, and the lures have certainly produced their share of big bass. Among the best-known firms are Castaic, Basstrix, and Osprey, and available patterns also imitate species like crappie, sunfish, and shad, in addition to the trout.

These swim baits are not only much, much larger than basic bass lures, but also much heavier. Some actually have small bills that cause them to dive to shallow depths, but others simply sink. They usually come rigged with a single hook, although some have two, but none have rattles.

What makes them effective is not their size or even their appearance, but their actions. When retrieved, these lures vibrate or "swim." In some, the tail wobbles from side to side, and in others the entire body is designed to vibrate as the lure is retrieved.

For the most part, swim baits are cast-and-wind lures, although as their use becomes more widespread, anglers are learning the lures are more versatile than most realize. In some lakes fishermen are catching big bass by vertically jigging swim baits in deep water, and in other lakes they're ripping them through vegetation. They're too heavy for Carolina rigs, and they seldom work in really muddy water, but beyond these limitations, the world is still learning how to fish these unusual lures.

"The basic way to fish a swim bait is simply to cast it absolutely as far as you possibly can, let it sink a foot or so below the surface, and then reel it back steadily," explains Nevada angler Byron Velvick, who has used swim baits for years throughout California and caught several 12- and 13-pound bass with them. "These are basically open-water lures that you don't cast to a specific target because they make such a huge splash when they land, so that's why you cast them as far away from your boat as possible.

"Originally, swim baits were considered to be late winter, early spring lures. That's because this coincided with the movement of trout from shallow water to deep, as well as the movement of bass from deep water to shallow. During this time when the bass and trout intermix, the bass feed heavily, so the swim baits can be very effective."

The technique of casting and retrieving just under the surface works especially well in rough, windy weather. When the water is calm, letting the lures sink

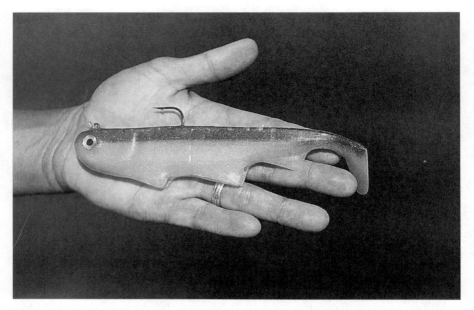

Swim baits are primarily designed to be cast and simply reeled back to make the bait "swim." Newer float-ing swim baits are often drifted quietly over deeper cover and structure in a technique known as flat-lining.

slightly deeper, such as 6 to 8 feet, often works better. And while a steady retrieve certainly produces its share of strikes, there are many times—such as when bass are feeding on or near the surface—that a really fast retrieve will produce truly bone-jarring hits.

In shallow water in spring, swim baits can be cast, then retrieved with an up-and-down rod tip action or by stopping and starting reeling so that the lure actu-ally skips along the bottom. When vegetation is present, swim baits can be reeled right into the greenery, then ripped out by jerking your rod tip. These are essen-tially the same types of retrieves that make lipless crankbaits so effective in spring, and they work just as well with the larger swim baits.

Another retrieve worth considering is simply to let the swim bait sit where it lands (holding your rod up to keep it from sinking), then twitching it once or twice. On a steady retrieve, the lure can also be stopped to let it sink slightly, twitching it, then resuming the retrieve. As always, the intent is to imitate some-thing injured that represents an easy meal for a big bass.

On some lakes, most notably San Pedro in California, fishermen have started jigging swim baits vertically in 20 to 30 feet of water, bouncing the lures off the bottom around rocks and other cover. Like fishing a jigging spoon, the lure is allowed to fall to the bottom, jumped upward by sharply raising your rod tip, then allowed to fall on a slack line so that it drops more erratically.

Again, this type of presentation imitates the actions an injured fish would likely make, and because the swim bait is much larger than any regular jig or plastic worm, it's attracting strikes from very big bass. Bass between 8 and 12 pounds are being taken with this deep jigging technique.

One interesting trick some fishermen have used successfully with the Castaic baits that have treble hooks is worth noting, simply because it is so unusual. In shallow water, a lure, such as their sunfish (bluegill) imitation, is reeled down to a log or perhaps a rock, and deliberately snagged. Then, with a treble hook holding the lure in position, the swim bait is made to vibrate by gently shaking your rod tip. In essence, the lure stays in position but looks totally alive; big bass feel the vibrations and simply swipe it off the log.

Because of their large size and heavy weight, as well as because they are used to attract monster bass, swim baits are fished with heavy action 7- and 7½-foot rods and 20- or 25-pound test line. Rod tips should be soft and flexible, however, to serve as a shock absorber and help in hook-sets. Strikes vary from smashing hits to simple butting, in which the bass appear to try to injure or stun the bait before eating it. Because of the large size of these lures and the single hook on most of them, a lot of fish are lost.

Where else can these big lures be fished? Practically anywhere you feel brave enough to cast one. Long, rocky points, steep bluffs, the outside bends of channels, along the edges of deep grasslines—all are potential hotspots. Surprisingly, although swim baits are usually large, they do attract occasional strikes from smaller fish, too, as well as from different species. Big spotted bass will hit them, as will striped bass in the 20- to 30-pound range.

"Swim baits are confidence lures," advises Velvick. "You can go a long time without getting a strike with one, but that doesn't mean there aren't any big bass around. I always have one tied on a rod no matter where I'm fishing, because they certainly work all over the country."

Spinnerbaits are among the most popular of all bass lures, and today they are fished in both shallow and deep water with a variety of techniques. Here Louisiana angler Eason Dowden shows off a nice bass caught with a spinnerbait.

3

USING SPINNERBAITS
AND BUZZ BAITS

HOW TO CHOOSE A SPINNERBAIT

At first glance, today's spinnerbaits look both simple and similar: most feature an open safety pin-type wire design, with one or two revolving blades on one of the wires and a molded lead head/hook on the other with a silicone skirt slipped on the head to cover the hook.

In truth, most spinnerbaits are quite similar, and the overall design is fairly simple. The trouble comes in learning to understand the relationship between the weight of that lead head and the size of the blades; these two components, combined with the speed of your retrieve, determine how your spinnerbait will act in the water. Choosing the wrong combination for the conditions you're fishing practically assures that you'll catch far fewer bass.

Blades are perhaps the most obvious feature of a spinnerbait and the two most common designs employed by manufacturers today are known as Colorado blades and willowleaf blades. Colorado blades are more rounded, while willowleaf blades are much narrower and pointed on both ends. Both are made in a variety of sizes, from smaller than a fingernail to more than three inches in length. Although blade sizes are listed numerically from a small size one to a huge size eight, there is no standardization in this size system in the lure industry, so blades differ accordingly. The average blade size on packaged spinnerbaits is about size four.

Colorado blades, by their wider design, catch more water and thus produce stronger vibrations when they rotate, which makes them excellent choices for slow-rolling, for extremely off-colored water, and for night fishing. The narrow willowleaf blades do not have as much vibration but they do produce more flash than Colorado blades and also come through vegetation more efficiently. Thus, they're excellent choices when fishing any type of greenery, thick brush, or extremely clear water.

Today, many professional anglers combine these two blade types on the same lure, normally putting a small, rounded Colorado blade ahead of a larger willowleaf. This provides a different type of vibration and adds flash to the lure, but in actuality, they do it more for personal confidence than anything else.

What's important to understand is the relationship of the blades to the weight of the lead head, because all spinnerbait blades, regardless of type, create lift. The faster the blades turn (the faster your retrieve) the more lift is created. When you want to keep your spinnerbait deep, you have to compensate for this lift by a) slowing your retrieve, b) using smaller blades, or c) changing to a heavier lead head.

Overall, a smaller (lighter) spinnerbait is better because it will bring more strikes. When you increase blade size, you start reducing the number of strikes you'll get because you'll start eliminating smaller fish. At the same time, changing blade size, up or down, or head weight, alters the lure's performance.

Normally, when you fish shallow water and fairly heavy cover, the most common spinnerbait situation, you can use a spinnerbait weighing between ⅛ and ½ ounce, with ⅜ ounce the favorite. The lighter the spinnerbait, the less chance it will get snagged, too.

A ½-ounce spinnerbait will cover most water down to about 10 feet efficiently, but deeper than that you'll want a heavier lure, such as ¾ ounce or heavier, depending how you're fishing.

Retrieve speed also must be considered when choosing a spinnerbait. If you want to fish deeper but retrieve fast, you'll need a heavy lure (see "Fast Rolling in Deep Water," page 43); even a slow, deep retrieve with large blades—a good selection for fishing in summer over deep vegetation—will require a heavy spinnerbait of ¾ ounce or more just to stay down.

If it all begins to get too technical and confusing, consider these basic guidelines:

Shallow water/slow retrieve: ⅜ ounce or less, with medium size blades to about size 4.

Shallow water/fast retrieve: ½ ounce most often, but some use ¾ ounce if reeling really fast with big blades.

Deep water/fast retrieve: 1½ ounces and heavier, smaller blades.

Deep water/slow retrieve: ½ ounce and heavier, larger blades.

The important thing to remember is that there are no specific rules about which blade size to use with which head size. The spinnerbaits some use in Florida's Lake Toho, for example, are big and heavy because they're fishing for trophy largemouths in heavy cover and vegetation but the same spinnerbait would be totally out of place in Lake Lanier in Georgia where water conditions are completely different.

Every bass fisherman needs to do some experimenting and decide which combinations perform best for him under different conditions.

If there is an all-around spinnerbait, it is probably either a ⅜- or ½-ounce model with a No. 4½ willowleaf and a No. 3 Colorado blade combination. From there, a bass fisherman can go up or down in both head weight or blade size, depending on how he wants to fish.

Slow-rolling a spinnerbait is a technique in which the lure is retrieved slowly and close to cover. One of the favorite places to make this presentation is over submerged vegetation, in which the lure just barely touches the top of the grass.

HOW TO SLOW-ROLL A SPINNERBAIT

Of the many different ways a spinnerbait can be fished, the technique of "slow-rolling" is probably the most misunderstood as well as one of the most difficult to master. It is also one of the most effective ways to reach bass when they're deeper than 10 feet, or when they are holding very close to cover and are not chasing lures well.

In slow-rolling, the lure does not turn or roll over, as the name implies. Instead, it refers to the fact the blades are barely turning or "rolling over" because the spinnerbait is being retrieved very slowly. You do not "drop" a spinnerbait in slow-rolling; rather, you cast shallow and slowly turn the reel handle so the lure swims and moves forward as it sinks. Once the lure is at the depth you want it, you continue to swim it slowly back to you.

The advantage of slow-rolling over other techniques like jigging or crawling plastic worms is that even though the spinnerbait is moving slowly, it provides both vibration and flash the others don't have. The real key in slow rolling is working the lure extremely close to cover and even bumping it, while at the same time continuing to turn your reel handle so the blades keep turning.

Two of the favorite places to slow-roll a spinnerbait are over submerged vegetation, and along fallen trees. Slow-rolling can be done in many other situations, however, such as around rocks or stumps, through standing timber, and even down points. Anytime you're fishing around good cover and bass don't hit your spinnerbait on a regular retrieve, you should consider slow-rolling; you can even try slow-rolling the same area you may have previously fished with a fast-moving crankbait because larger bass often prefer slower lures.

A lot of different types of spinnerbaits can be used for slow-rolling, but the favorite is probably a ½-ounce model with a No. 4 willowleaf and No. 3 Colorado blade combination. Over vegetation or in deeper water, a ¾-ounce, tandem willowleaf model is a good choice, while in shallow water (you can slow-roll in two or three feet) a lighter ⅜- or ¼-ounce spinnerbait can be used.

One special aspect of slow-rolling a number of anglers have learned to do is to click their reels into gear and begin reeling just before the spinnerbait lands. This causes the lure to start swimming immediately, and also gives you instant control. By keeping your rod tip pointed down toward the lure you can guide it more accurately, especially when you're fishing visible cover like laydowns. Once you begin reeling, however, don't stop. You can slow down so the lure gradually swims deeper, but you want to make certain the lure swims rather than free-falls.

One of the hardest, but also one of the most productive places to slow-roll a spinnerbait is over the top of emerging hydrilla or milfoil. If you ever happen to find yourself fishing Sam Rayburn or Toledo Bend Reservoirs in early February, for instance, this is one of the techniques you'll need to know. The trick is keeping the lure just over the top of the vegetation.

The way you do this is by feel and by trial and error. Experienced anglers can honestly feel the slight change in blade vibration when the lure first touches the

The best results in slow-rolling a spinnerbait normally come when the lure is retrieved just above the top of the vegetation.

hydrilla and they know then to raise their rod slightly and just keep reeling. Other anglers not quite so familiar with slow-rolling in this type of situation usually end up letting the spinnerbait fall too deeply into the grass and having to pull it back out.

The mistake many make when this happens is fishing the spinnerbait too far above the vegetation, simply to keep from getting it snagged. The result is far fewer strikes, as at this time of year the bass seem to be either in the vegetation or right over it; they'll hit a slow-moving lure passing right beside them but they won't move far.

Another prime place to slow-roll a spinnerbait is right along the trunks and through the branches of fallen timber, or "laydowns." These trees generally topple into the water because of soil erosion, and as a result the bases of their trunks are in very shallow water (perhaps even on land) but the top of the tree lies in deeper water. Bass may be anywhere along the tree, so the best tactic is casting shallow and slow-rolling the spinnerbait out into the deeper water.

Here you may find that it's best to keep your rod tip pointing up when your spinnerbait lands shallow, and then gradually lower it as the lure moves down the tree. Doing this allows you to keep the spinnerbait hitting the tree throughout its length, rather than swimming above it. Don't be afraid to bang the spinnerbait along the trunk, either; it's the type of erratic motion that frequently draws strikes.

Slow-rolling is not a new technique; in fact, professional bass fishermen have been practicing it for well over thirty years. There's a good reason for the technique's longevity, too—it definitely works.

The relationship between the size of the blades and the weight of the spinnerbait head is critical in obtaining success like this. Blades create lift, which is balanced against the overall weight of the lure to keep the spinnerbait at the proper depth.

FAST-ROLLING IN DEEP WATER

In case you may have been thinking that bass fishermen have learned all there is to know about spinnerbaits—after all, the lure has been around for more than half a century—be advised that one of the most exciting methods of fishing spinnerbaits was developed as recently as 1999.

The technique is known as "fast-rolling," and as the name implies, it is just the opposite of "slow-rolling." It is a method of fishing deep water quickly with a spinnerbait, allowing anglers to fish deeper cover and structure than with a crankbait and faster than with a Carolina rig.

The real key to fast-rolling is a heavy spinnerbait, which until 1999, was not being manufactured. That year, however, Lake Eufaula, Alabama anglers Jack Tibbs and Jackie Thompson began manufacturing a 2½-ounce lure that allowed them to work Eufaula's well-known deep ledges and breaklines. Thompson, a Lake Eufaula guide, had been adding slip sinkers to his spinnerbaits in an attempt to fish them deep and fast, and doing well enough that he caught the attention of Tibbs, a local tournament angler and lure manufacturer.

Fast-rolling is an easy technique to learn. The best way is by using a 7½-foot heavy action flipping rod and 20 pound test line, to handle the strain of casting and reeling such a heavy lure. After making a long cast and allowing the spinnerbait to sink, snap your rod tip upward just to get the lure off the bottom and make the blade start turning. Then, just start reeling.

"You can hit as much cover and structure as you like," explains Tibbs, "but don't worry about fishing it too fast because the lure's weight will keep it down. With lighter spinnerbaits, the spinning blades create lift so it's impossible to fish both deep and fast, but with this heavy spinnerbait, the blades don't generate enough lift to overcome the weight of the head."

Ideally, you want to keep the spinnerbait near the bottom, so you'll probably feel it hitting things as you reel it back. If the lure seems to be digging into the bottom often, reel faster or raise your rod slightly but not so high that you won't be able to set the hook when a fish hits. At Eufaula, anglers fish them over the ledges, by casting to the shallow side—which may still be 10 to 15 feet deep, and working the lure over the drop.

In some lakes, anglers are using fast-rolling to explore deep, rocky points (by casting shallow and retrieving deep) and other anglers are using the technique in flooded timber to catch suspended bass. In winter when vegetation may still be deep on the bottom, the heavy spinnerbaits can be fast-rolled right over the top of it, in much the same way slow-rolling is used at other times of the year.

Because of its heavy weight, this is not a lure to be used in shallow water. Tibbs' company, Strike Zone Lures, makes lighter spinnerbaits for that. If you want to fish water deeper than 15 feet, however, heavy spinnerbaits like this are needed.

Tibbs produces his heavy spinnerbaits with a choice of either willowleaf or Colorado blades; the willowleaf design is particularly effective when fishing around deep cover like stumps, rocks, and even vegetation; the more rounded

The technique of fast-rolling produces best when the lure is reeled fast and kept near the bottom. Working the lure over ledges is especially effective.

Colorado blade produces louder vibrations and has become a favorite for night fishing or fishing in heavily stained water.

What advantages does a spinnerbait like this have over other lures? First, it can be fished deeper than a crankbait, the traditional deep water lure; only a few diving plugs honestly reach 20 feet, and to get them that deep light line must be used. A heavy spinnerbait can easily be fished at depths of 25 feet on heavy line.

Fast-rolling is definitely easier than deep cranking, too. Anyone who has spent a day heaving a big crankbait across the water and then reeling the wobbling, vibrating lure back through deep water can also tell stories of aching wrists and sore muscles. Spinnerbaits do not have nearly the resistance in the water crankbaits do and thus are much easier to fish, especially with the stiffer rods (most crankbait fishing is done with lighter action rods).

Another advantage fast-rolling offers is that it is a fast technique with a lot of vibration. Carolina rig worms and lizards will also probe deep water like this, but they generally have to be fished slower and do not produce nearly as much vibration. There definitely are times when bass want faster moving lures, too; during the summer of 1999, fast-rolling was used to win three major bass tournaments on Lake Eufaula. In one of those events, won with four fish weighing just under 20 pounds, all the bass were caught between 18 and 20 feet of water.

RIPPING DEEP WATER FOR BIG BASS

Trophy bass guides have always been among the most ingenious of anglers when it comes to developing special techniques to fool big bass, so it should come as no surprise that the fishermen on Lake Fork in Texas have quietly been practicing and perfecting a spinnerbait technique that is producing fish in the 10- to 12-pound class.

The technique is known as "ripping," and it works on other lakes and with certain other lures like lipless crankbaits, but produces best with a ¾-ounce spinnerbait with a single No. 4½ willowleaf blade and 20-pound test line. When summertime bass are holding at depths between 20 and 30 feet and won't hit jigs and plastic worms anymore, ripping has certainly proven to be an alternative worth trying. There's no way to tell exactly where or when this technique was actually developed, but at Lake Fork, at least, is has become an accepted warm weather tactic.

Even though you're fishing deep water with a spinnerbait, you're not fishing it vertically like a plastic worm. The first step is making a long cast, and letting the spinnerbait fall to the bottom. Then, with your rod tip pointing at the lure, crank your reel handle as fast as possible for half a dozen turns or so, then stop and just let the spinnerbait fall. The moment it touches bottom, reel fast again, then stop. Do this for the entire retrieve.

What happens is that when you're reeling fast, the spinnerbait comes quickly up off the bottom, climbing at an angle toward the surface. When you stop reeling, the lure helicopters lazily back to the bottom. This is somewhat like the action an injured or dying baitfish makes, and it triggers strikes from waiting largemouths.

Strikes always come just after the bait stops climbing and begins falling back down, and they're vicious. A 10-pound bass just stops the lure, as if you've snagged a log, which is why you always keep your rod tip pointed at your lure rather than holding it high. When the strike comes, you have plenty of leverage in which to set the hook.

Over the years, the Lake Fork guides have determined that the single size 4½ willowleaf blade is the most efficient for this technique because it begins spinning quickly and easily when you start reeling, and that the ¾-ounce weight is best because it lets the spinnerbait fall slow enough for bass to get it. Heavier spinnerbaits fall faster and just don't seem to draw as many strikes, and the larger Colorado-style blades are more difficult to start spinning, especially when the lure is falling.

"Keeping your rod pointed at your lure is really the key," notes Lake Fork guide Richard McCarty, who has caught three bass over 10 pounds ripping spinnerbaits. "If you raise your rod tip and start reeling, you don't have anywhere to go to set the hook when you get a strike. You move the lure entirely with your reel.

"Ripping seems to bring reflex-type strikes," he continues, "because you can fish a spot with a jig or plastic worm—a spot you know holds bass because you can see them on a depthfinder—and not get a single strike, but you can make one

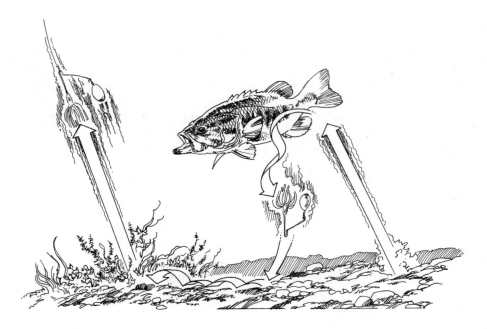

Ripping a spinnerbait works well in summer when bass are deep. The lure is cast, allowed to sink, then reeled quickly for half a dozen turns so the lure climbs suddenly off the bottom.

cast with a spinnerbait and get hit immediately. Bass definitely do not see many spinnerbaits at 30 feet."

The best places to try this technique are on creek bends, humps or long, falling points, and one of McCarty's favorite tactics is casting his spinnerbait into 15 to 18 feet of water and ripping it down into deeper water. That's what he was doing when he caught his first 10-pounder with the technique.

It was a warm September morning and he was just checking a spot for an upcoming guide trip to see if the bass were still in deep water or if they'd started their annual migration into one of Lake Fork's tributary creeks. On his first cast and about the third time he started ripping the spinnerbait, the big fish hit.

Ripping spinnerbaits is seldom effective along the edges of vegetation, primarily because most aquatic grasses don't grow in deep water. Ripping a spinnerbait with this technique brings the lure too close to the surface, but McCarty had used a large lipless crankbait instead, and enjoyed excellent success with it in water 12 to 14 feet deep.

Likewise, ripping rarely works successfully when you're targeting suspended bass, unless those fish have come to the surface to feed. Again, ripping a lipless crankbait through them usually produces better results.

In addition to keeping your rod tip pointed at the spinnerbait, it's important to really crank your reel fast to launch the spinnerbait up off the bottom. If the bass are not active and can't even be tempted with this technique, ripping can get tiring in a hurry. All it takes to make you forget that, however, is one strike from one big bass and at Lake Fork the guides have definitely proven that it can come with this technique.

FISHING SPINNERBAITS AFTER DARK

It was just after midnight when Bill Huntley eased his boat around a rocky point on Alabama's Pickwick Lake, entered a shallow cove, and made his first cast with a spinnerbait out across the calm water. Moments later, Huntley knew he'd just had a date with destiny, and lost.

The fish that hit his spinnerbait that bright, moonlit night was a giant smallmouth bass. Once hooked, the fish surfaced immediately with a series of jumps and splashes just out of reach of the net, but it came close enough for Huntley and his partner to see clearly. Both men feel it was a world record smallmouth weighing more than 12 pounds.

As suddenly as it struck, the bass disappeared. Calm returned to the cove, but in the boat Huntley's heart was pounding and his hands were shaking. In his lifetime, this Madison, Alabama angler has boated hundreds of smallmouth over 5 pounds and several over 8 pounds. In one night alone, he boated three fish over 6 pounds. Over the years, as a former lure manufacturer who spent tens of thousands of hours on the water, he defined the art of nighttime bass fishing with spinnerbaits.

Huntley's technique is simple and easy to learn and is based on the proven fact that bass, both smallmouth and largemouth, move into shallow water to feed on minnows, crayfish, and other creatures under the cover of darkness. A spinnerbait is perhaps the best lure choice to catch these bass because it attracts fish by vibrations, it is an easy lure to fish in shallow water (less than 10 feet deep), and it is basically weedless.

Learning to make the proper retrieve is critical to the technique, and it is best described as an up-and-down yo-yo presentation. Huntley casts, lets the spinnerbait fall, then raises it slowly with his rod tip to start the blade spinning. Then he lets the lure fall back on a tight line, reeling in slack line as it does. Throughout the retrieve, the spinnerbait is kept near the bottom, too; one way to envision its movement is like a flat rock skipping across the water in ultra-slow motion. Strikes, when they come, are usually sudden and vicious, and more than a few fishermen have literally had the rod yanked out of their hands.

"Strikes tend to come whenever the spinnerbait changes direction or blade vibration, such as when I bring the lure up from the bottom, or just as it starts to drop," Huntley explains. "Thus the reason for the yo-yo type of presentation. It provides more of these vibration changes than any other type of retrieve, so theoretically it gives me more opportunities to get a strike."

In many regions of the United States fishing spinnerbaits at night has proven to be extremely effective. Since most strikes occur as the lure is falling, anglers try to use a presentation that creates multiple falls during each retrieve.

Two aspects of this retrieve are extremely important. The first is that you establish a rhythm with your retrieve, and the second is that you make it as slow as possible. You don't want to jump your lure quickly off the bottom and then let it fall slowly. You want a smooth, even movement that lets the spinnerbait rise and fall at about the same rate of speed.

You can use several different spinnerbaits for this technique, although Huntley's two favorite sizes are ½-ounce with a single No. 5 Colorado blade, and ⅝-ounce with a single No. 7 blade. The key is being able to feel the blade moving, which is what attracts the bass. It's especially important that the blade spin as the lure is slowly falling, or half of every retrieve will be wasted.

Huntley's spinnerbait also features what is known as a short blade wire, which is generally considered to transmit vibrations to the angler better than a standard longer blade wire. These short-wire spinnerbaits are known as "drop baits," and they're manufacturered today by a number of firms. They are not really designed for casting and retrieving through brush or vegetation like a normal spinnerbait because they'll get snagged, but for scattered stumps and rocks with the type of retrieve Huntley uses, they're perfect. Most also feature large, single blades.

Huntley usually adds a small pork chunk (Uncle Josh No. 11 pork frog) to his spinnerbaits to provide a little added buoyancy so the lures fall even slower. He fishes with 20-pound test monofilament which not only provides strength but also helps slow the spinnerbait's fall.

This technique can be used around rocks, gravel, stumps, and sloping points—wherever bass might come shallow to feed. Huntley prefers shallow stump flats adjacent to deeper ditches and channels, and on his retrieves his spinnerbait frequently bumps into the stumps. Even when it does, Huntley still tries to maintain the slow, easy, up-and-down rhythm of his retrieve. Normally, hard gravel bottoms produce best for smallmouth, although this does not seem as important for largemouth.

Throughout much of the nation, night-fishing like this can begin in the spring and continue throughout the autumn. Autumn, when the water is beginning to cool, is probably the best overall season. Huntley likes the nights immediately before and after a full moon, but only because he can see better then; the actual phase of the moon does not seem to matter.

Neither does his lure color. While many prefer darker lure colors for darker nights, Huntley's spinnerbait skirt choices may range from green and yellow to chartreuse and white to black and yellow. Only on bright, moon-lit nights does he tone down slightly, often fishing a purple spinnerbait.

Anglers from throughout the United States have come to Alabama to fish with Huntley and learn his spinnnerbait techniques, and most are amazed at how simple they really are. His fish-catching record, however, proves without a doubt that it works, even if he did lose a probable world record that night on Pickwick.

Buzz baits attract bass by the amount of surface commotion they create. They are excellent lure choices around shallow brush, vegetation, rock riprap, and even during sudden snow storms.

UNDERSTANDING BUZZ BAIT VERSATILITY

Most bass fishermen know them as shallow water/scattered cover lures for active fish, but buzz baits can be used successfully in far more situations. In fact, these noisy, clacking surface baits are probably some of the most under-utilized lures in the sport today.

Because of the noise and commotion it creates, a buzz bait is an attractor-type lure that brings fish to it, in contrast to plastic worms and jigs that normally must be dropped very close in front of fish to generate strikes. In a flooded forest of standing timber, for example, a half-dozen casts with a buzz bait may not generate a single strike, but it has certainly gained the attention of any bass nearby; follow-up casts then with plastic worms and grubs often get hit immediately.

In clear water, buzz baits can sometimes be used to pull bass up from as deep as 15 to 20 feet; of course other topwater lures like Zara Spooks and Pop R's may do the same thing, but buzz baits are much easier to retrieve and with their large rotating blade have a completely different sound and action than other surface lures. All you do is cast them and retrieve them steadily. If you stop your retrieve, the lure will sink, and while a few fishermen have reported catching bass with "underwater" buzz baits, this is not what the lures were designed for and it's an inefficient way to use them.

In nearly all instances, the best retrieve is a slow one that just barely keeps the lure on the surface. This is not always true, however, and if bass aren't hitting a slow, chop-chop-chop retrieve, then by all means, start cranking it in faster until you begin getting strikes.

In truth, the sky is the limit on where, when, and how you fish buzz baits. Here are three completely different situations where buzz baits do excel, just to provide you with examples of how versatile this lure really is.

Shallow Shoreline Wiregrass

On many lakes, the shorelines may have different types of wiregrasses growing out to a depth of several feet, which, particularly in the summer, can be excellent buzz bait areas. Don't confuse this vegetation with hydrilla or milfoil; you're looking for vegetation with individual strands, and even if it's fairly thick, it can still be a good place to work a buzz bait.

"The reason is because the bass come into the grass to feed on grasshoppers and dragonflies," explains South Dakota angler Jimmy Crisp, who has fished for bass throughout much of the United States and found this particular situation on many different lakes. "The insects can land and rest on these types of grasses, and the bass come in and have a feast.

"We've opened up some of the fish we've caught and found their stomachs absolutely stuffed with grasshoppers."

Buzz baits can be cast back into this vegetation and reeled back as fast as possible. Even though the lure spends half its time out of the water climbing and rolling across the grass on each retrieve, the bass can still find it, and strikes are

In shallow water with heavy cover, noisy buzz baits may attract bass when other lures don't. The lures can be bumped into cover and guided by rod tip movement.

usually vicious. It's fun and exciting action, but it is often sporadic. The bass may be in the weeds one afternoon, but the next morning they may be gone.

Winter Snow Storms

If you happen to be caught on the water during a snow storm, don't worry. Just tie on a buzz bait and keep fishing. As unorthodox as it seems, certain winter storms initiate wild feeding sprees among bass, and buzz baits are usually the lures drawing the most strikes.

In all probability, the actual snow storm itself has little to do with the feeding. Instead, the activity is very likely triggered by a sudden fall in barometric pressure. The occasions where buzz baits produce best are normally early in winter when the snow begins falling quite suddenly, as from a fast-moving front. The bass feed most aggressively, also, when it's a wet snow, with big, heavy flakes.

Again, your best retrieve is a fast one, and the bass will be shallow, so concentrate on flats, points, and gently sloping shorelines.

Underwater Humps

The water is clear and deep, but somewhere out in the middle there is a high spot, or hump, where the water may be as shallow as 15 feet, even though it falls off steeply to 25 or 30 feet around it. You can fish the top of the hump with a Carolina rig, a jig, or a crankbait—or you can clatter a buzz bait on the surface.

The key to this situation is having active fish. Locations such as humps and ridges traditionally attract schools of bass, but, as every angler knows, the fish certainly aren't active all the time. When they aren't active, the bottom-bumping jigs and Carolina rigs are the best lure choices, but when they are, a buzz bait will certainly bring in plenty of strikes.

Once again, the best retrieve is a fast one. In fact, a proven tactic is to make a long cast but click your reel into gear while the lure is still in flight and start reeling the instant the buzz bait touches water, so it never sinks below the surface. Another way to quickly draw attention to the lure is to sweep your rod to the side when the lure lands, which instantly starts it moving across the water in a shower of spray and noise.

Schooling bass can be found on these high spots on many lakes throughout much of the summer and into the autumn, and when the bass do have baitfish trapped against the surface and are feeding, a buzz bait can be an excellent lure choice. While many fisherman will fish a slow chugger-type topwater, a buzz bait is much faster and can be retrieved with an erratic rod jerking motion that produces much more noise.

From these three instances, it's easy to see how versatile a buzz bait can be. Although the lure is best used as a surface lure, it still has a lot of applications and potential that most bass fishermen never utilize. The most common size is ½-ounce, but most manufacturers also make them in lighter ⅜-, ¼-, and ⅛-ounce sizes, which makes them even more versatile for different conditions throughout the year.

BUZZING BLUFFS

Steep-walled bluffs and cliffs can intimidate even the most experienced bass fishermen, but between late summer and mid-winter such structures can provide exceptional fishing action on clear water lakes. The trick is learning how to buzz them.

Buzzing bluffs can be done with both a spinnerbait and a buzz bait. It works because it draws reaction strikes from bass that suspend a few feet below the surface along the edges of the walls.

"The bluffs where this pattern generally works best are those that lead into a bay, or bluffs that actually circle and form the bay. Free-standing bluffs and ridges that don't connect to the shoreline can also be excellent, especially at each end,"

Buzz baits can be a possible lure choice on lakes with steep bluffs and cliffs because bass frequently suspend along the edges of these places. Abnormalities in the bluff wall such as cracks and bends are especially good places to try.

notes Missouri pro Denny Brauer, who uses this technique often on Lake of the Ozarks where he lives. "I believe the bass are attracted to the bluffs because this is where baitfish are located. The bass just suspend underneath them in the shade."

Just how effective is this technique? At times, it can be stunning. During a national bass tournament on Alabama's Lake Martin in December 1989, buzzing bluffs produced a catch of more than 53 pounds for the winner, but even more interestingly, it produced some of the heaviest largemouth bass (over eight pounds) fisheries biologists had ever seen caught in the lake, which is much more well-known for its spotted bass population and which are considerably smaller in weight.

The favorite spinnerbait for this technique is a ½-ounce model with a large No. 6 or 7 Colorado blade, and the retrieve is a fast one known as "waking." This means making long casts parallel to the face of the bluff (generally within 18 to 24 inches of the wall) and reeling very fast to keep the spinnerbait just below the surface. It creates a bulge and leaves a wake, but the lure itself never breaks the surface. A tandem Colorado blade spinnerbait can also be used

This pattern produces very well early and late on bright, sunny winter days, but may continue throughout the day under cloudy skies. The best bluffs are those with vertical faces that drop at least 15 to 20 feet straight down from the water's surface.

Buzzing bluffs works well throughout the country on clear water lakes but rarely does it produce good results in dingy or off-colored water, simply because bass don't use bluffs as much under those conditions.

When the bluffs do not fall quite as steeply and scattered brush and stickups are found along the edge, buzz baits may be more effective than spinnerbaits. Because bass holding in this type of cover will be more shallow, you'll have to make long casts to avoid spooking them. Both ⅜- and ½-ounce buzz baits can be used, and fished with a 7-foot or longer rod (to make long casts), and 20-pound test line.

The retrieve is similar to that with a buzz bait—fast, steady, and right through the stickups or along the bluff wall. The true secret of making this technique pay off is making long casts and keeping your lure rattling along right beside the bluff. Try not to bump the bluff or scrape the bottom with your boat because it may alert the bass to your presence. The lure itself, however, can bounce off anything in its path.

Because most buzz baits tend to come back in a straight line, this type of fishing sometimes requires a little lure modification to allow your buzz bait to track more to the left or right so it stays closer to the bluff. An easy way to do this is to bend the blade shaft off-center so that it doesn't line up parallel with the head shaft. You can also "guide" a buzz bait somewhat by pointing your rod tip where you want the lure to go.

As you fish along a bluff wall, pay particular attention to abnormalities in that wall, such as large cracks, rock slides, points, and of course, bends. Very often, bass will choose these types of places to hold rather than along a flatter, more featureless part of the wall. At certain times of the day, shade may also be an important consideration, especially in late summer when the water is still warm.

Normally, you will want your rod tip pointing directly at the buzz bait as you retrieve. This is to help in hook setting and control; when a bass hits, don't try to set the hook instantly because most of the time you'll miss the fish. Instead, you can hesitate a moment until you feel the weight of the fish on your rod (as it pulls the buzz bait down). You can also just keep reeling when the fish hits so that it hooks itself. Then, when you feel the weight of the bass, you can set the hook again.

Many bass pros believe a buzz bait looks like a school of baitfish as it comes through the water, and perhaps it does. The lure tends to generate more violent strikes, however, which lead others to believe it simply brings reflex strikes. These may also be a type of territorial defense strike, too. Or it may be that the lure's noisy, churning action simply aggravates the fish until it hits.

Whatever the reason, both spinnerbaits and buzz baits can be used very successfully along bluff walls in clear water lakes. Often, repeated casts across the same water may be required, especially with a buzz bait, but if the bass are there, sooner or later they'll hit.

Don't hesitate to try either spinnerbaits or buzz baits in this pattern at all hours of the day, regardless of weather conditions. On bright winter days bass may rise a little closer to the surface to take advantage of any available warmth, and thus become even more susceptible to these lures.

DON'T OVERLOOK THE IN-LINE SPINNERS

Although safety pin-style spinnerbaits have gained the most notoriety and are the most popular of all the "blade baits," there is actually another style of spinnerbait that has its own special niche in the world of bass fishing. These are the in-line spinners, in which the hook and blade are fashioned on the same shaft.

The most famous and well-known of these is a lure named the Snagless Sally, which has been manufactured since 1960 by the Hildebrandt Corporation. According to Alan Hildebrandt, who helped design the lure, he, his brother John Hildebrandt, company sales representative Charlie Hunter, and rod manufacturer Lew Childre all collaborated on the design, which originally derived from a weighted feather fly named the Yellow Sally being made then by the Peckinpah Company.

The primary use of an in-line spinnerbait is in vegetation or brushy cover or over flooded grass, which explains why more of these lures are used along the Gulf Coast than anywhere else. They are extremely snag resistant (the Snagless Sally has strands of wire that act as weed guards) and can be cast practically anywhere and retrieved fast or slow without a problem in getting them back. Because of its design, the lure is much less obtrusive than many other lures, and thus is also an excellent choice when fish are not aggressive.

Despite these advantages, in-line spinnerbaits will nearly always take a backseat to the more conventional safety pin spinnerbaits because they do not displace

In-line spinnerbaits work well in weedy-type cover and can be fished right over the top of flooded grass. These lures are often worked near the surface but they can also be crawled along the bottom.

as much water and thus are not considered as effective in generating reflex strikes. The most popular sizes of this lure for bass fishing, for example, are the ⅜- and ½-ounce sizes, which utilize single No. 4 and No. 4½ size Colorado blades, respectively. By contrast, conventional spinnerbaits in these same weights tend to have either a Colorado or willowleaf blade this same size, as well as an additional smaller blade of either design.

Nonetheless, many experienced bass fishermen prefer in-line spinnerbaits not only for thick vegetation and brushy cover, but also in tidal water conditions. The long, narrow profile of the lure may just look enough like a needlefish to fool bass into hitting.

There are an infinite number of retrieves possible with an in-line spinnerbait, but three specific retrieves seem to produce the most consistently. One is a fast and steady retrieve that keeps the lure just under the surface; another is a fast retrieve punctuated by stalls that cause the lure to suddenly start dropping to a deeper depth; and the third is a very slow crawling retrieve near the bottom.

Keep in mind that while the lure's primary use today seems to be in marsh-type environments with thick vegetation, such as in Alabama's Mobile Delta, in-line spinnerbaits can be used anywhere you'd throw a regular spinnerbait. Well-known angler Paul Chapple of Birmingham, Alabama, has used a Snagless Sally very successfully for years in the Coosa River impoundments (particularly Logan Martin and Lay Lakes), where he fishes them along the bottom around stumps and logs in shallow tributary creeks, as well as around the rocky bluffs in much deeper water.

Alan Hildebrandt remembers that when he and his friends were designing the Snagless Sally, they wanted a lure that could actually be cast up on shore and crawled into the water without making any commotion, and then retrieved very slowly through cover. Today, when many of the bass pros fish these lures in competition, they may cast up on the bank and crawl the lure into the water, particularly if the fish are extremely shallow and spooky, but most of the time they don't stop the lure and let it fall when they hit a stump or piece of brush. They simply bump it and keep retrieving.

"The stall-and-fall retrieve works better for spotted bass, which are normally found in slightly deeper water," notes Gainesville, Florida, pro Bernie Schultz. "I think one of the reasons we tend to keep an in-line spinnerbait moving after we bump cover is because we're generally fishing it very, very shallow and there really isn't any reason to drop it. Conventional spinnerbaits, with their tandem blades, can be fished over deeper water because they create stronger vibrations that reach deeper fish."

In-line spinnerbaits, like their safety pin brethren, can be fished with or without pork or plastic trailers. In its earliest days, the Snagless Sally was always fished with one of the small Uncle Josh pork chunk trailers, but today many anglers fish the lure without anything attached.

A trailer, of course, makes the lure larger, but some feel this may actually make the lure less appealing to bass. The in-line spinnerbait, for the most part, is not a big bass lure. Instead, it is usually classified as a "numbers," bait, which means it draws strikes from smaller, more aggressive bass. Increasing its size with a trailer, some believe, may actually make the lure more intimidating to these smaller fish.

Other anglers, who have fished a Snagless Sally for years, say just the opposite, pointing out that the lure is actually made in heavier sizes of ¾, 1, and even 1¼ ounces, which makes it not only larger but also better suited for deeper water.

Whichever size you choose, don't neglect these special in-line spinnerbaits, especially if your fishing takes you into shallow, weed and brush-filled water. They're easy to use, and the fact they have survived in the marketplace virtually unchanged for four decades says much about their dependability.

Some soft plastics, particularly those with a swimming tail design, can be used to locate bass, since they can be fished fairly rapidly and at a variety of depths. Some swimming-tail grubs work well both as top-water lures and as crankbaits.

4

USING SOFT PLASTICS

FINDING BASS WITH SOFT PLASTICS

It's a crisp, clear morning in the flooded timber just north of the Highway 147 bridge on Sam Rayburn Reservoir, and Gary Yamamoto is doing what he does best: swimming an eight-inch black/blue tail plastic grub through the trees. Rigged with a 5/0 hook and 20-pound test fluorocarbon line, the big plastic lure has already produced four quality bass.

On this day, however, Yamamoto is not trying to finish a five bass tournament limit. Instead, he's using the lure to find bass for the next three days when competition will be underway. Very few professional fishermen use soft plastics to locate bass, but Yamamoto does it all the time, and he does it very well.

"Many soft plastic lures, particularly those with a swimming tail design, appeal to bass through both their appearance and their actions," explains the veteran angler, "and when they do, the lures actually become excellent fish-finding baits.

"This is one of the major advantages soft plastic lures have over many hard baits. Not only do some of them have very good tail actions, they also look very natural in the water, like something a bass eats regularly. And with good tail actions, plastic lures become much more versatile than most anglers realize."

One of the most versatile is a larger 4- to 8-inch plastic grub, which can literally be fished from top to bottom. On the surface, when rigged with a light screw-in sinker, a fast retrieve turns the grub into a tail-churning buzzbait, while a slower retrieve lets the lure sink slightly where it can be used as a weedless crankbait, two lures often being used to locate bass.

You can also rig grubs Texas-style with a ½-ounce sinker and pitch them into weeds just as you'd pitch or flip a jig; or you can rig them with a football-style leadhead and use them as a drop-bait around ledges and steep rocks.

Deciding which type of soft plastic lure to use and when is a question that deserves careful consideration, because while differences between many soft plastic lures may seem subtle, often they're not.

Single tail grubs, for instance, are best used on lakes where the bass are known to be feeding on baitfish, while grubs with double tails (generally known as "twin tails") are more effective when the bass are feeding on crawfish. The twin tail lures can be crawled and bounced along a fairly smooth bottom to imitate crawfish but they're not that effective in thick hydrilla because the double tail will frequently snag in the vegetation.

On many of the deeper lakes of the western United States where the bottom is generally clear of vegetation, a twin tail grub rigged with a one-ounce football-style leadhead with the hook exposed often works well as a fish-finder. While many would chose a lighter-than-normal weight for such conditions, remember that the heavy weight lets you cover water quickly because the lure sinks faster. At the same time, a faster-falling lure tends to generate more reliable reflex-type strikes than a slower falling lure, which is what you're basically trying for when you're initially searching for bass.

The technique for using grubs this way is to pitch or cast the lure to steeper, bluff-type shorelines and then gradually work it into deeper water by raising your rod tip to pull the lure out, then lowering your rod so the grub falls again into deeper water. Bluff-type banks often are actually a series of small ledges descending into deeper water, and these are the places you want the grub to fall.

Larger single tail grubs and plastic worms can also be used very effectively around standing timber and flooded brush in shallow water. These lures penetrate thick cover very easily when you rig them with a screw-in sinker rather than a slip sinker, and the larger size of the lures allows them to swim as they fall and continue to swim as you retrieve them. Because they imitate a baitfish, the lures will often actually pull bass away from cover to strike.

Yamamoto experienced this very response during a national bass tournament on Oklahoma's Lake Eufaula in the spring of 2000. For two days the bass could be caught by flipping a worm directly into the flooded brush and jigging it once or twice, but that bite died entirely the last day. He started pitching an eight-inch swimming tail grub just beyond the bushes and slowly swimming it back beside each target, and the bass actually left the bushes to hit it. His last-day catch of five bass weighing 22 pounds, 4 ounces was the heaviest of the event.

A 6-inch grub or worm can be used anytime for this technique; an eight-inch version is effective when larger bass are likely to be present; and a ten-inch lure is best when truly big bass are present. Yamamoto's presentation technique, while simple, is certainly one that's worth trying, too. He usually presents the lure with a soft pitch, lets it fall, then slowly swims it back by gently raising his rod tip. Then, holding his rod tip up, he stops so the lure swims back to the bottom.

The Carolina rig lizard is one soft plastic lure many anglers use to locate bass, and when bass are on points or around scattered grass in the spring, crawling a lizard along the bottom is hard to beat. The most popular rigging technique is to slip a ¾- or 1-ounce sinker on the line, tie on a swivel, then add a 2- to 4-foot leader and a hook.

The lizard is rigged with the hook imbedded, but contrary to what many believe, it does not float or swim above the bottom. When you jerk your rod to move the lure, the lizard will jump off the bottom a short distance, but then

When fishing pressure is heavy and bass move tighter to cover, soft plastic worms and grubs are among the most effective lure choices because they can be presented right in the heart of that cover and kept there.

quickly settle back down; the line, which is held to the bottom by the heavy sinker, keeps the lure from floating.

Leader length is generally a matter of preference, although one general rule does apply: the thicker the cover, the shorter the leader so you have better control over the lure. Leader line size can be any weight you choose; although many anglers use slightly lighter line than their main line, others use the same size and occasionally even stronger line.

In the spring, soft plastic jerkbaits can be effective lures for locating bass. One advantage they have over hard plastic jerkbaits is their erratic action when jerked; hard jerkbaits dive and move from side to side in a fairly predictable manner but you're never quite sure if a soft plastic one is going to roll back on itself in a big loop, jump, dive, or twitch when you jerk it. It is this erratic action that most often triggers the reflex strike you're looking for.

Certainly one of the major advantages in using soft plastic lures to locate bass is that all of them can be rigged weedless. As such, they can be cast or pitched into places where other lures will quickly snag—the very places bass live.

"We have all begun to realize that bass move tighter to cover and become more and more reluctant to leave that cover as fishing pressure increases," explains Yamamoto, "so if you can't get a lure to the fish, there's no way you can catch it.

"With a soft plastic bait rigged weedless, you can go straight to where the bass live, with a lure that not only looks but also acts completely realistic. I'm sure that in the years ahead, as more and more anglers realize how effective soft plastic lures are in finding bass, that they'll start using them that way."

HOW TO FINESSE A BOAT DOCK

Fred Bland smiled as he rounded the point and looked into the cove ahead of him, for practically as far as he could see boat docks lined both shorelines. He was home for the rest of the day.

Guiding his boat slowly and methodically around the first boathouse he came to, the Birmingham, Alabama angler began sending his tiny plastic "finesse" worm underneath the structure from every conceivable angle he could find. When he finished fifteen minutes later, he'd caught one largemouth of about three pounds, a spotted bass weighing two, and missed a third fish.

His secret? A four-inch plastic worm, a ⅛-ounce jighead, and six-pound test line.

Say what you will about boat docks—they're boring, they only produce small bass, they get fished hard, they're not very challenging—and anglers like Bland will prove you wrong every time.

The two primary advantages of boat docks are that the majority of lakes have docks on them so there are plenty of places to fish, and that the docks attract and hold fish throughout the year. If your other patterns fall apart or you just can't seem to locate bass anywhere else, you'll generally find at least a few around boat

Boat docks are excellent places to look for bass because of the cover and shade they provide. Many consider a finesse-type presentation with a small plastic worm and a light sinker as one of the best ways to fish these structures.

docks. This is especially true on clear lakes, on lakes that have a lot of pleasure boat and ski traffic, and on lakes that do not have much natural shoreline cover.

Light lines and small lures are often effective around docks because the bass are suspended, either around the support pilings or underneath the main body of the structure itself, and smaller lures fall slower and thus remain in the strike zone longer. At the same time, smaller lures always bring more bites than larger ones.

A good starting point with this type of tackle is a ¼-ounce round jighead with a 2/0 hook, 6- or 8-pound test line, and a very thin, 4- to 6-inch plastic worm. A round jighead provides more action to a worm than a Texas rig because the weight of the jighead remains right at the head of the worm. Each time you twitch your rod, the worm moves instantly. With a Texas rig, the sinker slips down the line and kills a lot of the worm's action.

One technique to tempt these suspended fish into striking is a presentation known as "shaking" or "doodling." The worm is counted down to a certain depth, and then the rod is simply shaken by moving your wrist. The worm stays at the same depth but jumps and dances actively to gain the attention of any nearby fish.

Small, thin plastic worms appear very natural in the water. They maintain their action with light jigheads and lines, but when conditions are extremely tough, consider changing to an even smaller 4-inch size and downsizing to a ⅛-ounce jighead.

Another effective finesse technique for boat docks is a presentation known as "skipping," a tactic Bland himself developed more than thirty years ago.

The key to skipping is making a short, fast underhand cast that keeps the lure traveling very low to the water. You want the lure to touch down close to the edge of the boat dock so the skips will take it further underneath. It's like skipping a rock across a pond. The harder and flatter the rock hits the water, the further it skips over the surface. Skipping is easiest with a 5½- to 6-foot spinning rod, but skilled anglers can also do it with baitcasters.

As soon as the lure stops skipping and begins to sink, you can begin shaking your rod to give the worm action. Don't swim the worm out or crawl it back along the bottom. If the lure isn't hit during the fall, shake the worm a few times on the bottom and then reel back for another cast.

"With the round jighead I use, the worm stands straight up when it's on the bottom," Bland explains. "When I shake it, the worm dances and curls and jumps but it always lands standing straight up.

"I've watched bass in an aquarium to learn how they react to this. They swim up to within a foot or so of the worm and just watch it. Three or four fish may surround it and study it, and then, if you twitch it again, one of them will dart in and take it. What I do is imagine this happening when my worm is on the bottom."

Boat docks on the points leading into coves tend to have the deepest water around them, but not necessarily all the deep water. Some docks may be located right along the edge of a channel while others may have a ledge, a hump or a ridge a few yards away. Look for depth changes and structure like this because these are among the factors that help attract bass to a particular boathouse.

Floating docks tend to be over deeper water simply because that's the easiest way to build them. Permanent pilings are always nice to fish but the water around them is usually more shallow. Docks that extend far from the bank also tend to be in more shallow water.

On many lakes, an entire cove will be lined with boathouses and docks on both banks, and it would be difficult and impractical to fish them all. Boathouses at the entrance to the cove or creek should always be fished because they may attract bass migrating into the cove. These docks may also have deep water, or be the closest to deep water.

When you first begin searching for bass, start with these and then fish perhaps the next three or four docks. If you haven't had any success, skip several and move further into the cove. Work your way to the back and then fish the same way going out until you locate fish.

GAINING CONFIDENCE IN THE CAROLINA RIG

Of all the fishing "systems" bass anglers have to use today, few are as misunder-stood as the Carolina rig. Many disdain it because they feel the technique catches only small fish; others believe it to be suitable only for deep water; and still others simply give up trying to decipher all the different combinations of weights, leaders, and lures that are possible with it.

For those anglers who have overcome their doubts, however, the Carolina rig has become one of the most successful fish-finding techniques in all of bass fishing. While its most efficient use comes in depths between 5 and 20 feet, a Carolina rig can be fished as shallow as 1 foot and as deep as 50 or 60 feet. It is not only a fish-finding tool, but also a fish-catching one as well, and it definitely accounts for its share of trophy-class bass. In deep water a Carolina rig frequent-ly outperforms a crankbait, and in the shallows it's often better than a Texas rig.

"Carolina rigging is a structure fishing technique rather than a technique for heavy cover," notes Mark Davis, a former guide on Lake Ouachita and the 1995 world bass fishing champion. "It is best used on a fairly clean bottom because as you drag the lure along that bottom, you are constantly receiving information about what's down there, which in turn will help tell you where the bass may be."

A standard Carolina rig consists of a ¾- or 1-ounce sinker (either bullet or egg-shape may be used), a swivel, a leader, and a hooked lure. Heavier 17- or 20-pound test line may be used as the main line, and the preferred rod is a medium/heavy action 7- or 7½-footer with a fairly soft tip. Options include plastic or glass beads, and a wide choice of lure types.

To put it together, slide the sinker on your main line, add the small glass or plastic bead (used for noise), and then tie the line with a Palomar knot to one ter-minal of the swivel.

The Carolina rig, which places the lure away from a sinker at the end of a leader, works well for structure fishing. By retrieving the lure quickly, a Carolina rig can also be used to locate bass on points and flats.

The leader is quite possibly the most important part of the Carolina rig package. In stained to muddy water, you can often use the same size line as your main line. More often, however, pros like Davis drop several sizes (sometimes as light as 10-pound test), depending on water clarity and depth. A standard leader length ranges from 3 to 4 feet, but may be as short as 2 feet or as long as 6 or 7 feet, depending on the conditions. If you're fishing shallow water, or around stumps, fallen trees, or even scattered brush, a shorter leader will provide better lure control; the clearer and deeper the water you're fishing, the longer you should consider making your leader.

Some anglers like to fish Carolina rigs along a shoreline, and for this both lighter lines and sinkers normally perform better. A ⅜-ounce sinker is a good choice but in very clear water, a ¼-ounce size may be better to avoid spooking bass. Lighter sinkers mean you can use lighter lines, too, with some using lines as light as eight-pound test.

In 1955, when Gastonia, North Carolina, bass fisherman Lloyd Deaver developed his famous 4-inch, two-hook Fish Finder Worm and began using it on a Carolina rig, it quickly became the standard lure for the technique. Deaver did not originate the Carolina rig but he definitely helped spread its early popularity, and he also made the first experiments with heavier sinkers and various leader lengths that began to show the system's versatility.

Today, however, the most popular lure choice for a Carolina rig is a 6-inch plastic lizard, rigged with a 2/0 or 3/0 hook. This choice is closely followed by the short, stubby French fry–type plastic lures (used with a 1/0 hook). Other popular lures include a 10- or 12-inch plastic worm (shorter leader for easier casting and a 5/0 hook); plastic tube jigs (good for spring spawning bass); and imitation crawfish. In truth, virtually any soft plastic lure can be used with a Carolina rig. It is possible to use hard plastic lures like crankbaits and jerkbaits on Carolina rigs, but seldom are they as successful as the plastics.

The true keys to fishing a Carolina rig successfully are fishing it slowly, and keeping the sinker on the bottom. The sinker, not the lure, is what feeds you the information about the bottom, and it is often what first gets the attention of the bass. After they see the lure crawling along behind the sinker, they may follow it for a while before actually picking it up, so the slower it moves, the more natural it appears.

To keep your sinker on the bottom, don't lift your rod tip as you do with other lures. Instead, sweep it to one side to drag the sinker, reel in your slack line, then sweep your rod again. Even your hook-set is more deliberate; it's like a reverse golf swing in which you use your entire body to sweep your rod to the side. Point your rod tip at the fish, then bring the rod across as you rotate your body with it. Long sets like this are necessary because of the leader; often you don't actually make contact with the bass until the very end of your sweep.

Contrary to popular belief, the lure you use on a Carolina rig does not float freely above it. Instead, it remains on the bottom, especially if you use the rod-

The length of leader used in a Carolina rig often depends on the cover, with longer leaders preferred in vegetation and shorter leaders used around stumps or standing timber.

sweeping method to keep your sinker on the bottom. The one exception to this is when you may be fishing thick, submerged vegetation that actually stops the lure from continuing to the bottom behind the sinker.

The importance of using the sinker to interpret the bottom cannot be over-emphasized. To do this well, of course, requires a skill developed from hours on the water, but it truly is the key to Carolina rigging. Bass prefer something different on the bottom, such as an open patch of gravel along the edge of a grassline, a stump on an otherwise clear bottom, or a slight depression cutting across a flat, level bottom. As you drag the sinker across these types of places, it will change its vibration or "feel," and these are what you're searching for.

Davis remembers a 10-pound bass he caught that illustrates the importance of his sinker's "feel." It was during the spring on South Carolina's Lake Murray, and Davis thought the bass might be spawning along the very edge of the lake's hydrilla. He positioned his boat over the grass so he could cast his Carolina rig (with a green-pumpkin plastic lizard) into the open water beyond and retrieve it back toward the vegetation. Once he felt his sinker enter the hydrilla, he would simply stop and let the lizard sit motionless for up to half a minute. On about his 12th cast, he felt the lizard get picked up, and when he did, he set the hook. On his scales, the bass weighed 10 pounds, 2 ounces.

Catches like that will inspire anyone's confidence in the Carolina rig, but it's more important to understand how to rig and use the system for all those other casts that don't bring in giant bass. With that understanding will also come confidence, and with confidence will definitely come more fish.

SPLIT-SHOTTING, DROP-SHOTTING, AND DEAD-STICKING

When bass fishing is especially difficult, either because of poor weather, heavy angling pressure, or unusual water conditions, three techniques with soft plastics can be tried. These techniques are split-shotting, drop-shotting, and dead-sticking, and although all three first gained acceptance among bass fishermen in the western United States, they are now widely used throughout the country, and each has contributed to various national bass tournament victories.

Split-Shotting

Split-shotting is often described as a light-line version of the Carolina rig, although this is not entirely accurate. In its most basic form, a split-shot rig consists of a very light split shot weight ranging from ½2 to ⅛ ounce clamped on your fishing line between 12 and perhaps 36 inches above your hook. Line size generally varies from 6- to 10-pound test, so split-shotting is normally considered a finesse tactic for clear water; in dingy water conditions, however, some may use line as heavy as 14-pound test and weights as heavy as 3⁄16 ounce. Favorite lures include small plastic worms up to about 4 inches in length.

The split shot itself serves two purposes in that it provides weight for casting and then allows you to stay in contact with the bottom if you do crawl the lure back to you that way. In contrast to regular Carolina rigging in which a larger weight is used, the smaller split shot allows you to work your lure through bottom rocks and brush more effectively. In clear water where bass rely more heavily on their vision to find food, the smaller weight size is also much less intrusive to fish.

The most common retrieve is bottom-crawling your worm in a very slow, deliberate stop-and-go motion, moving the lure only a couple of feet at a time. Former San Diego guide Dean Rojas, now a full-time tournament pro living in Arizona, often employed this split-shotting retrieve with his less-skilled clients because it produced fish so reliably, but it certainly is not the only retrieve option you have.

One variation that has produced a lot of big bass for some anglers is a retrieve known as "stitching," in which the lure is moved just 5 or 6 inches at a time along the bottom. This is done as it is in fly fishing, by pulling the line through the rod guides with your fingers. The reason for such a slow presentation? To better feel the sometimes almost imperceptible pickup of big bass, which usually want their lures moved very, very slowly.

Split-shotting is generally considered a horizontal presentation, meaning that you cast the rig, but you can also fish it vertically. In fact, split-shotting gained much of its early fame through a presentation technique known as "shaking" or

The technique of dead-sticking, in which a plastic worm or grub is allowed to lie motionless on the bottom, works well in cold water conditions when bass are lethargic.

"doodling." Here the worm is presented more vertically by short pitches or even dropped directly over the side of the boat beside cover like pier pilings, bridge abutments, or standing timber. As the worm falls, the rod is shaken to give the lure extra action, and the shaking continues even after the lure reaches the bottom. Of course, you can stop the worm at any mid-range depth and shake it there, too, a technique worth trying around deep cover when you're still trying to determine the exact depth range of the bass.

Drop-Shotting

Drop-shotting originated in Japan where bass fishermen frequently must contend with extremely heavy angling pressure, and made its way to the United States in the late 1990s. It is an absolutely deadly technique in both shallow and deep water where a lot of fishermen are working the same water, as well as in lakes where cold water has pushed the fish deeper and made them lethargic.

The main feature that distinguishes a drop-shot rig from any other rig is that the sinker is tied to the very end of your line and the hook is tied 6 to perhaps 12 inches above. This is essentially a rig for vertical fishing because it positions your lure slightly above the bottom. Sinker weights range from about ⅛ to about ¼ ounce, and a small circle (live bait) hook such as a No. 4 wide bite, short shank J hook is tied in place with a Palomar knot. Lures include any soft plastic creation from 2 to as much as 6 inches long, but the most popular are small, thin worms that are simply hooked through the head leaving the hook exposed.

"Lure choice depends really on your own preference," says Rojas, who uses the drop-shot rig often when he's fishing western tournaments. "All you do is drop the rig to the bottom and then start shaking your rod. The sinker stays in place on the bottom but the worm dances and moves as if it's alive and literally calls bass to it."

It is actually possible to "walk" a drop-shot rig along the bottom by making a short cast toward the bank, letting the sinker find bottom, and after shaking, simply raising your rod tip to lift the sinker and move it toward you in a slow, looping hop. Once the weight has touched the bottom again, begin shaking your rod until you're ready to move it once more.

Falling bluffs and points are among the best places to use a drop-shot, but in truth, it can be used just as effectively in shallow water around rocks, scattered vegetation, and vertical structure. Professional tournament angler Mark Rizk nearly won the 2000 Bass Masters Classic world championship in Chicago by drop-shotting (he finished second by 18 ounces), and another California angler, Kotaro Kiriyama, used drop-shotting to finish tied for fourth in the same event. Both were fishing areas that received extremely heavy pressure from other contenders.

Dead-Sticking

The technique of dead-sticking is a bottom-fishing presentation that works best in cold water conditions when bass are lethargic. It is not a specific method of rigging a soft plastic lure because it can be used with plastic lures on a Texas rig, Carolina rig, and even when fished weightless.

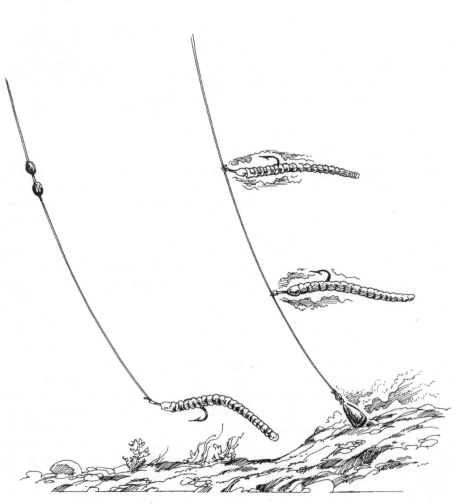

Split-shot (left) and drop-shot rigs (right) are finesse tactics that work when conditions are tough. The drop-shot technique has quickly gained wide popularity because of its effectiveness.

All you do is cast your lure, let it sink to the bottom, and leave it there absolutely motionless—sometimes for as long as half a minute. Needless to say, it is a very tedious way to fish, but the results can certainly be worth the effort. Sometimes bass just pick up the lure and begin swimming away but other times they strike with sudden fury.

How long do you let your lure sit there? There's no specific answer; normally the bass will tell you. Start with ten seconds, then gradually increase the amount of time until you begin getting hits.

Dead-sticking is not a good technique when you're trying to locate bass. Instead, it is a presentation that works after you have already found fish because it allows you to work an area so thoroughly. Any plastic worm, lizard, or similar lure can be used, and preferred line choices range from 10- to as heavy as 17-pound test, depending on water clarity, the amount of bottom cover, and the size of the fish. Remember, heavier lines cause your lure to fall even slower, which can be part of this technique.

Most pros cast toward shallow water, let the lure sit in perhaps 2 feet of water, then slowly move it deeper and let it sit some more, until they're down to 10 or 12 feet. Dead-sticking can be used along barren, rocky banks, around scattered stumps or boulders, and even in brush and light vegetation. Once the proper depth range is known, casting 45 degrees to the bank may work better than casting straight in, since it will allow you to keep the lure in the proper zone the entire length of the retrieve.

Although the lightest sinker weight possible is usually used, dead-sticking also works with weightless worms. It is best in shallow water, and may even require actually casting your lure on the shore, crawling it into the water, and then letting it settle to the bottom.

WEIRD, WONDERFUL WACKY WORMS

The moment Lee Bailey Jr. saw the conditions at Missouri's Table Rock Lake—clear water and a gravel bottom with shallow bass preparing to spawn—he knew exactly the technique he could use to catch them. It was a style of plastic worm fishing he employs often in the lakes and rivers near his home in Connecticut, and as it turned out, it was the perfect technique for Table Rock. In three days, Bailey boated more than 47 pounds of fish.

The rig Bailey used is known as the wacky worm, and it consists of practically any type of plastic worm hooked through the center of the body rather than at its head, as in a Texas rig. The hook (usually a 1/0 or possibly 2/0) is left exposed, and a weight is inserted into the worm itself instead of put on the line. Companies like Lunker City Products sell a special wacky worm weight (which Bailey uses), but other anglers make their own weights by snipping the head off an ordinary roofing nail and pushing the nail shaft into the plastic.

"Wacky worming is a very slow presentation that works well between early spring and late fall," notes Bailey, "and it can be used in a wide variety of water conditions, from ultra-clear to dingy. Wacky worming was developed by guides on Toledo Bend Reservoir in Texas in the late 1970s for spring bass fishing around vegetation but even there, where heavy lines were the norm, light lines were used with this rig. I rarely use lines of more than 10-pound test, and have used as light as 4-pound test."

The reason for such a light line is that it allows you to get more action out of the worm, for wacky worming produces best with a shaking presentation when the worm is on the bottom. Because it is hooked in the middle, the worm undu-

The wacky worm technique utilizes a plastic worm hooked in the middle, which allows a totally different type of action when the rod is shaken. It works in many different water conditions between spring and autumn.

lates and flutters at each end, just like a live night crawler does. Originally on Toledo a wacky worm was cast and slowly reeled back about a foot below the surface, but continued experimentation by anglers across the country have pretty well eliminated this particular presentation.

Naturally, using such light line discourages many anglers who might otherwise try this technique; Bailey often practices for tournaments with 4-pound test line, then switches to 6-pound test once competition begins. With the 4-pound test line, he will get more bites and will be better able to gauge the mood of the bass and determine just exactly what type of presentation he'll need to use.

In early spring, smaller plastic worms in the 4-inch range tend to produce better results, but as the bass become more active and begin feeding on larger baitfish, longer worms can be used. Regardless of worm size, a weight heavier than ⅛ ounce is rarely if ever considered. Wacky worms will catch larger bass, too; Bailey's best is a 7-pounder from Sam Rayburn Reservoir, but he's lost heavier fish simply because he likes to use such light line.

Wacky worm rigs can be fished around vegetation like milfoil and hydrilla, and are especially effective along the edges rather than up on top of surface matted greenery. Because they are rigged with such light weights, the worms will not penetrate heavy vegetation the way a Texas rig or Carolina rig does. Thus, the wacky worm can be particularly productive around deeper submerged grass because it will actually sit on top of that vegetation.

The advantage a wacky worm offers is that you can keep the lure in one spot while shaking it and generating a lot of action. This is why many prefer it when sight-fishing for bass in shallow water; even if the worm's initial splash into the water spooks bass away, the fact the lure remains in one spot but wiggles as if it's alive frequently brings bass back to investigate more thoroughly.

Wacky worms can also be fished along bluffs and steeply-falling shorelines, as well as along offshore breaklines—in fact, the technique is effective down to about 15 feet. When fishing spots like this, the worm is often at its best when cast, allowed to sink to the bottom, and then shaken at 4- or 5-foot intervals along the bottom as it crosses that break.

"To me, wacky worming is also a good fall-back technique to try when conditions suddenly change and the fish become more hesitant to bite," notes Bailey. "For example, after a cold front hits and lowers the water temperature overnight, you can fish a wacky worm right beside sunken brush or the edge of a grassline and catch bass that probably wouldn't hit many other lures or presentations.

"Very often at times like this I will also insert a small rattle in one end of the worm to help attract fish. I have watched bass come in to a wacky worm, and they'll hover just above it and watch, as if they're trying to decide what to do about it. Then, suddenly they'll just dart in and take it."

Strikes are not always violent rod-benders with the wacky worm. Many times, the fish pick up the worm very subtly and just begin swimming away with it. In clear, shallow water, of course, you can often see this occur, but when fishing the worm deeper, line watching is critical.

Bailey also notes that under adverse conditions the wacky worm system can be a good presentation to try on new lakes you may not have fished before. He suggests studying a map and locating several long points that gradually drop into deeper water and shaking a wacky worm down them.

MORE VERSATILE GRUB FISHING

Few bass fishing lures are as frequently overlooked for both their versatility and their fish-attracting qualities as the plastic grub. Typically measuring 2 to about 4 inches in length (some grubs are much longer) these miniature plastic worms might seem to have extremely limited applications on today's lakes, but such is not true at all.

Originally developed in 1960 by well-known Eufaula, Alabama, luremaker Tom Mann as a short and stubby flat-tailed imitation minnow, today's grubs have been transformed so completely that they can be fished from the surface to the bottom to imitate not only minnows but also frogs, baitfish, and crawfish. They can be crawled, hopped, jumped, bounced, buzzed, and cranked by flipping, pitching, and casting.

Ironically, few bass fishermen now even use grubs as they were originally designed. Today the vast majority of these lures feature a single curled, swimming tail (some have double curled tails), and one of the most popular designs also fea-

Plastic grubs can be cast or jigged, and used anywhere between the surface and the bottom. They're extremely versatile lures and can be rigged a variety of ways to match the conditions.

tures a multi-strand skirt on the opposite end. These are generically known as Hula grubs (a la Hawaiian dancing skirts) and were first developed by Gary Yamamoto.

Any of these designs can be rigged various ways, depending on their intended use. Perhaps the most commonly used rigging is with a ¼- or ⅜-ounce round leadhead in which the hook is left exposed. The weight of the leadhead used can vary greatly, however; some anglers use a leadhead as heavy as a full ounce because it makes the grub fall faster and allows them to cover more water quicker.

With the hook exposed, the grub is generally limited to open water with a clean brush-free bottom. In such conditions on certain impounds like Table Rock and Bull Shoals, the skirted grubs are cast to plain gravel shorelines and simply crawled out toward deeper water. It's just a slow, steady retrieve without any hopping; the lure is imitating a crawfish and both smallmouth and largemouth attack them readily.

A variation of this retrieve, in which the grub is allowed to sit motionless on the bottom for a half-minute or so, may also produce surprising results. As has been observed frequently in tanks and aquariums, bass frequently follow moving lures but refuse to hit them. When the lure sits motionless, fish crowd around it watching, until one suddenly darts in to grab it.

With a lighter ⅛-ounce leadhead, a swimming tail grub (usually one without the hula skirt) can be fished very effectively as a topwater lure. In effect, the grub becomes a buzz bait, with the vibrating tail churning the water like a frog swimming over the surface. With a long shank hook, the grub can also be rigged weedless so it can be buzzed through brush and weeds without snagging the way a regular buzz bait would.

By letting your grub sink several feet, it can easily change from a buzz bait to a crankbait. The swimming tail still provides plenty of action so bass can find the lure, but in contrast to a crankbait that will float to the surface when you stop reeling, a grub will sink. That means you can crank it right to a stump or rock pile, then stop and let it fall straight down beside the cover. Rigged weedless with the hook imbedded, you can let the grub drop into the very heart of a brushtop where bass live and still get it back.

Bass often suspend around vertical stucture like bridge and pier pilings, and in these situations, both casting and vertically jigging a grub can bring strikes. Instead of simply letting your grub fall straight toward the bottom, however, try snapping your rod tip several times to make the lure jump, fall, jump, and fall again as it descends. This more closely resembles how an injured minnow acts, and often this is what triggers a bass to hit.

A grub can also be one of the most effective of all lures to use for schooling bass, both when they're thrashing and feeding on the surface and also after they descend. With a ¼-ounce leadhead and fished with 10-pound test line on spinning tackle, a grub can be cast a long distance to avoid spooking the fish. Then, with your rod tip high, the lure can be skipped and sashayed over the surface just like a jumping baitfish. You can also let your lure sink a foot or two, then rip it through the school, and you can let it it fall deeper and work it with a pull-and-drop retrieve.

Certainly one of the most productive places to fish grubs is in fast water, either in creeks and large tributaries, or in the tailraces below power dams. In such spots, grubs drifted and washed along by the current may get hit not only by large-mouths but also by smallmouths, spotted bass, stripers or hybrids.

This technique is easy to do. In tailraces, anglers can either anchor in one spot or drift with the current if conditions permit. The grub is cast to the edge of the fast current, allowed to sink nearly to the bottom, then simply washed downstream. If you're anchored when you do this, cast upstream, then hold your rod tip up to keep the grub above the bottom, and rotate in your seat as the lure is swept past.

Tailrace fishing often requires heavier leadheads because of the current. Often ½-, ⅝-, and ¾-ounce sizes are used, and slightly larger grubs are usually more productive. In creeks and tributaries where the current is not as swift, lighter heads and smaller grubs should be used, and again, the key is letting the current wash the lure downstream naturally around points and shoreline pockets.

Even though most grubs in use today feature swimming-action tails, these smaller lures provide even more action when fished with spinning tackle and eight to 10-pound test line. For the larger Hula grubs, or when heavier leadheads are used, baitcasting equipment will be better. In all cases, use a rod with a sensitive tip that not only aids in casting but also helps you work the lures and feel light strikes.

FISHING FLOATING WORMS AND RATS

Bass fishermen around the nation will tell you hardly anything compares with the sudden, jolting strike of a bass smashing a topwater lure, but surprisingly few of those same anglers seriously consider fishing a soft plastic lure on the surface.

Actually, plastic worms can be used very successfully as topwater lures, and a small but specific category of soft plastics known collectively as "rats" are designed for use only as topwaters.

Worm Fishing

When plastic worms are used on the surface, they're generally known as "floating" worms, but in truth, many who do use them really work them from the top down to perhaps 12 inches underwater. The technique gained its first followers around North Carolina's Currituck Sound in the early 1970s, but owes much of its present popularity to a Kinston, North Carolina, angler named Danny Joe Humphrey, who gained national publicity with his topwater tournament successes in 1987 and '88. Today, Humphrey manufactures special plastic worms designed for topwater fishing, but practically any worm can be fished this way.

Floating worms offer several distinct advantages over other topwater lures. First, they're weedless, so you can pitch and cast them into weeds and brush

Hollow-bodied frogs or "rats" are worked over the top of matted vegetation or around thick, wooded cover with a series of quick jerks that often draw vicious strikes.

without much threat of getting snagged. Secondly, with a slow, steady retrieve, they provide a distinct side-to-side swimming action similar to a small snake. They don't disturb a lot of water, but they do imitate a favorite bass food. And third, floating worms do just that—they float—which means you can keep them in a potential strike zone for a long time.

The most popular size for topwater worm fishing is a 6- or 7-inch straight-tail model, although longer worms can and are used on occasion (when especially large bass are being targeted, for example). A wide gap 2/0 hook works well with a 7-inch worm, and most anglers use 10-pound test line. Rig it with the hook imbedded, as you would Texas-style. Larger, heavier hooks will actually tend to drag the worm under, which means you have to retrieve the lure faster to keep it on the surface—and one of the keys to this technique is fishing slow.

With the light line, most prefer open face spinning tackle. To prevent line twist with spinning gear, tie in a swivel 12 to 14 inches above the hook, as with a Carolina rig, but leave off any weight. Your best rod selection will be a medium action 6- to 6½-footer.

Floating worms really shine in shallow water with heavy cover, around boat docks and piers, and over scattered vegetation. Like nearly all topwater fishing, most success seems to come when you establish a cadence to your retrieve—a steady, repetitive series of jerks and pauses—rather than a straight cast-and-wind back presentation.

Woo Daves, winner of the 2000 Bass Masters Classic world championship, also recommends working a floating worm with your rod 90 degrees to one side, rather than pointing the rod tip directly at the lure.

"There are two reasons for this," explains Daves, who has made a career of plastic worm fishing, "which are that it's easier to establish that retrieve cadence when your rod is pointed to one side—you're moving your rod side to side rather than up and down—and also that it forces you to pause before you set the hook.

"You can't set the hook immediately with a floating worm because bass often hit the lure in the middle where a fast hook-set will miss them entirely. Instead, when a fish does strike, point your rod tip down at the fish, let the bass swim away until your line tightens, and then set the hook with a sweeping set rather than a quick jerk."

Not surprisingly, the techniques of grassbed fishing that made the floating worm so popular at Currituck Sound more than thirty years ago can still be used today. The best places to aim your casts are where the vegetation makes a point or where there is an open hole or channel leading into the greenery. If the vegetation is still below the surface, consider letting your worm slowly sink until it is just above the grass before you begin your retrieve.

Rat Fishing

When the vegetation is thick and matted on the surface, another type of plastic lure often comes into play. These are the floating, hollow-bodied "rats" or "frogs" that are scooted across the top and which often account for huge stringers of bass. In the South, rat fishing usually starts in late June and just gets better until late fall, and if there are no hard freezes, the lure can be used through the winter.

Actually, vegetation is not a prerequisite for using one of these lures. In many western waters, plastic rats are regularly fished around heavy, shallow stumps,

The plastic frog or "rat" can be an effective lure choice when fishing vegetation that has matted on the surface. These hollow, weedless lures, however, also work well in open water around other types of cover.

stickups, laydowns, and other cover. It's unusual, because southern bass fishermen tend to use spinnerbaits in these types of places, while in the heavy, matted vegetation western anglers often prefer jigs.

In the summer months, the best rat fishing takes place early and late, but as the water gradually cools, the lure can be productive throughout the day. Most serious rat fishermen use line testing at least 20 pounds, and a 6½- or 7-foot medium/heavy or heavy action rod. The rat is simply cast back over the vegetation, or right into the middle of the stumpfield, and then retrieved with a series of jerks or pulls that move the lure quickly but erratically in a stop-and-go pattern at different speeds. Because it floats, you can stop a rat at any time right beside a likely-looking hideout, twitch it slightly, or really rip it quickly over the top. By their design, these lures are essentially weedless, with most having two hooks protected by the lure's soft body.

Half the fun of fishing a rat is anticipating a strike, which can come at any place. In vegetation, especially, the strikes tend to be violent explosions that send water and grass flying, and as likely as not, the fish will be a heavy one. Rat fishing is known for producing trophy-size fish.

As with a floating worm, however, you have to hesitate just a moment to make certain the bass has fully engulfed your lure before setting the hook. You'll also get a lot of complete misses when you fish this lure; it's as if the bass are following underneath it and simply hit it to knock it out of the way.

Plastic rats and frogs have been around for many years, but their use, like the floating worm, was originally much more regional than national in scope. Among those who have helped give the technique national publicity are Loyd Tallent of Huntsville, Alabama, an early manufacturer who spread the lure's popularity around Lake Guntersville, where rat fishing is still considered one of the primary summer and fall bass patterns over the milfoil; and Harry Ehlers of the Snag Proof Co. in Cincinnati, who for years has manufactured a wide variety of rats and frogs for bass fishing.

USING MONSTER WORMS AND PLASTIC JERKBAITS

Few lure designs lend themselves as well to modifications, both in design and fishing techniques, as the plastic worm, and during the past half-century, the lure has certainly undergone its share of changes. These new designs, in turn, have led to several very specific fishing techniques that can be used effectively in lakes and rivers across the country; two of these techniques involve using monster worms and soft plastic jerkbaits.

Monster Worms

Monster worms are generally classified as those plastic worms measuring longer than 10 inches in length, and, in fact, some anglers know them as "snakes," because that's what they look like. The DeLong Lure Manufacturing Company produces plastic worms 16 inches long and actually lists them in their brochures as snakes,

Extra-large plastic worms, often termed "snakes," are a favorite choice among trophy bass anglers. Some fish them as floating worms while others rig them with a slip sinker or split shot and crawl them along the bottom.

while Hawg Caller, Berkley, Luck E Strike, and a number of other firms produce plastic worms in 10- to 12-inch sizes.

Monster worms can be used throughout most of the year, depending on the region of the country. They are essentially lures for warm water, and also lures for larger-than-average bass. California fishermen often use monster worms during the winter months in Southern California as the bass begin staging prior to spawning, while in states like Arkansas, Texas, and Georgia big worms are more frequently used between June and September when bass tend to be feeding on larger prey.

Monster worms can be rigged several different ways, including as a basic Texas rig with a slip sinker (use a 4/0 to 6/0 hook with a ⁵⁄₁₆- or ⅜-ounce weight); a Carolina rig (1-ounce weight but only an 18-inch leader to make casting easier); or as a split shot (⁵⁄₁₆- to ⅛-ounce weight clamped 10 to 14 inches above the hook).

Whichever way you decide to rig, the presentation is nearly always the same, which is very slow and deliberate. This is not a lure to use when exploring the water looking for bass; instead, it is a technique that allows you to thoroughly cover an area you already know holds bass because you just crawl the worm along the bottom. Big bass like large meals, and they often prefer them to be moving slowly, which is exactly what a monster worm provides.

Two slight variations in presentation have proven particularly effective in different regions of the nation. One is known as "stitching," in which the worm is moved just 2 to 10 inches at a time by pulling line through the guides with your fingers and then reeling in the slack. Trophy bass expert Bill Murphy is the angler who made this presentation famous; he uses 10- to 12-pound test line with a heavy action spinning rod in the clear California water he fishes.

Another presentation is sometimes known as the "lift and glide" because instead of crawling the worm along the bottom, it is lifted by raising your rod tip, then allowed to float back down on a slack line while your rod is still pointed up. When the worm touches bottom again, lower your rod and reel in the slack line.

The effectiveness of this particular presentation cannot be over-emphasized, and it works well not only for most categories of plastic lures but also for spinnerbaits and jigs. Bass hit lures most often as they are falling, so you try to create as many falls as possible during each retrieve.

Sloping points, the edges of grasslines, lily pads, and even scattered brush are all excellent places to fish monster worms. They can also be very effective at night during the summer (three or four days before the full moon) when you're fishing clear water. Angler Ron Shuffield of Arkansas often fishes at night during the warm weather months, and has caught largemouths of nearly 10 pounds by crawling big plastic worms down stumpy points.

The key to fishing a lure of this type is keeping contact with the bottom, which means that when you lose that contact a bass has picked up the worm. When that happens, don't set the hook immediately. Instead, peel line from your reel and let the bass take the worm for several seconds. When the fish stops, then reel in any slack and set the hook. It's an exciting way to fish because practically any bite you get will be from fish weighing more than 5 pounds, even though strikes may be extremely light.

Soft Jerkbaits

The term "soft jerkbait" refers to that category of plastic lures that look much like long, slender minnows and are fished like hard plastic jerkbaits. Some know them as soft jerkbaits, others call them flukes or jerkworms, and still others simply call them a Slug-Go, since that was the name of the first lure of this type introduced in 1988 by Connecticut angler Herb Reed.

Soft jerkbaits are usually fished without a weight, which is one of the reasons they're so effective. They are easily rigged weedless—many soft jerkbaits are designed with a special body cavity that helps hide the hook—and allowed to sink, which they do very slowly. Once below the surface, the lures can be jerked with your rod tip to make the lure dart forward, glide, and then slowly begin sinking again. Establishing a slow but steady cadence that keeps the lure moving continually is usually the most effective retrieve.

"There are probably an infinite number of ways to fish these lures," explains Reed, who made thirty-nine prototypes of his Slug-Go before he settled on a design he liked. "The actions soft jerkbaits have are very erratic, which helps trigger a reaction strike, but at the same time, the lure's basic minnow-type appearance also helps generate feeding strikes. And, because you rig them weedless, you can cast them into heavy cover where bass like to hide.

"You can fish soft jerkbaits over submerged vegetation with a series of jerks that moves the lure rapidly and brings bass up out of the vegetation, but when you're fishing around stumps and isolated brush, you can jerk it quickly up to the cover and then stop it so it settles slowly down beside that cover."

Your imagination really is the only limiting factor on how you can use these lures. Some put them on Carolina rigs and fish them deeper, while others keep them weightless and simply let them fall longer before they begin twitching them —particularly around rocks and sloping riprap. When bass are schooling in the autumn, soft jerkbaits can be rigged on a light leadhead to increase casting distance and fished fast or slow, depending on how the fish want it. If you're fishing another type of lure such as a topwater plug and get a strike but miss it, a quick cast back to the spot with a soft jerkbait often brings another quick strike.

Most anglers rig them with a 4/0 or 5/0 wide gap hook, and use lines testing between 12 and 17 pounds. They are excellent lure choices in the spring and fall, but produce equally as well at other seasons, too.

POWER TUBES

When brothers Gary and Bobby Garland introduced a strange new plastic fishing lure on the market in 1975, even they admit they had no idea it would become one of the most legendary lures of all time. Their creation was basically a short, hollow

Power fishing with tube jigs has become one of the most popular of all bass fishing techniques. Heavier, slightly larger tube jigs can be pitched or flipped into thick brush cover just like regular jigs and plastic worms, and provide something different for bass to see.

plastic worm with a stringy, squid-like tail they named the Gitzit, but because it looked like a small tube, that's how these lures were described.

In short order, dozens of manufacturers copied the Garlands' idea, making subtle changes in both length and thickness, but the original concept of a small, light-line lure for clear water that sank slowly and erratically did not change.

It did not change, that is, until the early 1990s when a group of professional bass anglers from Arkansas developed a larger, thicker tube to suit their particular style of fishing in heavier cover. The original Garland design of 2½ inches was lengthened to 4½ inches and the walls strengthened to accommodate a much larger hook. In effect, the Arkansas pros created a tube that allowed them to flip and pitch into thick, heavy cover with much heavier line, a technique generally described as "power fishing."

Even with heavier lines and rigged with a light slip sinker, the lure still sashayed through the water like its smaller Gitzit cousin. It was about the same size as a regular jig, and it penetrated thick cover as easily, but it offered a totally different type of action bass hadn't seen very often.

How effective was the oversized tube jig? So effective the Arkansas pros tried to keep it a secret, which they managed to do until 1997 when one of the pros, Doug Garrett, won a national bass tournament with it and a sportswriter wrote about it. A year later, another pro named Denny Brauer won the Bass Masters Classic world championship with the lure, and ever since, the big tube has been one of bassdom's "must-have" lures.

The most popular method of rigging a power tube is Texas-style, with either a 3/0 or 4/0 wide gap hook and a ³⁄₁₆- or ¼-ounce slip sinker. In extremely thick, brushy cover, a screw-in type sinker can be used. Smaller, 3½ inch tubes (used with the smaller hooks and lighter sinkers) can be fished on spinning rods with 10- to 14-pound test line, while the larger tubes are used with baitcasting gear and 20-pound test line.

With either set-up, you can pitch or flip the lure into brush, holes in the vegetation, or around any type of vertical structure such as bridge pilings, standing timber, or boat docks. Allow the lure to fall on a slack line in order to take advantage of its side to side swimming action, but watch your line carefully for any indication of a strike as it does fall. Once the tube has reached the bottom, you can jig it, hop it, or swim it to attract bass.

When you're using the smaller tube, skipping the lure underneath boat docks or beneath overhanging tree branches can be effective (skipping is much easier with open face spinning rods than with revolving spool baitcasters). Again, once the tube has stopped moving across the water, give it plenty of slack line so it will fall freely.

Tube jigs can be fished deeper on Carolina rigs, and around surface-feeding schooling bass the lure can be skipped across the surface like a baitfish, or allowed to sink slightly and then pumped up and down through the school with your rod.

One thing you have to be aware of when rigging tube jigs is not to over-weight them, because if you do, the lure loses its action and will sink just like a jig. Even with 20-pound test line, which helps slow the lure's rate of fall, a ¼-ounce sinker is just about the heaviest weight to use. Because the lure is light, changing to a slightly lighter rod action may make presentations easier for you.

Whereas normal jigs are most often fished vertically, power tube fishing can easily involve horizontal presentations. That is, these lures can be pitched or cast to a distant target, allowed to sink, and then retrieved with hops, a stop-and-go swimming action, or even a non-stop swimming motion. With its tail of individual strands of waving plastic, the lure looks and acts remarkably like a baitfish.

Tube jigs can also be rigged with a leadhead and fished like a plastic grub, simply crawled along the bottom, or drifted freely in current. They are spectacular smallmouth bass lures and are used frequently by anglers in Lake Erie and Lake Champlain, who let the tube bounce along the bottom as they drift with the wind.

In water deeper than 5 feet, a tube jig can be an effective lure to use with a Carolina rig. Each time you jerk your rod tip, the tube will jump into the air, then swim erratically back to the bottom—an action similar to those often exhibited by a dying shad.

In each of these applications, of course, any number of different soft plastic lures might be used. The tube jig is simply another option to consider. Because it has not been used in these ways very long, many feel its greatest advantage is simply that bass have not seen very many of them. When Denny Brauer won his world championship in 1998, he actually located his fish along the shallow, wooded shoreline by pitching a regular jig into the cover. When actual competition began, however, those same bass simply would not bite a jig, but they readily hit Brauer's tube.

When the Garland brothers first developed their Gitzit tube, they fished it most often in the clear water lakes of the west, where it is still a popular lure today. Power tubing the larger tube jigs has proven to be more effective in off-colored and stained water conditions. The overall characteristics of the lure itself lend itself to practically any situation, and the years ahead will likely provide additional new and imaginative ways to fish them.

5

HAVING FUN WITH TOPWATERS

TEN TIPS FOR BETTER TOPWATER SUCCESS

Bass fishermen generally describe topwater fishing as the most exciting type of fishing because the action occurs in full view on the surface, but they also describe it as a very fragile type of fishing. That's because so many different conditions influence topwater fishing, and a change in any one of them can stop the action almost instantly. A shifting breeze, cloud movement, and even something as innocent as starting an outboard engine can make each bass change their behavior.

Here are ten tips describing various aspects of topwater fishing, which when followed, can help improve your fishing success.

1) Choose the Proper Lure

Topwater lures are made in a wide variety of shapes, sizes, and actions, many better suited for specific conditions than others. Smaller, quieter minnow-type lures usually work better in early spring, for example, while larger prop baits and chuggers are a better choice in summer, because of how the bass are feeding. Quiet lures tend to produce best in quiet water, noisy ones do better in rough water. Poppers and chuggers are good summer/autumn lures because they can be presented so many different ways, both in open water as well as around shallow cover. Later in autumn when bass are really feeding heavily, larger noisy prop baits are among the best choices.

2) Retrieve Speed Is Critical

The speed at which you retrieve a topwater lure is often more important than the lure choice itself, because a surface lure can attract bass both by sight as well as noise. Although there are no specific rules about what speed to use under certain conditions, generally speaking, a slower retrieve is often the best. This is particularly true when the water is unusually cold or hot.

Many topwater pros start with a slow, quiet presentation, then change to a faster one—often on the same retrieve—until they finally get a strike. In shallow water, a slow retrieve should be tried first (to avoid spooking bass), but very often, a slow retrieve works best over deep water, too. When bass

Oklahoma angler Jim Morton proudly holds up a 13-pound largemouth that hit his Big Bug topwater lure. At certain times of the year, especially in spring and fall, topwater lures can be very effective trophy bass lures.

are schooling and feeding on the surface, a faster retrieve often is better. At certain times, bass may only hit a lure after it's been sitting absolutely motionless on the water for fifteen or twenty seconds.

3) Watch the Time of Year

Topwater fishing can be productive year-round, but it tends to be best between late spring and early summer (March to June) and again from late summer into autumn (August through October). These are transition times for the fish during which they are moving from shallow water to deep and back again; they are often suspended, which makes them the most susceptible to a surface lure.

In the summer when bass are relating more to structure and cover than to food, and are more scattered, larger lures that create more commotion may be needed to bring a strike. The same is true later in the autumn when bass are feeding on large shad; use a large topwater lure to tempt larger bass. In the winter, look for vegetation if you want to fish a topwater lure. Bass will hold in moss, hydrilla, and other greenery, and can often be brought out with a slow but noisy topwater lure.

4) Fish Shallow and Deep

Don't limit your topwater fishing to just shallow or deep water; work both. In shallow water, bass will either be cruising the shallows looking for food (generally at night and early in the morning) or they will be holding around shade and cover (throughout the day), and in either case, a small chugger or popper can be used. These are not suspended bass, and the fish may be spooky, so make long casts and work your lure slowly.

In deeper water, you'll be targeting suspended bass. Key places to look are over points, around channel breaks, the mouths of creeks, and near special underwater structures like roadbeds, humps, and ridges. Large topwaters that can be "walked" or "waked" on a long retrieve often work best.

5) Watch for Changes in the Water

Changing water conditions frequently dictate how bass react to surface lures. On calm, slick water you may need a quiet, minnow-type lure that swishes over the surface, but if the wind starts blowing and causing a surface chop, you'll want to change to a prop-type lure that creates more commotion. Remember, you want the bass to see, hear, and feel your lure, but at the same time, you don't want to overdo it, either.

Watch for changing cloud conditions, too. Typically, overcast skies make bass more active, while clear conditions push them tighter to cover. Bass

Topwater fishing does not have to be limited to shallow water. Suspended bass are also susceptible to a surface lure, particularly a noisy one that makes a lot of commotion.

react very quickly to these conditions, which usually means you'll need to change lures just as quickly to continue catching them.

6) Listen to the Bass

While it is true that any type of strike indicates you're in productive water, studying the type of strike you get may tell you how to get even more hits.

For example, if a bass hits your topwater lure very lightly and not aggressively, consider changing to a slim profile lure like a minnow bait, and retrieve it very slowly. On the other hand, a huge, explosive strike usually indicates bass are more aggressive and that you can use a faster retrieve and possibly a larger lure, especially if you're fishing a lake known for big bass. A jumping/skipping retrieve is often effective during these times because aggressive bass are also very easily excited, which is what this type of retrieve is designed to do.

7) Choose Your Lure Colors Carefully

Topwater fishing is based in large part on bass being able to see your lure in clear water, so it follows that you want to use colors that may appeal to the fish, or at least colors the fish can most easily see. On dark, overcast and rainy days (which produce excellent topwater fishing) consider a black lure. It will show as a silhouette, no matter how dark the sky becomes. On bright, sunny days, consider using shad patterns or possibly even clear lures.

Interestingly, many early fishing lures, including topwater plugs, were painted with white bodies and red heads. This combination caught a lot of bass, as many oldtimers can readily attest, but today these colors are seldom used by bass anglers. Red and white do remain a popular and productive combination for northern pike and muskie, however.

8) Don't Neglect Open Water

Because most fish that hit topwater lures are suspended and roving bass, it pays to cast to open water as well as to visible cover. This means making a lot of blind casts, but remember, topwater lures attract fish by the noise and vibrations they make, and bring bass to them. Depending on the depth of the water you're fishing, consider fishing open water with one of the walking lures, or a prop bait.

9) Use the Proper Rod

Using the proper rod is critical to the success of your topwater fishing because it will allow you to work the lure properly and impart maximum action. That action is generally controlled by the rod's tip, so choose a rod with a light or medium/light action and a flexible tip. Most bass pros use a shorter rod, as well, measuring from 5½ to 6½ feet. This is because most of the action is done by twitching or jerking the rod downward, and a longer rod will hit the water each time you jerk. Either a pistol grip or straight handle may be used, depending on your own preference.

10) Wait to Set the Hook

This may be the most difficult aspect of topwater fishing, but it is also one of the most important. You should wait an extra instant—until you feel the weight of the bass on your rod—before setting the hook. This is to insure the bass actually has the plug in its mouth and that you don't jerk it away from the fish. When bass are hitting actively and aggressively, they may not be taking the lure at all but instead, simply slapping or butting it. Leaving the lure in the water after an attack like this frequently results in an almost immediate second strike if you don't move it.

SHOULD YOU BE NOISY OR QUIET?

Each time bass fishermen take to the water, they're confronted with a number of problems they have to solve in order to catch fish that day. Most of these problems vary from lake to lake and season to season, but one question remains constant, no matter where or when they're fishing or which lure they're using: what type of retrieve to use. This is especially critical in topwater fishing, since surface lures attract bass primarily from the amount of noise or commotion they produce, rather than any specific action they may have. While some topwater lures do "walk," "spit," and "pop," their main attraction to fish comes from the amount of noise (water movement) they produce.

It is easy to think that the more noise a lure makes, the more attractive it would be to bass, but this is not the case at all. There are many times when bass, both largemouth and smallmouth, will not hit a moving topwater lure. They prefer it to be sitting perfectly still on the surface, and sometimes it has to sit there unmoving for fifteen or twenty seconds before they hit it.

On the other hand, there are occasions when bass prefer just the opposite. They want a lure making so much noise and commotion you'd think they'd be spooked immediately. There is no way to determine beforehand how the fish want a lure presented; you simply have to try different lures and retrieves until the bass start responding.

There are, however, some basic guidelines that can often shorten this experimentation.

One consideration is the water condition itself. If the water is calm, slick, and clear, consider a silent retrieve, regardless of the time of day. Unless you are actually seeing bass chasing baitfish, or seeing bait flick on the surface, you can guess that bass are not feeding very actively at the time. When you cast a topwater lure

Lures with dual propellers like this Gilmore Special, used by Texas angler Cody Bird, create a lot of surface noise and are often more productive when the water surface is rippled and baitfish are active.

and simply let it sit motionless where it lands, you can try to attract a strike from curious fish.

Any bass in the immediate area will certainly hear your lure land, and some of them will probably swim up under the lure just to see what has dropped into their living room. Sometimes, after a few seconds of watching (to a fisherman it seems like hours), you'll get a sudden and vicious strike. There is no way to determine just what makes a bass strike under these conditions, but the strikes are nearly always loud and violent.

Occasionally you can encourage a strike by barely moving your rod tip so the lure quivers slightly. This is particularly effective with lures that have a tinsel, bucktail, or feather trailer attached, for just the slightest lure motion causes this trailer to move and gives the appearance the lure is alive.

Large topwater lures do not normally produce the interest and strikes that smaller lures do when the bass are acting this way. Many fishermen, in fact, resort to clear, transparent lures under these conditions, since these baits tend to appear even smaller than they really are when viewed from underwater.

One possible scenario to keep in mind when this is the presentation you have to use is that you may be in an area that does not contain a lot of fish, or at least not a school of bass immediately nearby. Bass are very competitive in their feeding and when many fish are present, strikes usually come quickly. It isn't unusual to get several strikes per retrieve and even to hook two bass at the same time.

The opposite retrieve from a silent one, of course, is a noisy one, and certainly some of the noisiest of all topwater lures are those that have one or two propellers on them. These "prop baits" whir, buzz, sputter, and churn the water like lawnmowers, and some topwater pros have one tied on and ready at all times.

When there is just a little ripple on the water, or when you do see baitfish activity, these are good lure choices, as they draw attention to themselves because of their noises. When the surface is rippled and choppy, bass can locate them much easier, and certainly when bass are active and aggressive you want them to locate your lure as quickly as possible.

Between late August and October when bass are usually feeding actively in preparation for winter, prop baits tend to be good topwater lure choices. They're also excellent early spring lures—start with a single propeller model in colder water and gradually change to one with both front and rear props as the water warms. Later in spring after bass have spawned, prop baits are excellent choices for attracting roving fish.

Retrieves with prop baits are as varied as the lures themselves, but most anglers agree the best retrieves incorporate a series of jerks rather than simply casting and winding back without a pause. You might try two jerks and a pause followed by three jerks and a pause, and then one long, fast jerk that rips the lure across the surface. Again, your retrieve is going to be a complete trial and error until you get a strike.

The size of the prop bait you use should be dependent on both the water conditions as well as the size of the bass you expect to encounter. The rougher the

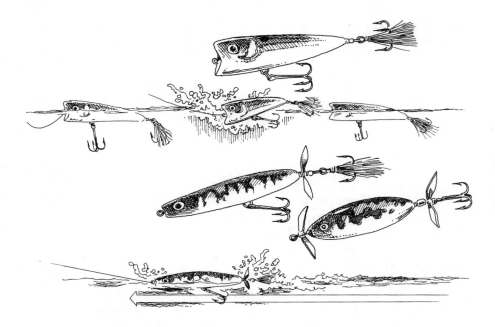

When fishing topwater lures, let the fish tell you the retrieve they want. Use a variety of presentations until fish begin hitting.

water, the larger the lure to use, because it will create more noise and be easier to locate. Likewise, if you're on a lake known for producing big bass, you should use a larger lure.

Normally, lines testing between 14 and 20 pounds can be used satisfactorily with topwater lures. If you're using a prop bait that you're jerking with your rod, a shorter, medium action rod will generally be a better choice.

The question of a silent or noisy retrieve is not always an easy one to answer, and the answer may change during the course of a day as the mood of the fish changes. The important thing to remember is that there are going to be days when one or the other of them is the only way you're going to get a strike.

HOW TO WOBBLE UP A BASS

Would you ever consider fishing a topwater lure in water 50, 100, or even 150 feet deep? Would you do it under a bright, hot sun, or perhaps in the wind?

The technique is known as "wobbling," and it has been in use for many years on certain lakes throughout the United States. Wobbling is most often practiced on deep, fairly clear impoundments, and is believed to have originated on Bull Shoals Reservoir in Arkansas where anglers were actually fishing for striped bass

99

rather than largemouths. It's a tactic designed to draw strikes from suspended bass, which is why it works best on deep water reservoirs.

Wobbling is easy to learn, and it is probably most effective when bass are suspended in late spring, but it can be used from early spring throughout the entire summer.

To wobble up a bass, you'll need a large, jointed jerkbait, such as a Storm ThunderStik or Cordell Red Fin, although in a pinch you can try a Heddon Zara Spook (although not jointed, it is a large plug). Spool a reel with 14-pound test line and use a medium action rod, and you're ready.

All you do is cast and retrieve very slowly so the lure "wobbles" across the surface, creating a distinct wake. Don't stop-and-go, don't retrieve fast so the lure dives under the surface, and don't twitch or jerk your rod to make the lure move erratically. The key to this entire technique is making a slow and steady retrieve.

This type of retrieve imitates the action of an injured or dying shad, and it will bring bass up from as deep as 12 to about 15 feet. Remember, even though you may be fishing water over 100 feet deep, the bass are suspended only a short distance below the surface.

The best place to try this is out in a big cove or bay, letting the wind drift you across. You won't see any targets to cast to and you may not see any of the suspended bass on your electronics, but don't worry. If they're anywhere around, they'll find your lure. Other excellent places to try this are along the edges of steep bluffs, as well as over points and underwater islands.

Wobbling also works in shallow water in the early spring, especially around points leading into coves or tributaries that might be spawning areas. In shallow water, however, cover like stumps, rocks, and standing timber becomes much more important since the bass aren't as deep. The retrieve remains the same, however.

The retrieve must be slow and deliberate when other types of lures are used, as well. Prop baits, poppers, and chuggers are not particularly effective, but "walking" lures like Zara Spooks and Chug Bugs may be tried.

Wobbling works on practically any lake where bass gather in large schools. The primary way to fish for schooling bass is to wait until they come to the surface and cast to them with topwaters, jigs, spoons, and other lures. Normally, after a few casts the fish submerge again, and this is when wobbling is a good technique to try. If you know a general area where bass do tend to school, you can try wobbling before they come to the surface.

Other good places to try wobbling are over any type of well-defined structure, such as humps, ridges, islands, and channel breaks. These are the types of places where bass do suspend in schools, and good lake maps will show their locations.

Surprisingly, wobbling can also produce good results around boat docks, particularly those that are floating rather than those anchored by pilings. Floating docks tend to be over deeper water anyway, and of course, the fish have to suspend because there isn't any vertical cover for them to use.

Although on most lakes schooling bass tend to be fairly small, larger bass frequently may be holding below them, and wobbling is a good way to catch them. The big jointed jerkbaits represent a large meal that seems to be more attractive to larger bass.

Wobbling is an unusual topwater technique that doesn't work everywhere, such as on shallow lakes with abundant cover. It produces best over deep, clear water—the least-likely places most bass fishermen ever cast to. It's a surprising technique, but one certainly worth trying on these types of lakes.

FISHING SHALLOW IN SUMMER

Topwater fishing is synonymous with summertime and shallow water, but the pattern (as are all topwater patterns) is a particularly fragile one and often depends on a number of circumstances over which the angler has absolutely no control.

There are certain lakes, however, where a shallow topwater pattern can be very dependable, not only during the prime early morning and late afternoon hours, but throughout the entire day. The types of lakes where this occurs are those that have a shallow shoreline shelf extending a few feet out from the bank which then drops steeply into deeper water.

This shoreline shelf, in which the water depth is seldom more than 3 feet, may extend 10 to 20 feet off the bank. It does not have to have a lot of visible cover, although the more it has, the better it may be. The drop itself is completely visible, although the bottom generally is not.

Bass relate to this break exactly the same way they relate to a breakline in deeper water. In this case, the fish use the deeper water as a hiding/ambush area, a sanctuary, and even a resting zone, even though they may only be 3 to 6 feet deep. Baitfish will hide and feed on the shallow shelf, and later in the summer bream will spawn on it, so the bass do not have far to go when they're feeding.

A truly good topwater lake will have an abundance of this type of structure along much of its shoreline. Likewise, a lake that has a large population of bass in excess of 3 pounds will also be a good topwater lake when structure like this exists because these fish are separating themselves from larger bass that have claimed much deeper habitat.

Two quick examples of lakes like this are Caney Lake in Louisiana, which has produced several bass over 15 pounds, and Lake Mead in Nevada, which now ranks as one of the top "numbers" fisheries in the western states. Both of these impoundments offer very clear water conditions, too, which is also important in topwater fishing.

Lakes like these are definitely worth looking for because of the quality of fishing they can offer, and the best way to fish them is by retrieving your lures right along the edge of the breakline. Poppers, chuggers, and the shallow-running minnow baits or "twitch baits" are among the best lure choices because not only must you impart a specific action and speed to these lures, you can also

Lakes that have a shallow shoreline shelf that drops steeply into deeper water often offer good topwater fishing throughout the summer. The immediate access to deep water gives fish the security they need when moving into the shallows.

change these actions as you retrieve the lure. Instead of a pop-pop-pause retrieve, for example, you can easily speed up or slow down with faster pops or longer pauses.

This is important to consider whenever you're still trying to figure out which specific topwater retrieve the bass may want. Even though a buzz bait may be your favorite topwater lure, it actually does not offer that many retrieve variations, because if you stop moving it the lure sinks. After you learn what the bass want, you may decide a buzz bait will work, and you can change then.

Consider this basic rule of thumb when you're still trying to determine how the bass want a lure served to them. If you notice fish following but not striking your lure, your retrieve speed is probably too slow. The bass are getting too good a look at the lure as they follow and are deciding against it. In contrast, if you get strikes but the bass repeatedly miss the lure, you're retrieving too fast. Normally in clear water, a faster retrieve is best, as it also is in a lake that has a lot of baitfish. In more stained conditions, or on a lake without a lot of bait, you'll need to slow your retrieve.

In addition to changing your retrieve speeds, it's important to keep your retrieves moving right along the edge of the break. You may see bass cruising on the shallow flat and they may chase a lure, but you can rest assured far greater numbers of fish are hiding in the deeper water. These fish are generally much easier to catch, too.

While you're moving along this break, study the water ahead for additional cover, such as rocks, stumps, fallen logs, points, and ditches. Bass will use all of these when they come shallow to feed, and they won't stray far from them when they move back to deep water.

Because so much of topwater fishing is vision-oriented, and especially so in shallow water, studying the size of the available forage and matching it with your lure can be an important consideration. For example, in early spring after bass have spawned, a lot of tiny fry may still be present on the shallow flat, so a smaller lure will often work better. Later in summer after the fry have grown and the bream may be spawning, a larger lure can be used.

Smallmouth bass can also be caught on topwater lures throughout much of the summer. This is particularly true in lakes where they are the dominant species. In clear water impoundments like Lake Champlain in Vermont the fish suspend off weedy points. Even though they may be 15 to 20 feet deep themselves, the smallmouth will rocket to the surface to hit a big popper or chugger-type topwater lure.

In the particular case of Lake Champlain, where this type of surface action lasts from June to September, the smallmouth apparently are chasing alewives, the principle forage there, and they prefer the lures moving fast and creating a lot of commotion. Much of the smallmouth behavior, of course, is dependent upon the action of the forage they're feeding upon, which is why on Champlain the fish relating to vegetation rather than rocks.

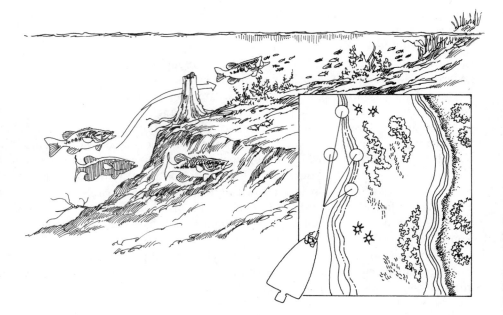

When fishing lakes that have a shallow shoreline shelf that drops into deep water, work your lure along the edge of that dropoff as much as possible.

In other lake systems, especially those that do not have as much vegetation, the smallmouth do relate to the rocks. Sometimes a fast retrieve will generate strikes, but other times the lure has to be kept completely still and the fish may only strike after the bait has been kept motionless for ten to twenty seconds.

You've probably heard the phrase, "Let the bass tell you how they want the lure." What this means is that you need to constantly keep changing your presentation until you start getting strikes. This is important in all types of bass fishing, but especially so when you're fishing topwater lures during the summer. Overall, the bass are not feeding as actively as during other seasons, and they must truly be tempted to strike.

No doubt you can think of many times and places where topwater fishing has been productive in shallow water during the summer. It definitely is a prime time to enjoy surface fishing, and it can be even more productive if you remember the types of lakes where it works best, and learn to use different presentations until you start to get strikes.

TWITCHING TACTICS

Ever since 1962 when *Life* magazine published an article describing a thin, minnow-like fishing lure made in Finland by Lauri Rapala, American bass fishermen have enjoyed an on-going love affair with what have since come to be known as "twitch baits." Rapala's lure, which is still produced, opened the door not only to the production of an entire category of fishing lures, but also to a host of innovative techniques on how to use them.

Today these slim diving plugs are made in a variety of styles and sizes by practically every major lure manufacturer in the United States. All feature a thin, narrow body profile, two or possibly three treble hooks, and an angled lip to make the lure dive. The deeper diving models are generally known as jerkbaits (see "Advanced Jerkbait Tactics," page 26); the lures that stay very shallow are more often described as twitch baits or minnow baits, and are usually classified as topwater lures.

The name "twitch bait" refers to the way these lures are retrieved, which is through a series of short, erratic twitches imparted by the rod. Essentially, twitch baits imitate injured baitfish, which immediately makes them appealing to both active and inactive bass. These lures not only trigger hard, slashing strikes from feeding bass, but they can also be used to tease non-feeding fish into hitting when they seemingly ignore every other type of lure.

Spring ranks as the favorite season for twitch baits, primarily because these are shallow running lures and bass are shallow during this season. If the water is still cold, or if the bass are somewhat inactive, one presentation to consider isn't even a true retrieve. Because these lures float, just cast to shallow water cover such as a boulder, fallen log, or even a man-made brush pile, and let the lure sit there. After a few seconds, wiggle your rod tip slightly from side to side to make the lure vibrate in place. A variation of this presentation might be to then swim the lure to another piece of cover, stop it, and then wiggle it again.

When you're looking for bass in more open water, twitch baits are excellent lure choices to fish around shallow rocky points or along the edges of vegetation. These are good places to start by moving your lure with a series of twitches and pauses, such as twitch-twitch-stop, twitch-twitch-stop.

Your own imagination is really the limit on how you might retrieve a twitch bait in situations like this, and opinions are divided among anglers on whether establishing a regular, repeating cadence is best or whether you need to be completely erratic and refrain from ever repeating the same pause/halt sequence.

Probably the best advice is to try both, and keep experimenting with different presentations of all types until you generate a strike. Because the lure will dive slightly with each movement of your rod tip, you generally want to let it float back to the surface before you move it again. Overall, however, a slow presentation tends to trigger the most strikes, regardless of whether it's erratic or steady.

"Twitch baits" are thin-bodied, shallow-running lures that imitate injured baitfish. They're excellent choices for spring fishing around brush, rocks, and along the edges of vegetation.

Sometimes, however, just the opposite is true. In the summer on extremely clear lakes, a truly fast, ripping retrieve can be extremely effective when you fish around boat docks, riprap, or along rocky bluff banks. In these conditions, you're trying for reflex-type strikes so you don't want bass to be able to see your lure very well.

These twitch baits can be fished over submerged vegetation, too. Here, your best presentation may be fast or slow, depending on the mood of the fish. During the summer and autumn months bass will often cruise in the thin layer of water between the top of the vegetation and the surface, and these fish normally get tempted first by an erratic retrieve rather than a static one.

Consider sweeping your rod hard to one side so the twitch bait moves a longer distance just below the surface, then stop so it floats back to the top, then sweep it along again. Another presentation might be a twitch-twitch-pause, twitch-twitch-pause action, with practically no true pauses; in other words, you make a long cast, and just start twitching the lure back to you, only stopping periodically.

Because of the small size and light weight, many prefer to fish these lures with spinning tackle and with lines of 6- and 8-pound test. Some also prefer to attach a small snap to the line-tie eye of the lure to insure full freedom of movement with each twitch. The small size of these lures generally—but not always—also limits their use to calm water. In choppy conditions, they simply get lost in the wave action.

In recent years, several Japanese lure makers have introduced lipless twitch baits, which have also proven effective for shallow water bass. These lures are extremely erratic when twitched—some even roll from side to side when moved —and some of their best uses have been around the edges of shoreline weeds and tules or in calm coves with a hard gravel and rock bottom.

The Japanese introduction of their lures is just part of the continuing verification of the effectiveness of the twitch bait types of lures. Even Rapala has continued to expand on their original design and now has well over a dozen models available.

OLD RELIABLES: ZARA SPOOKS AND JITTERBUGS

Imagine, if you will, a lure whittled from a piece of broomstick with part of a spoon attached across its nose. The lure was originally intended to be a diving plug, but although it did not dive properly, it did work pretty well on the surface. It was named after a popular dance of the time, the jitterbug, and eventually became one of the most popular topwater lures of all time.

The Jitterbug was introduced by the Fred Arbogast Company in 1937, and while it is one of the best-known of all topwater bass lures, it has shared the spotlight with another topwater lure, the Heddon Zara Spook, for more than sixty years. Originally introduced in 1922 as the Zaragossa Minnow—named after a well-known street in the red-light district of Pensacola, Florida—it became the Zara Spook in 1939 when Heddon began manufacturing the lures in plastic and painting them with scale-like patterns that produced a spooky, ghostly appearance.

Today, both the Fred Arbogast and James Heddon companies have been purchased by Pradco, one of the largest and best-known lure manufacturing firms in the United States, and both the Jitterbug and Zara Spook are not only still being made, they are used regularly by tens of thousands of bass fishermen worldwide.

Both lures could hardly be more different. The Jitterbug has its own built-in action and requires little fishing skill beyond being able to cast, while the Spook has no built-in action and demands exceptional skill to use. Each, however, has a long-proven record of catching bass.

Because of its design, the Jitterbug wobbles noisily from side to side as it is retrieved through the water, but even with all its side-to-side motion, it always tracks in a straight line. Thus, it's easy for bass to zero in on and hit, regardless of where you fish it. The most effective retrieve is usually a slow, deliberate one with occasional pauses beside visible cover.

The Jitterbug can be fished practically anywhere, although with its two dangling treble hooks it is not weedless so it is not a lure to fish over the top of vegetation or in brush. Primarily, this is a lure to fish beside cover, along the edges of vegetation, across shallow points, and over shallow flats. It's an excellent lure for creeks and small rivers where its wobbling vibrations can be heard and felt over the pull of current; and of course, the same noisy wobble also makes the Jitterbug an exceptional night fishing lure.

The modern Zara Spook, right, retains many design similarities with the original Zaragossa Minnow, left, which was introduced in 1922. The Zara Spook is known as a "walking" lure because of its action.

Night fishing is probably where the Jitterbug still sees the most use today. A long cast followed by a slow, steady retrieve that just chugs and gurgles the lure across the surface has probably created more fishing memories and dreams than any other lure. Jitterbugs probably represent frogs or other large creatures that big bass feed on frequently, which is why the lure seems to attract strikes from a lot of trophy-class bass.

Zara Spooks are equally well-known as big-bass lures for the same reasons as the Jitterbug. They are fairly large in size, and when retrieved properly, create a lot of disturbance. When a school of fish is present, it is not at all unusual to hook two bass on the same cast.

A Zara Spook has essentially only one retrieve, which is known among anglers as "walking the dog." The lure darts (pivots is probably a more accurate description) to the left, then the right, to the left again, the right, and so on all the way back to the boat. By pointing your rod tip further to one side or the other a Spook can be guided toward a specific target, and the lure can be "walked" at any speed, as well as stopped right beside an object. Many seasoned pros use a variety of speeds during each retrieve.

All of this is accomplished by holding the rod tip down toward the water and twitching the rod quickly with short downward jerks with your wrists. At the same time, the reel is cranked half a turn with each jerk to make the Spook move forward at the same time it is pivoting from side to side. Many anglers fish Spooks with shorter 5½- or 6-foot rods so they don't hit the water with the tip, and some still use the older style pistol grip handles instead of the newer straight handles.

It's easy to walk a Spook a few feet; it's much more difficult to continue walking one at the same cadence for a full retrieve, and even more difficult to maintain that cadence on cast after cast. It takes practice and more practice, which is why it is an absolute joy to watch anyone who has truly mastered a Zara Spook.

Zara Spooks work best in clear water, and while they are extremely effective when fished around visible cover like boat docks, standing timber, and brush piles, they can also be fished over extremely deep water where they attract suspended bass. The choice of ideal conditions for a day of Spook fishing vary with different fishermen. Some prefer heavy overcast with perhaps a light rain or drizzle but calm water with heavy logs and brush in water less than 10 feet deep, while others prefer a bright sky with a slight ripple on the water. Either way, the Spook "season" begins in early spring and continues well into the autumn.

Interestingly, the harder to use Zara Spook is promoted quite widely today while the easier to use Jitterbug is not. Several sizes of each lure are now manufactured, and although both lures are well-known, few of today's professional bass tournament pros use Jitterbugs while all of them carry a selection of Spooks.

Both lures, however, deserve a place in anyone's tackle selection, because both Jitterbugs and Zara Spooks are time-proven topwater lures, even if one was originally designed to be a diving lure and the other was named after a street famous for its ladies of the night.

A Zara Spook can be "walked" by pointing your rod tip down and twitching the rod with short jerks. With each jerk, the reel is also cranked half a turn to move the lure forward.

6

LEARNING TO USE JIGS

DEVELOPING JIG AWARENESS

When it comes to using a jig in bass fishing, anglers usually fall into one of two distinct groups: they either love the lure and do very well with it, or they dislike the lure intensely and avoid using it whenever possible.

The most often-cited reason for poor performance with a jig (which automatically leads to a dissatisfaction with the lure) is a problem known as "jig awareness." This is a catch-all term that basically defines how to fish a jig; to be truly good with this lure, you have to know what it is doing all the time it's in the water, and because the majority of jig bites are whisper-light, you have to learn to recognize when a jig suddenly feels a little heavier that it should. Jig awareness, then, is developing a sense of "feel" for the lure.

There is no fast way to develop jig awareness, but there definitely are ways to do it. Most accomplished jig fishermen describe their own learning process as "time on the water," and indeed, jig fishing certainly exemplifies the motto of experience being the best teacher. Even then, however, more than a few pros will still tell you they literally forced themselves to learn jig fishing by leaving all their other lures at home.

Mark Stevenson, a veteran guide at Lake Fork in Texas, started his jig awareness education not only by fishing in area lakes but also by fishing in a swimming pool, and this is definitely a technique worth considering. Stevenson anchored a small tree in the deep end of his pool, then started working his jigs through the limbs.

"One of the secrets to successful jig fishing is being able to visualize what your jig is doing on the bottom, and identifying by feel each object it bumps into," he explains. "By putting the tree in my pool, I could not only feel my jig hitting the limbs, I could watch it happen.

"It made the visualization process much easier and quicker for me, and it was especially helpful when I began comparing jigs of different weights. I even fished the pool at night when I couldn't see my jig, to help me learn to concentrate on feeling the lure."

Another way to develop jig awareness, continues Stevenson, is learning to present the lure properly to a piece of cover. Jigs are cover-specific lures, which means that you pitch or flip them directly to a bush, tree, or some other object. Rarely do you cast them into open, featureless water.

One of the most important elements in successful jig fishing is developing jig awareness: learning what the lure is doing in the water and when you have a strike.

Jigs are often hit as they fall on the initial presentation, which is why line watching is so important. When a bass strikes, the line often jumps slightly.

"If you don't have access to a swimming pool," he says, "just start pitching toward the shoreline in shallow water and simply work your lure back. Just park your boat out in deeper water and fish the same spot over and over."

In some respects, learning to fish a jig is similar to learning to fish a plastic worm; the biggest problem is recognizing when you have a strike or when the lure has simply bumped into a stick or rock. Most jig pros advise setting the hook whenever in doubt; over time, you'll learn to tell them apart.

Another tip to developing jig awareness is learning to focus your attention on your rod tip and your line, rather than in your hands. Bass inhale jigs most often as the lure is falling; when this happens, you will not necessarily feel it through the rod handle, but if you're watching your line just where it enters the water, you will see your line stop moving, and sometimes you'll see the line actually twitch or jump slightly. If the strike is a little harder, your rod tip may dip slightly.

After making a presentation to a target, some anglers hold the line very lightly with their thumb and forefinger as they work the jig up and down with their rod. This is certainly something worth trying; cradle the rod in the palm of your left hand just above the reel, with the line between your fingers and using your right

Jigs are effective bass lures because they can be presented into the thick cover where bass live, and kept there. Some anglers believe the best way to learn to fish jigs is by leaving all your other lures at home.

hand to control the reel. This way, you can actually set the hook without moving either hand.

Learning to fish a jig is also much easier if you start in shallow water, such as between 3 and about 7 feet. This is an excellent depth range for bass holding in heavy cover, and will almost guarantee at least some strikes if bass are present. The deeper you fish, the easier it is to lose control of your jig, especially if you're still learning how to feel it. By staying shallow, you not only learn more about control but also gain confidence at the same time.

Still another way to learn jig awareness is by fishing with another angler who is already an accomplished jig fisherman. Such a partner will be able to coach you through the various steps of lure presentation and hook setting, and hopefully, also be able to guide you quickly to productive water where the bass are biting. A few hours spent working jigs over a stumpy point loaded with bass is worth days of casting to a swimming pool tree.

When you begin jig fishing, it's critical to begin with the proper rod, which will aid you in presenting the lure correctly, increase your feel for the lure, and certainly, make hook-setting easier. Most pros agree that a 7- or 7½-foot graphite rod with a medium/heavy to heavy action (a flipping stick) but with a sensitive tip is best. Nearly all rod manfacturers today produce rods especially designed for jigs.

It's important to realize, also, that jigs of different weights fall at different rates of speed, and part of developing your jig awareness is learning the different fall rates. When you're first learning to fish a jig, start with one weighing ⅜ ounce. This is an excellent jig for shallow water and can also be used very successfully down to about 15 feet.

Even though fishing in a swimming pool or repeatedly pitching to the same piece of shallow cover in a lake will certainly help you develop jig awareness, it is still a process that takes time, dedication, and above all, concentration. The payoff, however, is definitely worth the effort, for of all the lures a fisherman has at his disposal for catching bass, few can match a jig in overall productivity.

FISHING JIGS IN HEAVY GRASS

The history of bass fishing is filled with notable dates, and certainly one of the more significant dates has to be November 20, 1981. That's when a Texas fishing guide named Tommy Martin won a national tournament on Toledo Bend Reservoir with a total of 81 pounds, 10 ounces of bass.

Martin, who at the time was a fishing guide on the massive Texas-Louisiana lake, won by fishing a jig through the thick hydrilla that covered much of the water's surface—a feat that stunned the fishing world at the time. Until his victory, no one recognized how many fish lived under the hydrilla, nor had they figured out how to catch them.

Martin's win not only opened the door to a technique that has since become standard in bass fishing—grass jigging—it also laid the groundwork for a new lure specifically designed for this technique, the grass jig.

Special jigs like this one by angler Terry Oldham have been designed to penetrate thick hydrilla and other vegetation. These heavier jigs typically have a different head design, a wide gap hook, and a stiffer weed guard.

Today grass jigs are specialized jigs designed to penetrate the thick hydrilla present on lakes throughout the South, but they can also be used around rocks and standing timber. They are not really suitable for use in thick brush because they are heavier than other jigs, regularly weighing ¾ ounce and some as much as 1½ ounces.

Other characteristics of grass jigs include extremely wide gap hooks to handle big bass, stiff weed guards, a line-tie eye specifically positioned so it doesn't collect vegetation when retrieved, and rattles. Because no manufacturers were making jigs heavy enough to break through the matted hydrilla when Martin began perfecting this technique, he had to add a ¼-ounce slip sinker to his line ahead of his ½-ounce jig.

Because grass jigs are fished in such heavy vegetation, anglers use them with heavy lines and stout rods. Terry Oldham, another Texas-based bass pro and one of the earliest grass jig manufacturers, uses 80-pound test braided line and a 7-foot, 3-inch heavy action rod that bends evenly from tip to butt. Martin and others regularly use monofilament lines testing between 20 and 30 pounds, and 7½-foot flipping sticks.

The majority of strikes on a jig come as the lure is falling so Oldham tries to create multiple falls on each presentation. He pitches his jig into the vegetation and lets it fall freely to the bottom. Then he snaps his rod tip upward to make the jig jump about two feet, then lets it fall again. He does this repeatedly for fifteen to twenty seconds, and then if he hasn't had a strike, he reels in and pitches to a new location.

Martin doesn't hop his grass jigs quite as actively. Instead, he likes to shake them, and he starts shaking them the moment he feels them break through the hydrilla. Once the jig reaches bottom, Martin may shake it in place, or hop it; he tries different presentations until he learns what the fish want.

This is one reason virtually all grass jigs have rattles. Most anglers feel the added noise helps bass locate the lures in the dim light conditions. Most veteran grass jig anglers also add a pork or plastic trailer to their jigs, primarily to give it extra action when they're hopping or shaking it.

Most of the fishing is a near-vertical presentation with very short pitches. Longer casts are not only harder to control, they also make it practically impossible to bring a fish out, since any bass hooked is going to collect several pounds of vegetation around it before it comes to the surface. Vertical presentations give you the most control over your lure and the fish.

Sometimes the surface mat is too thick for even a heavy grass jig to penetrate on a normal pitching presentation. When he's in these types of conditions, Oldham pitches his jig straight up, rather than out, and jerks his rod down hard to increase the speed of the jig and literally crash it through the vegetation. Sometimes it works, he says, and sometimes it doesn't.

Grass jigging is possible because vegetation like hydrilla and milfoil only mat on the surface; one to two feet below this mat the water is fairly open, which is why bass are present. It's shady and it's also full of baitfish. Martin had discovered this on Toledo one day when he donned mask and fins and jumped overboard just to see if it was fishable.

Hydrilla grows very distinctly along bottom contours to form fingers (which are actually high spots on the bottom) and cuts (which are low spots), and bass may gather in either area. Thus, it's important to know what you're fishing and once you catch a bass to immediately pitch back to the same spot.

During the summer when hydrilla has matted on the surface, it is easy enough to slowly move along the outside edge of the grassline to identify these formations. At other times of the year, the edge may be less visibly definable and depthfinder study may be needed to follow the vegetation.

Overall, however, most hydrilla fishing is a long process of elimination, patiently moving along the edge of the vegetation and making pitch after pitch through the greenery. Many anglers don't like the technique at all because it can be so tedious, but those who have learned the technique and have confidence in it describe it as one of the most exciting of all ways to fish for bass.

ULTRA-DEEP JIGGING

During the winter months when bass move into deep water, they are still susceptible to at least two lures, a jigging spoon, and a regular jig. Of these, the jig may produce better results, particularly if the fish are holding in standing timber or if they're very close to the bottom, both of which are common occurrences.

The biggest problem is not actually locating bass. Rather, it is finding locations that have the potential to hold bass, and this means a lot of depthfinder study. In standing timber, neither bass nor the baitfish that often provide a clue to the whereabouts of bass will be recorded.

In winter, your search should center around deep creek channels or ditches, preferably those leading to wide flats and points where bass might spawn. On quality lake maps, these flats and points should be fairly easy to identify, and once you do find them, simply look for the primary channel leading into them. These channels, if they're deep enough and have the right cover, often become the winter holding areas for bass after they leave the shallow flats in the autumn.

Georgia angler Mickey Bruce, who is very good at this type of jigging, believes the best way to actually fish a channel full of deep, flooded timber is by fishing parallel to it, casting along the edge of the channel rather than across it. This puts his jig in the potential strike zone for virtually all of his retrieve.

The secret is fishing very, very slowly. Once your jig is on the bottom, start reeling it up very slowly until you feel it hit its first limb. With your rod tip, crawl the lure over that limb, then put your reel back into freespool and let the jig fall to the bottom again.

"This is the way I do it," says Bruce, who has won two national tournaments using this technique in water 60 to 70 feet deep. "Sometimes it takes me ten minutes just to get my lure back on a single cast."

Putting out marker buoys to outline a fishing area helps casting accuracy, and can be especially helpful in keeping your boat properly aligned on the spot.

The majority of strikes occur as the jig is coming over a limb or starting its fall back toward the bottom, and strikes are solid hits so you don't have any trouble identifying them. The problem is having the patience to continue this slow technique over and over.

"You can help yourself two ways when you try deep jigging like this," adds Bruce. "First, a ½-ounce jig is heavy enough. You don't need a heavier jig. In winter, bass normally want a slower falling lure, and a really heavy jig will fall too quickly.

"Secondly, you should use a 7- or 7½-foot rod but not a stiff, heavy action rod. I like a very light tip action that increases sensitivity, and I also use light 10-pound test line, which also improves sensitivity."

Bruce has taught this technique to a number of his fishing friends, some of whom—once they've mastered it—say that it's easier than fishing in shallow water, because the bass haven't been pressured by as many anglers. Indeed, quite possibly the very best way to learn this technique is to spend time in the boat with someone who already has mastered it.

Deep jigging works in the summer, as well. On deep lakes that stratify and form a thermocline, baitfish gather in huge schools right along the upper edge of this thermocline. The actual thermocline is where two different layers of water meet but do not mix. The two layers form such a distinct line that it even shows up on depthfinders. The deeper water is many degrees colder and contains much less oxygen than the upper zone, which is why baitfish gather where they do above it.

Once you determine the depth of the thermocline, don't fish it in open water. Instead, move toward the shoreline and try to locate ditches, channels, and other structure where the bottom corresponds to the thermocline depth. This is where you want to drop your jig, and you don't necessarily need to have timber or brush around.

Key places will be outside channel bends and edges, and you may be able to locate these with a map. If not, another way to possibly locate them is by cruising along the shoreline until you find a tributary. Instead of turning into that tributary, turn out and follow its channel into the main lake. Keep in mind that you're looking for a channel bend (underwater point) at the same depth of the thermocline.

If timber is present, you can use the same slow retrieve Bruce recommends in the winter months, crawling the jig up over limbs one at a time. If timber is absent, consider popping your jig after it touches the bottom. Do this by snapping your rod sharply upward just a few inches—you don't want the jig leaping violently through the water, just jumping slightly above the bottom.

After the jig settles back to the bottom, crawl it a few inches by slowly raising your rod tip, then pop it another time. Strikes tend to come just after you pop the jig and it begins falling, or just after you start crawling it.

This type of presentation seems to create interest in fish because of the three different types of erratic activity it presents in a very short distance, but of course,

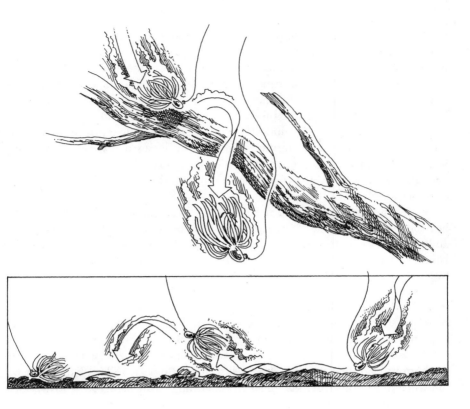

When jigging in deep timber, let the lure fall to the bottom, then begin reeling it back very slowly, crawling it up and over each limb and letting it fall back again.

it isn't the only retrieve you can use. If popping and crawling doesn't bring any results, consider a variation of more hops or longer crawling along the bottom.

Although the technique of deep jigging sounds difficult, it really is not. The hardest part is locating the right area in which to do it. If you know this is the technique you're going to be using, spend some time seriously studying a good lake map and try to pinpoint several potentially good spots before you get on the water.

FISHING THE FLY 'N RIND

No one knows when jigs first appeared in the bass fishing world, but most agree the earliest ones that did appear were constructed with some type of animal fur or hair. Often, the material used was from a deer, which led to the name "bucktail." A more common name, however, the "hair jig," eventually evolved, especially for smaller jigs. This, in turn, later evolved into the "fly and rind," a term describing a small, lightweight hair jig adorned with an equally small trailer of pork rind.

Names aside, the fly and rind became the staple of smallmouth fishermen, particularly in Tennessee, where small lures and light lines were commonly used to catch big fish on Dale Hollow and other impoundments. While its luster has dimmed somewhat with the introduction of other jig skirt materials, most notably silicone, the hair jig remains an integral part of the bass fishing scene and today is used not only for smallmouth but also for largemouth and spotted bass, as well as for other species of gamefish.

Today, many bass anglers limit their use of hair jigs to clear, cold water where temperatures range from the mid-40s to mid-50s, and while this is where the lure excels, it is certainly not the only application. Hair jigs are an excellent lure choice in clear water anytime, in deep water anytime, and certainly in cold water anytime. Basically, when bass fishing conditions are tough, this is a lure that will usually catch some fish.

The standard weight for a hair jig is ⅛ ounce, although both lighter and heavier models are made. The dominant colors tend to be reddish brown, black, and olive green—natural hues that more closely approximate a baitfish. These jigs have a very small, slim profile, even when a trailer is used, and they attract strikes by sight more than anything else.

Because the hook is exposed and because the jig is so light, its primary use is in fairly open, rocky water. It is not a jig that can be flipped, nor is it a jig that can be retrieved well through wood or grass cover. Points, bluffs, sloping shorelines, and underwater ridges are among the very best places to use them.

Probably the most common retrieve used is simply to cast the jig, let it fall to the bottom, and then slowly reel it back so the jig appears to be a baitfish swimming near the bottom. Because the jig is small and usually fished on 4- to 8-pound test line with spinning gear, strikes are generally easy to detect.

An alternative presentation that often works well around rocky points is to cast and let the jig sink to the bottom, then to retrieve it with a series of hops. You can do this by snapping your rod tip upward sharply, which causes the jig to jump up from the bottom. How high you snap your rod determines how high the jig will jump; normally, you want the jig to rise only 6 to 10 inches at a time.

As with other presentations with similar bottom-type lures, this retrieve creates multiple falls, and because bass seem to hit jigs most often when they are falling, this offers more opportunities for strikes. Sometimes an aggressive presentation like this also triggers reflex-type strikes that a slower, more casual swimming presentation does not.

A lot of anglers like to fish hair jigs around bluffs, and on many of today's big impoundments, this is where the hair jig probably sees its heaviest use. The idea is to let the jig fall as close to the rock face as possible, which usually means parallel casting along the side of the bluff. How long you let the jig fall depends on the depth of the water, and certainly, the location of the bass.

Casting bluffs like this can be effective because bass very often suspend beside them, perhaps as shallow as 4 or 5 feet down, even though the water may be 20 or

30 feet deep. It's important to pay attention to your strikes so you can determine just how deep the bass are holding.

On many lakes, bluffs are everywhere, so you may have to do a lot of casting before you encounter bass. First, however, consider fishing the ends of any bluffs, bluffs that are located near the mouths of tributary creeks and coves, and also those bluffs that are free-standing in open water. Don't forget to consider wind direction, either, since several days of steady wind from the same direction will blow plankton against a bluff wall that will attract baitfish and eventually bass.

Once you cast a hair jig along a bluff wall, you can do a lot of things with it as it falls. Certainly, giving your rod tip an upward twitch now and then to make the jig suddenly dart in a new direction, may attract a bass. Likewise, letting the jig sink for several seconds, then twitching your rod tip down and reeling so the jig starts coming back to you, then stopping to let it sink some more, is another option.

On many western lakes, the bluffs do not actually fall as steeply into deep water as they first appear. You may see flooded brush along the water's edge, and while hair jigs are not good lures to fish through woody cover, you can certainly fish around it. Consider throwing beyond the brush, letting the jig sink several feet, then retrieving it slowly with slight twitches of your rod around the outside edge of the cover.

Attaching a small pork or plastic trailer to a hair jig adds bulk to the lure and increases its action. If you encounter aggressive bass, by all means use a trailer since it may help attract larger fish. Normally, trailers like this also slow the lure's fall, which is usually desirable in colder water. Certainly, adding a trailer makes the jig easier to cast.

More than half a century ago when the old-timers on Dale Hollow Lake fished hair jigs they nearly always fished them with a trailer, as much as anything to give smallmouth more to chew on. Obviously, the tactic worked, for their fly 'n rind entered the lexicon of bass fishing and has remained there ever since.

JIGGING IN CURRENT

As unusual as it may sound, the most stable water conditions in any lake when the weather itself is unstable are in the far upper reaches where the lake is actually a river flowing with current. This may be literally within sight of a dam impounding the next lake upriver, or simply the rocky, log-strewn region where the water is continuously moving.

The conditions are stable in the sense that the water is moving steadily and does not fluctuate that much in temperature, since it is generally already colder than main lake water. Because of these two factors, this colder, moving water is an excellent place to fish in summer, autumn, and winter, but especially in later autumn and early winter when the first cold fronts begin coming through.

One particular lure of choice for these conditions is a jig. It is a fairly compact lure that can be presented very naturally right to the bass. Its speed can be controlled by its own weight—lighter jigs move faster and heavier ones go slower—

When fishing jigs in current, make your cast upstream so the lure is washed downstream naturally. You can help guide the jig by moving your rod tip from side to side as necessary.

and its direction and depth are easily controlled by rod tip action. Jigs are proven big bass lures, and in cold water they are among the most effective of all lures because they can be controlled so easily.

Bass stay in current because moving water contains more oxygen; in the summer it is cooler and in the winter the water is actually a little warmer. Moving water also presents a constant stream of food to the fish. Because a wide variety of items is steadily washing down before them, all the bass have to do is dart out from behind their rocks and logs and snare whatever they choose.

Therein lies the key to fishing jigs successfully in current. The lure should be pitched upstream and allowed to wash downstream so that it appears as just another food morsel. Your task is to guide it into the proper places. You're not bouncing the jig along the bottom, but rather, following it with your rod as the current pushes the lure along. If the jig continually hits the bottom, you should probably change to a lighter model; normally, a ¼- or ⅜-ounce jig works best, but in faster current a ½-ounce model may be needed.

The more a jig hits bottom, the more likely it is to get snagged and ruin your presentation. You want to keep it off the bottom but close to it, which is the most natural presentation. Don't try to control depth by raising your rod tip higher because when a strike comes you won't be able to set the hook.

The most difficult aspect of swimming a jig in current like this is staying in contact with, or "feeling" the lure. Strikes may be very subtle and hard to detect in the force of the moving water, so concentration and line-watching are important. Whenever your line stops moving and you feel any resistance at all on the jig, it's time to set the hook.

Largemouth bass are rarely in strong current, but rather, along its edges where they can be hiding behind rocks and logs or the small points formed by cuts and shoreline breaks that offer some protection from the current. In this calmer eddy water the fish do not have to expend as much energy staying in one position, but they still have a front-row seat to all the food being washed past them.

Keep these places in mind as you pitch your jig upstream. Sometimes the current will take the lure right into these hideaways naturally, but other times you may need to guide the lure with your rod tip. Normally, short pitches are the best type of presentation because with less line out you'll have better control. In some areas, flipping may also be possible.

While rocks and fallen logs are obvious places to present your jig, don't overlook any type of current break near the shoreline itself. The mouths of small feeder creeks in this upriver area may be the real bonanza spots because they can offer two-way water movement. When water is being released from an upstream dam, these creeks flood with incoming water, but if that water flow stops and water is then released from the downstream dam, water will flow out of these creeks.

When water is flowing into these creeks, the inside edge of the upstream point at the creek mouth frequently holds bass, while the downstream point holds bass when water is flowing out of the creek. When water is flowing into the creek, pitch your jig upstream into the main current flow so it will wash around the upstream point; when water is flowing out of the creek, pitch into the creek itself and let the current pull the lure out around the downstream point.

If you're fishing a lake that contains either smallmouth or spotted bass, you're more likely to find both of these species closer to the main current instead of along its edge. These fish seem to naturally be more acclimated to colder water and in some areas you will probably find them not behind rocks and logs, but out at their edges. Sometimes, they'll even be in front of the structure.

The best solution to catch these fish is still to present your jig upstream, but to gently guide it into all of these places until you catch your first fish. That bass will likely give you a very positive location you can then use to help pinpoint others.

For this type of fishing, you'll probably want a 7- or a 7½-foot rod with a soft, limber tip that lets you pitch lighter jigs and which is sensitive enough to help you detect light strikes. Lines testing 14 to 20 pounds should be satisfactory.

Fishing jigs in current is just one more way to take advantage of these versatile lures. Sometimes, just getting to the area where current is present may mean a long boat ride, but once there, the results will usually justify it.

HOW AND WHEN TO SWIM A JIG

The stereotyped image of jig fishing is usually one of an angler gently raising and lowering his lure in shallow flooded brush or timber, and indeed, this is certainly one of the most common and productive ways to fish a jig. Another totally different technique that also produces surprisingly good results is swimming a jig above the bottom.

Swimming a jig is not practiced very often, and it probably works much better than most anglers think it does. Many bass fishermen believe you swim a jig only when you have to, not when you want to.

There are at least three primary conditions throughout the year when swimming a jig should definitely be considered. The first occurs in the late fall and early winter months when the water temperature ranges between the mid-50s and high 60s, and bass are frequently suspended around objects like bushes, logs, and even pier and dock pilings. If you pitch or flip a jig to these bass and work the lure on the bottom, you're going to be fishing under them, and strikes will be few and far between.

The swimming presentation in this situation is simple and easy. Cast past the intended target, and begin a slow to medium retrieve so the jig swims a foot or so beneath the surface. As the lure passes your particular target, or any potential fish hideout, you can pause for just a split second to let the jig fall slightly, but then just start reeling again.

The depth of the water you're fishing determines the weight of the jig you should use. Consider ⅜-ounce as a starting point, and use a lighter jig in shallow water, a heavier one in deeper water. Adding a trailer is recommended, too, to give the lure added vibration.

In early spring another condition for swimming a jig exists on lakes that have abundant hydrilla, milfoil, or other sub-surface vegetation. Basically, you try to swim the lure just over the top of this vegetation. Other lures, including both spinnerbaits and lipless crankbaits, are most often used in this situation; a jig provides more of a finesse-type presentation and does not advertise its approach nearly as loudly. As a result, a swimming jig may generate strikes over vegetation when these other lures do not.

You want to keep your jig just barely touching the top of the grass, so most of the time a steady reeling retrieve can be used. The standard rule of thumb to remember is that if you're feeling the vegetation, speed up your retrieve to raise the jig slightly, but if you can't feel anything, slow down your retrieve. As a result, most of your retrieves will need constant adjustment because the top of the grass won't be even.

When you're swimming a jig over grass, keep your rod pointed down but not directly at the jig. Instead, point it about 45 degrees to one side; the reason is because you want your rod to work for you and flex when a bass hits. If your rod is pointed directly at the lure, it cannot flex as much unless the bass pulls straight down or swims quickly to one side.

Swimming a jig works well in the early spring on lakes that have abundant sub-surface vegetation. It provides a finesse-type presentation that may be more effective than other lures.

Swimming a jig over submerged vegetation works well in spring; as you retrieve the lure, keep your rod tip pointed to one side so the rod will flex when a bass does hit.

Again, a ⅜-ounce jig should be your basic starting point for this retrieve, with lighter or heavier jigs used depending on the water depth. Keep in mind, too, that a slow, steady retrieve usually works best, and that if you're having to reel unusually fast just to keep the lure from getting snagged in the grass you should tie on a lighter one.

A third condition where swimming a jig can be especially effective is when fishing thick shoreline vegetation. Around Lake Dardanelle in Arkansas where this technique is believed to have originated, and in many other lakes throughout the Southeast, shorelines often have a thick vegetation known as water willow. It's not a tree, but a heavy emergent vegetation that grows to a height of as much as 18 inches and out to a depth of perhaps 5 feet. It's too thick for buzz baits or spinnerbaits, which is how the swimming jig presentation was started.

The jig itself (a ½-ounce model works best) is cast into the greenery near the shore, and while a jig does sink into the water, your line catches on the grass and keeps the jig from sinking completely to the bottom. Your retrieve is a series of jerks that makes the jig actually skip through the weeds. It's a fabulous big-bass technique, for when you get the jig to any type of opening or hole in the water willows, you can stop and let it sink.

In this presentation, the jig appears more like some type of fleeing creature than a minnow or crayfish. Bass are usually lurking in weeds like this, but there's no way to reach them effectively except with a presentation of this type. It works between early summer and late fall until the first freezes kill the vegetation.

On the upper ends of some lakes where conditions are more riverine, you can also swim jigs around log jams that occasionally form along the shorelines. Here, the key is swimming your lure parallel to the longest logs and trees, and at a depth just below them. Because most of these jams are at least semi-permanent, they quickly attract bass, and a jig swimming right along one of the logs looks just like a small minnow to them.

Alton Jones, a former fishing guide who lives in Waco, Texas, has been a swimming jig fan for many years, and can certainly vouch for its effectiveness. He particularly likes to recall a June trip on Lake Waco during which he visited one particular log jam up the Bosque River by the Highway 185 bridge. He and his partner already had five bass weighing about 18 pounds in the livewell, but within half an hour they'd replaced them with five larger fish weighing more than 28 pounds— all caught by swimming a jig just under the outside logs.

What makes Jones' story even more impressive is that while they were swimming their jigs, another angler was fishing the same logjam by flipping jigs down between the logs, and he never had a strike.

Swimming a jig is largely a learning/feeling process that many consider one of the most difficult of all fishing techniques. The retrieve may not have many applications, but when it works, it also has to be considered one of the best.

INDEX

B

Bailey, Lee, Jr., 75–77
bass by the numbers, 1–3
Bird, Cody, 20–23
Bland, Fred, 64–67
boat docks, finessing, 64–67
Brauer, Denny, 55, 89
Bruce, Mickey, 118–20
buzz baits, 51–56
    buzzing bluffs, 53–56
    versatility, 51–53

C

California swim baits, 32–35
Carolina rig, 62–63, 67–71, 87, 89
casting angles, 16–17
Chapple, Paul, 58
choosing a tributary, 3–6
clear water, 8, 51
Clunn, Rick, 1, 11–13, 20
Cochran, George, 20
cover, 15–16
crankbait fishing, 11–35
    advanced jerkbait tactics, 26–29
California swim baits, 32–35
    deep cranking tips, 13–17
    in winter, 23–26
    lipless crankbaits, 17–20
    power cranking shallow brush, 20–23
    shallow flats, 29–32
    speed reeling, 11–13
Crisp, Jimmy, 51
currents and jigging, 123–25

D

Daves, Woo, 82
Davis, Mark, 67–69, 71
dead-sticking, 73–75
Deaver, Lloyd, 69–70
deep cranking, ten tips for, 13–17

deep water, 43–47, 93
depthfinder, 16
dingy water, 8, 28
drop-shotting, 73

E

Ehlers, Harry, 84

F

fast-rolling, 43–44
floating worms. *See* worm fishing
flukes. *See* soft jerkbaits
fly and rind, 121–23
Fritts, David, 29–31
frogs. *See* rat fishing

G

Garland, Gary and Bobby, 87–89, 90
Garrett, Dout, 89
grass jigging 115–18
grub fishing, 77–80

H

hair jigs, 121–23
Hildebrandt, Alan, 56–58
Hildebrandt, John, 56
hula grubs, 79, 80
Humphrey, Danny Joe, 80
humps, 53
Huntley, Bill, 47–49

I

in-line spinners, 56–59

J

jerkbait fishing, 26–29
jerkworms. *See* soft jerkbaits
jigs
    deep jigging, 118–21
    fly and rind, 121–23
    grass jigging, 115–18

how and when to swim, 126–29
    in current, 123–25
    jig awareness, 111–15
    learning to use, 111–29
Jitterbugs, 107–9

K
Kiriyama, Kotaro, 73

L
lipless crankbaits, 17–20
locating bass
    by months of the year, 2–3
    by the numbers, 1–3
    by water color, 6–9
    choosing a tributary, 3–6
    with soft plastic, 61
lures
    colors of, 95
    noisy versus quiet, 96–97
    picking the right, 16

M
Mann, Tom, 77
Martin, Tommy, 115–17
McCarty, Richard, 45–46
monster worms, 84–87
muddy water, 8
Murphy, Bill, 86

N
night fishing, 47–49
Nixon, Larry, 8–9

O
Oldham, Terry, 117
open water, 95

P
power tubes, 87–90
Pruitt, Bud, 17

R
Rapala, Lauri, 105
rat fishing, 82–84
Reed, Herb, 87
Reese, Skeet, 26–29
Rizk, Mark, 73
rods, using the proper, 95–96
Rojas, Dean, 71

S
Schultz, Bernie, 58
seasons of the year, 2–3, 9, 15, 23–26, 31
shallow brush, 20–23, 25, 28, 49
shallow flats, 29–32
shallow water, 100, 101–4
Shuffield, Ron, 86
shoreline, 51–52
slow rolling, 40–41
soft plastics, using, 61–90
    at boat docks, 64–67
    Carolina rig, 62–63, 67–71, 87, 89
    dead-sticking, 73–75
    drop-shotting, 73
    finding bass with, 61–64
    grub fishing, 77–80
    monster worms, 84–87
    power tubes, 87–90
    rat fishing, 82–84
    soft jerkbaits, 87
    split-shotting, 71–73
    wacky worming, 75–77
    worm fishing, 80–82
    speed reeling, 11–13
spinnerbaits, 37–49, 53–59
    basic guidelines, 38
    choosing, 37–38
    fast-rolling in deep water, 43–44
    fishing after dark, 47–49
    in-line spinners, 56–59
    ripping, 45–47
    slow-rolling, 40–41
    split-shotting, 71–73
stained water, 8
Stephens, Bill, 23, 26
Stevenson, Mark, 111–13

summer fishing, 9, 101–4, 120
swim baits, 32–35
swimming a jig, 126–29

T
Tallent, Loyd, 84
Texas rig, 73, 75, 76
Thompson, Jackie, 43
Tibbs, Jack, 43–44
topwater fishing, 91–109
    Jitterbugs, 107–9
    noise, 96–99
    shallow water, 101–4
    tips for success, 91–96
    twitch baits, 105–7
    wobbling, 99–101
    Zara Spooks, 51, 107–9
tributaries
    and channel bends, 120
    choosing, 3–6
    in crankbait fishing, 15
    twitch baits, 105–7

V
Velvick, Byron, 33–35

W
wacky worming, 75–77
water color
    for locating bass, 6–9
    seasonal patterns, 9
water conditions
    categories of, 8
    changes in, 93–95
winter fishing, 9, 23–26, 52–53, 118–20
wobbling, 99–101
worm fishing, 80–82

Y
Yamamoto, Gary, 61, 79

Z
Zara Spooks, 51, 107–9

ABOUT THE AUTHOR

Steve Price has been an award-winning writer and photographer for more than twenty-five years, specializing in outdoor recreation and travel. Formerly the outdoor editor of *Southern Living* magazine and the south regional editor of *Field & Stream*, he has been a senior writer for *Bassmaster* magazine for more than twenty-two years. He has written more than 2,500 magazine articles and sold photographs to many national and international magazine and book publishers, including *Field & Stream*, *Outdoor Life*, *Sports Afield*, *Reader's Digest*, Rand McNally, the National Geographic Society, the Brunswick Corp., Ford Motor Co., and others. Assignments have taken him throughout the United States and much of Canada, as well as to Africa, South and Central America, India and Asia. He has also written numerous video and television scripts and has served as the producer and host of a nationally syndicated radio show. This is his sixth book, his fourth about bass fishing. A graduate of the University of North Carolina at Chapel Hill, he lives in Granbury, Texas.